# Uncovering Mysteries of the Parables
# with Haggadic Midrash

*To you [my followers] it has been granted to know the mysteries
of the Kingdom of Heaven (Mat 3:11)*

## Anne Kimball Davis

BibleInteract
UNCOVERING THE MYSTERIES OF THE KINGDOM OF GOD

All Scripture quotations, unless otherwise noted, are taken from the *New American Standard Bible*®, Copyright © 1960, 1962, 1963, 1968, 1971, 1972, 1973, 1975, 1977, 1995 by The Lockman Foundation. Used by permission. (www.Lockman.org)

The *NASB* uses italics to indicate words that have been added for clarification. Citations are shown with small capital letters.

The Reconstructed Temple drawing (page 79), © Leen Ritmeyer, is used by permission.

Published by CreateSpace for BibleInteract, Inc.

ISBN-13: 978-1492724933
ISBN-10: 1492724939

BibleInteract, Inc.
865 Los Pueblos Street
Los Alamos, NM 87544

http://www.bibleinteract.com

# Table of Contents

# Acknowledgments

I want to thank those who helped me on my journey of exploring the parables as haggadic midrash. Eunice Filler and Kaaren Craig reviewed the manuscript and made thoughtful and helpful suggestions. Pat Rose formatted the book both for printed publication and for the kindle edition.

# Preface

I first suspected that the parables were a form of haggadic midrash when I was preparing to teach the Parable of the Prodigal Son. Haggadic midrash is a form of commentary on some passage in the Hebrew Scriptures for the purpose of instruction in practical living.

I was planning to demonstrate that the Parable of the Prodigal Son contained various linguistic devices that produce an artistry of language. These starting and thought provoking words led to a rich understanding beyond the simple story. I remember being drawn to the heartbreaking words spoken by the prodigal son not once, but twice. "Father, I am no longer worthy to be called your son." These words cut deeply into my heart, and I agonized together with the one who had wasted his inheritance in reckless living. I was especially curious about the repetitive word "worthy" because there was a dichotomy between the unworthy yet repenting son on one hand, and the father who obviously perceived his wastrel child as worthy on the other. I was also puzzled by the eldest son who seemed to be the worthy one, but who was apparently unworthy in his father's eyes.

My curiosity led me to the Old Testament for the concept of being worthy or unworthy. I discovered Jacob, who was returning from twenty years of exile after he had left his father and his father's house. In his prayer to God, Jacob humbled himself and spoke these words. "I am unworthy of all the lovingkindness and of all the faithfulness which You have shown to your servant" (Gen 32:10). Thus, the Parable of the Prodigal Son seemed related to, and was probably even, a commentary on this account of Jacob.

Once I suspected that the New Testament parables were a form of haggadic midrash, which is a type of commentary on some passage in the Hebrew Scriptures for the purpose of instruction in practical living, I began methodically working through one parable after another to see if there were other connections to the Old Testament. I let the various linguistic devices and startling elements become my clues.

My suggestion, that all the New Testament parables are a form of haggadic midrash, will likely be new to many. As for what

I call first century methods, you may recognize my approach as a literary analysis. However, the concept of "listening to the text," the suggestion that a citation precipitates a memorized block, the prevalence of repetition and chiasm, and the presence of intentional startling elements will likely appear as an innovative approach.

The purpose of this book is first to share with you the deeper meaning I have uncovered by perceiving the parables as haggadic midrash. More important, I wish to demonstrate how you too can search the Scriptures for its depth of meaning. You must first consider something I have already concluded, namely, that the New Testament is intimately connected to the Old and is, in fact, a kind of commentary on the Hebrew Scriptures. After all, there are over 300 citations in the New Testament of the Old Testament. That alone should prompt some serious thought. However, perceiving the parables as haggadic midrash, which all comment on the Hebrew Scriptures in some way, reinforces this suggestion of the intimate relationship between the two testaments. Viewed together, the Old and New Testaments reveal powerful messages from God.

I have written this book for lay people who have an earnest desire to learn how to search the Scriptures as people in ancient Israel would have heard Jesus teach. Furthermore, because I have found the parables (in fact all of the New Testament) to be very Hebraic in thought and linguistic style, I have chosen to use the Hebrew name of Jesus, which is Yeshua. I will also begin referring to the Old Testament as the Hebrew Scriptures.

I offer one last suggestion. You may be tempted to jump ahead and read the parables out of order. However, I have placed them in a careful sequence of five sections. The three parables in each section are followed by a concluding chapter. So, my suggestion is that you resist deviating from the order, and take extra time to consider each of the five concluding chapters when you come to them.

I trust you will enjoy what I call "my great adventure of discovery." As you proceed through this book you will undoubtedly be confronted with many new ideas. However, I trust you will be as excited as I was as you travel through this adventure of uncovering mysteries from Scripture.

# Introduction
## A New Approach to the Parables

The New Testament parables are pillars of Christian tradition. They are provocative tales that activate our imagination, evoke an emotional response, and proclaim a meaningful message of godly living.

When I first realized that all the parables were a form of haggadic midrash, I discovered an incredible new depth of meaning that midrash uncovers from the Hebrew Scriptures.[1] The message of Christian tradition had not changed significantly. However, the new depth of understanding was so intense that my excitement was overwhelming. How much more was my growing relationship with God through midrash than through Christian interpretation that relies, in large part, on a simple reading of the story or a traditional theological interpretation.

What, then, is midrash and how is haggadah a form of midrash? The people at the time of Yeshua believed that the inspired Word of God had both a plain meaning and a deeper hidden meaning that could be uncovered with methods of midrash. Haggadah is a specific form of midrash that has three characteristics. First, there is a connection to the Hebrew Scriptures because each parable is a creative commentary on some account from the Hebrew text. Second, the resulting message instructs us how to walk in the ways of God in His kingdom. Third, these short haggadic narratives are teeming with provocative language that is indirect, artistic and slowly emerging, which is different from our western tradition that is direct, analytical and immediate. Until we learn to "think with a first century mind," it will be difficult to penetrate the rich depth that the parables are poised to present.

---

[1] Protestant tradition uses the title "Old Testament." Because the order of the Hebrew books at the time of Yeshua was the Torah, the Prophets and the Writings, some have begun to use the Jewish acronym Tanach, which stands for Torah, Nevi'im (Prophets) and Ketuvim (Writings). I prefer to use the term Hebrew Scriptures.

## Think with a first century mind

I am pursuing what has become an exciting journey to recapture first century methods of searching the Scriptures. My adventure started with a growing curiosity that eventually became a burning passion.

It all began when I was working on Paul's letter to the Galatians. When Paul declared "I speak these things allegorically" (Gal 4:21), he followed with five metaphors that make no sense and four contradictions of Scripture.[2] That was certainly strange. So, I followed Paul's startling markers to the Hebrew Scriptures where I uncovered a remarkable understanding about the nature of the inheritance by the children of Israel. This inheritance is called the birthright because God declared them to be His firstborn son (Ex 4:22).[3] That discovery of intentional linguistic anomalies merely whetted my appetite in Galatians.

I turned next to Galatians 3:6-14 where I pondered no less than six citations from the Hebrew Scriptures that Paul condensed into eight verses. This startling cluster of citations led me to read everything I could find on ancient methods of midrash. I learned that midrash penetrates a depth of understanding from the Hebrew Scriptures.[4] And that was merely the beginning of what has become an exciting journey of discovery and adventure as I continue to recapture first century methods of searching the Scriptures.

My heart desires to bring you with me. However, first you must learn to think with a first century mind. There are five basic principles, which may sound easy, but it isn't. You must leave an approach to Bible study that I have described as "direct, analytical

---

[2] Anne Davis, "Allegorically Speaking in Galatians 4:21-5:1," *Bulletin for Biblical Research*, 14.2 (2004). A metaphor is an implied comparison between two things that are literally dissimilar but nevertheless have a subtle relationship.

[3] Anne Kimball Davis, *The Law is not a Curse: Paul's Midrash in Galatians* (published by BibleInteract, 2012).

[4] See, for example, Michael Fishbane, ed., *The Midrashic Imagination: Jewish Exegesis, Thought and History* (NY: State University of New York), 1993.

and immediate" and adopt a new approach that is "indirect, artistic and slowly emerging."

Let us start with the first principle. In the first century at the time of Yeshua, the life of God's people, Israel, was God-centered. When was the right time to plant and harvest? What was the meaning of sickness and death? How did one please God? God had disclosed all the answers to life and godliness in His Word, and every aspect of daily living was regulated by a desire to live in harmony with God. Again, this may sound simple, but it isn't. Our modern, western mind is filled with material intrusions that stimulate complexity. Our lives are no longer God-centered. So, to pursue first century methods of searching the Scriptures we must identify with the Jews of the first century who were indeed God-centered.

The second principle logically follows the first. The people of Israel were Scripture-centered, that is, the Holy Writings were an integral part of their lives. After all, God had made Himself known through the words of His prophets, which meant that Jews not only viewed the Scriptures as inspired by God but they also relied on God's Word for all matters of life and godliness.

My family tradition helps me understand the intensity of this second principle. I come from New England where oral history is strong and pervasive. I spent my teenage summers working at an old resort hotel on an isolated island ten miles out from Portsmouth, New Hampshire. There I became fascinated with the life of the early settlers - first fishermen, then guardians of the lighthouse that protected the dangerous waters, and finally the gilded life of Victorian visitors to the old resort hotel. One thing that captured my imagination was the pivotal role that the Bible played in their lives. In fact, for the fishermen and lighthouse keepers it was typically the only book they owned. On cold winter nights, with the wind howling and the only light cast from a single candle, the father would read the Bible and expound on its moral lessons. As the children grew and learned to read, their only textbook was the Bible. Memories as a child recapture this heritage because my family has preserved the well-worn Bibles of my ancestors where births and deaths are recorded. These cherished Bibles must have been the center of their lives.

The third principle is an extension of the preceding two;

the Holy Writings were memorized at an early age. After all, people of the ancient world did not have books as we do today. So at night, after work had ended and the evening meal was finished, the father would gather his children to recite memorized portions of the Holy Writings. This was followed by his expounding on moral principles and practical applications for daily living.

Written documents on scrolls were expensive and scarce. In ancient Israel the Holy Writings were arduously copied by hand on vellum, which was made from the skin of goats and calves. These vellum parchments were carefully rolled and typically stored in the synagogue. Hence, learning Scripture first began at an early age in the home where the father would have been the teacher. As a result, the children came to memorize the Holy Writings as their ancestors before them had also internalized the Hebrew Scriptures. Thus, the third principle of the memorization of Scripture is especially important in our journey to think with a first century mind and to recapture first century methods of searching the Scriptures.

Again, I have a personal experience to share that will help you capture the tradition and impact of memorization. When I was learning to read biblical Hebrew, a senior member of our local Jewish community agreed to instruct a friend of mine and me. My friend was a Jew who wanted to better understand the Hebrew liturgy of the synagogue. I was a Christian who desired to read the Hebrew Scriptures in the original language. Little did I know when we started that our teacher would adopt the same method of instruction that he had experienced as a child in Eastern Europe. He had us take turns reading the text in Hebrew, not verse by verse, but a certain passage or block of Scripture at a time. When we were done reading, he would expound on the meaning of what we had read...in Hebrew.[5]

In ancient Israel there were no books in the home. So at

---

[5] My daughter gave me invaluable advice on how to learn and understand what I was hearing in Hebrew. I prepared questions in Hebrew to ask my instructor. When he answered my questions in Hebrew, I knew the topic of his answer and could follow some of what he was saying.

night, after work had ended and the evening meal was finished, the father would gather his children to recite memorized portions of the Holy Writings followed by his expounding on moral principles and practical application for daily living. As a result, the children came to memorize the Holy Writings.

The third principle, then, is the memorization of Scripture, which is especially important in our journey to think with a first century mind and to recapture first century methods of searching the Scriptures.

As you read the New Testament, a first century composition, you will discover literally hundreds of citations and allusions to the Hebrew Scriptures.[6] C. H. Dodd, the respected theologian, is known for promoting realized eschatology (the belief that Yeshua's references to the Kingdom of God meant a possible present reality as well as the expectation of something future). He was the first to suggest that a brief citation would have caused the early listener to recall memorized portions or blocks of Scripture. So today, after identifying a citation in the New Testament, we must return to the Hebrew Scriptures to identify, and carefully read, the entire passage in which the citation is located before returning to the New Testament to reconsider the citation there. This basic principle, that Scripture was memorized in blocks of verses, has allowed me to unlock many New Testament passages that cite only one small verse or part of a verse but stimulate the entire memorized passage. Failing to see the cited verse in its memorized block has challenged Christian understanding and led to numerous conflicting interpretations.

The fourth principle will become especially important when we begin to address the fundamentals of midrash. Once again, it may sound simple. However, you must realize that employing first century principles can be a new way of viewing Scripture. For example, those who first heard the words of Yeshua, who were Jews, understood "truth" as synonymous with

---

[6] Archer identifies 337 citations and allusions to the Hebrew Scriptures in the New Testament. Gleason Archer and G. C. Chirichigno, *Old Testament Quotations in the New Testament: A Complete Survey* (Chicago: Moody, 1983). For every citation there are also numerous allusions.

God. Thus, all true knowledge and understanding resided in God and emanated from Him. His words of truth are recorded in the Holy Writings. So far this sounds simple. But how did mortal mankind comprehend these immortal truths?

We turn now to the fourth principle. We must accept that truth resides in God, and that truth is expressed in the Word of God which is as infinite and deep as God Himself. In the first century way of thinking, one could only stretch and reach to grow closer to God through His Word. Then, with a hungry heart the journey would continue to bring a person closer and even closer to God. However, God is infinite, so the Holy Writings reflect the infinite nature of the Heavenly Father. Most important for our understanding of the first century, the journey to know God through His Word, and the truth that resides in these words, will never end. Mankind cannot arrive at the final truth, but can only continue to grow closer to the truths that reside in God Himself.

Compare this image of continually stretching to comprehend the truth of God's inspired Word with our modern, western world where each Christian denomination has a creed that identifies and defines "the truth" as interpreted by that denomination.[7] Thus, our western tradition views mankind as capable of capturing the meaning of truth. According to Jews in the first century (and even in Judaism today), truth resides in an infinite God. It is no surprise, then, that Judaism does not have thousands of denominations as Christianity does.[8] So, according to the fourth principle we must learn to acknowledge that truth resides in God, and we can only stretch to grow closer and even closer to that truth.

We are now ready for the fifth and final principle, which hangs on the first four. The people of first century Israel believed that the one true God had chosen them to be a holy people, and

---

[7] According to *The Dictionary of Christianity in America* Downers: Grove: Intervarsity Press, 1990), David B. Barrett identified 20,800 Christian denominations worldwide.

[8] There are three main branches of Judaism - Orthodox, Conservative and Reformed. Only recently have splinter groups emerged.

had given them His Word so they could walk in His ways. Furthermore, they viewed the Holy Writings as reflecting the nature of this mighty God. Therefore, as God is infinite and mysterious, so His Word is also infinite and mysterious. People of the first century acknowledged a plain and simple meaning in Scripture which they called the *p'shat*.[9] Yet, beneath the *p'shat* was a depth of meaning as deep and infinite as God Himself. Therefore, the fifth principle recognizes hidden mysteries in the Holy Writings just waiting to be uncovered in God's time. It is important to our goal of thinking with a first century mind that there were methods of midrash that could uncover these hidden mysteries.

## Midrash penetrates the depth of Scripture

When I talk about "midrash" I am referring to *methods* of ancient exegesis that penetrate the Hebrew Scriptures to uncover a depth of meaning that lies behind the plain and simple words.[10] These methods of midrash were in use during the Second Temple Period, which includes the time of the New Testament.[11]

There is general agreement that there are two basic forms of midrash in the ancient Jewish literature. These are commonly called *halachah* and *haggadah*. However, to facilitate an introduction to what is likely a new concept for many, I have chosen to use the more descriptive terms, legal midrash (*halachah*) and artistic narrative (*haggadah*). I will give only a brief synopsis of legal midrash since this method does not play a role in the parables.

Legal midrash begins with the understanding that God is infinite, and therefore His infinite nature is embedded in the Holy

---

[9] *Pesher* is a Hebrew word meaning "interpretation" in the sense of "solution." However, the use of *p'shat*, which is deriveed from *pesher*, means the plain and simple meaning of Scripture.

[10] Exegesis is a critical explanation and interpretation of Scripture.

[11] The Second Temple Period refers to the time between the return from exile in Babylon (538 BC) and the destruction of the temple by the Romans (70 AD).

Writings that He has given to mankind. This infinite wisdom penetrates far beyond the plain and simple meaning of a literal reading. Furthermore, legal midrash proceeds from the understanding that God has placed everything in His Holy Writings that mankind will ever need to know. Thus, Scripture is filled with hidden mysteries just waiting to be uncovered in God's time.

The Talmud records seven methods of legal midrash used by the great sage Hillel, which could uncover this hidden meaning. I have found Paul using some of these methods of legal midrash in his letters to the Galatians and the Romans.[12] I have also uncovered methods of legal midrash in the divorce passage in Matthew (Mat 19:3-11) and the introduction to the Letter to the Hebrews (Heb 1:5-14).

The second form of midrash I call "artistic narrative," which is a rather simple but useful description of haggadic midrash. The creator of the artistic narrative selects a verse or passage from the Hebrew Scriptures and re-tells the story in a way that expands and applies the message to our daily lives.

The connection to the Hebrew Scriptures can sometimes be quite obscure for those of us who have not memorized Scripture. So, we have tended to see the parables as isolated narratives with a moral message. However, I have found that every parable in the New Testament refers back to something in the Hebrew Scriptures in a way that gives meaning for everyday living. Without processing the underlying connection to the Hebrew Scriptures, much of the rich meaning and impact of the parable is lost, and occasional misinterpretation can occur.

---

[12] Davis, *The Law is not a Curse*, 93-117.

## Key Concept: Hebraic Sense of Time

In the gospels, the parables frequently refer to the Kingdom of Heaven.[13] We hear that "the Kingdom of Heaven is like...." and then the parable follows.

There is general agreement in Christian tradition that the Kingdom of God, or Kingdom of Heaven, refers to a time of peace and harmony with God when mankind will be in a righteous condition in order to come into His presence. However, there is confusion as to when this condition will occur. I suggest that the confusion stems, in large part, from our perception of time. Our western, analytical thinking originates from the ancient Greco-Roman world, which is now embedded in our lives. This modern sense of time is linear, and perceives points on a line. Therefore, past events are behind us. The past may have consequences in the present but what occurred in the past is essentially over. Future, then, is ahead of us, and has not yet happened.

How, then, are we experiencing time today according to the Greco-Roman concept? The past can only be experienced second-hand, so we have history textbooks and oral history and artifacts from the past. We experience the future through our imagination. Therefore, our only real and immediate experience is in the present.

Not so with the Hebraic sense of time that is quite different from our modern, western concept. Yet, before explaining the Hebraic sense of time let us ponder a passage in Scripture that may suggest that all is not compatible with our western tradition. Perhaps this verse will peak your curiosity to know more.

In 2 Peter we read a puzzling proclamation. "With the Lord one day is like a thousand years, and a thousand years like

---

[13] The Kingdom of God and the Kingdom of Heaven refer to the same thing. Tomson explains that 'the kingdom of heaven' is a normal phrase in Judaism, which is a discreet appellation of God. Peter Tomson, "Jesus and his Judaism," in *Jesus*, ed. Markus Bockmuehl (Cambridge: Cambridge University, 2001), 29.

one day" (2 Peter 3:8).[14] This verse is a commentary on Psalm 90:4, so let us look at the cited verse in its context.

> Before the mountains were born or before You gave birth to the earth and the world, even from everlasting to everlasting, You are God.
> You turn man back into dust and say, "Return, O children of men."
> For a thousand years in Your sight are like yesterday when it passes by, or *as* a watch in the night.
> You have swept them away like a flood, they fall asleep. In the morning they are like grass which sprouts anew. (Ps 90:104)

We see that God is present in all aspects of time, even before creation when everything came into being. "Before the mountains were born," declares the psalmist. But what about mankind, we ask. We are thrilled to learn of the special relationship between God and His created beings because God has been our place of refuge, not from time to time, but in all generations. And then, with sad certainty, we know that we will "turn to dust." But wait! We also hear God declaring, after mankind turns back to dust, "Return, O children of men" (Ps 90:3). Who will return to God? In Hebrew it is *b'nai adam*, that is, the descendants of Adam, which is all mankind, God's created beings. And when is mankind alive? Both before returning to dust, which is likened to sleep, and again when they are like grass that sprouts anew.

We must be careful to perceive our original verse in 2 Peter through God's eyes. "With the Lord one day is as a thousand years and a thousand years as one day." Since God is ever-present in all aspects of time, and God is life, then life must be ever-present also. In any case, one thing is certain. This verse does not convey a linear sense of time. So, if not linear, then what is it?

---

[14] 2 Peter 3:8 deletes "or as a watch in the night" from its citation of Psalm 90:4. The ancient ear would have heard this and considered it significant.

I like to explain the Hebraic sense of time this way. Since God created all things, and because God did not separate Himself from His creation, then we can perceive God in time, or we might conclude that God *is* time. Since God is infinite and ever-present, then time must also be infinite and ever-present. With God, "one day is like a thousand years and a thousand years is like one day."

Let us take the Hebraic sense of time one step farther. For those who know biblical Hebrew, they understand that the language of the Hebrew Scriptures has essentially two aspects of time - complete and incomplete. However, with God something might be expressed as complete when the process of completion has not yet ended. Take, for example, the creation.

> By the seventh day God completed His work which He had done, and He rested on the seventh day from all His work which He had done. (Gen 2:2).

The completed sense of time is puzzling because we know there is still more to be done before God's creation is complete. What about the new heavens and the new earth?[15] Then there is mankind, which God created in His own image (Gen 1:27). Certainly there is more work to be done to fulfill the completed work of God toward His creation of the new earth, and mankind whom He has created in His own image. That is the Hebraic sense of time, which cannot be described as points on a line. Instead, the infinite nature of God is the very essence of time.

Since God *is* time, and time is *in* God, we might consider God's still incomplete perfection (expressed in Gen 2:2 as "rest") as a promise of future fulfillment. As I sometimes explain, if God says it will happen, then we can consider it done! We can live in the promise as a completed act. This is the Hebraic sense of time. We can bring the past perfection of the Garden of Eden into our lives today when we walk in the ways of God. We can bring the future perfection of the end of times into our lives today when we keep our eyes fixed on Yeshua.

---

[15] Is 65:17; 66:22; 2 Peter 3:13.

Let us look at another example. Righteousness is a condition that is completely free of sin, thus in perfect harmony with the Righteous God. At some time in the future God's creation of mankind will be completely righteous as Isaiah depicts in the following passage.

> Your sun will no longer set, nor will your moon wane; for you will have the LORD for an everlasting light, and the days of your mourning will be over.
>
> Then all your people *will be* righteous; they will possess the land forever, the branch of My planting, the work of My hands, that I may be glorified. (Is 60:20-21)

With the Greco-Roman sense of time we would stop here and imagine a future time with God. However, with the Hebraic sense of time we are only beginning to penetrate an understanding. We have just seen God's perfection in the beginning of time and again at the end of time. That concept of perfection applies to mankind as well as to the heavens and the earth. In the beginning God created mankind in His own image (Gen 1:27), so God sees His children as righteous at the time of creation. However, this initial righteousness is followed by a *process* of righteousness in our lives now, and followed again by what we have just read in Isaiah about something still future.

Christians are familiar with this concept of God's perception of righteousness in His children because of Paul's citation of Genesis 15:6.

> Then he [Abraham] believed in the LORD; and He [God] reckoned it to him [Abraham] as righteousness. (Gen 15:6)

Abraham was a Gentile, that is, he was not a Jew.[16] So, when a Gentile first believes in God's son Yeshua, God reckons that faith as righteousness just as He did to Abraham. Thus, God sees that person as righteous when he or she first believes in His son.

---

[16] The term "Jew" derives from Judah. But Jews as a distinct "people" originates biblically with the Exodus from Egypt.

The same principle applies to the children of Israel whom God sees as righteous. "Israel is My son, My firstborn," declares God in Exodus 4:22. Then in Deuteronomy we read,

> Do you thus repay the LORD, O foolish and unwise people? Is not he your Father who has bought you? He has who made you and established you [caused you to stand]? (Deut 32:6)

Thus, God is a Father to the children of Israel and they are His son.

Does God see His children Israel, as righteous when they first become His? The Jewish sages answered "Yes," pointing to the account of Abraham's circumcision. How, they asked, could God expect Abraham to "walk before Me and be perfect," that is, righteous (Gen 17:1), even before he was circumcised as a sign of God's covenant (Gen 17:10-11)?[17] This understanding of the initial righteousness of God's children makes perfect sense according to the Hebraic sense of time. All of God's children are righteous when they first belong to Him, and they will be made righteous at some time in the future.

However, what about now, the present time? Here we come to the most important aspect of the Hebraic sense of time for our study of the parables and for our lives today. Now we have righteousness in us (a gift from God when He made us His) so that we might *walk* in that righteousness. When do we walk in righteousness? We walk in righteousness when our hearts are focused on God. Unfortunately that does not happen all the time. So, perhaps we could say that a righteous walk is possible in part now because we have God's righteousness in us, although the completion of our walk of righteousness is still future.[18]

---

[17] Gen 17:1-14.

[18] The New Testament attributes the Holy Spirit as the guide to a righteous walk (John 14:26).

## Hebraic Sense of Time and the Kingdom of God

Now we turn to what is important in this study of the parables as haggadic midrash. Many of the parables begin, "The Kingdom of Heaven is like...." We remember that the Kingdom of Heaven (or the Kingdom of God) is a time when mankind will be in a righteous condition in peace and harmony with God. So, when is the Kingdom of Heaven according to the Hebraic sense of time? It existed in past linear time in the Garden of Eden. It will be completely complete at the end of time, which is still future. It was present in Yeshua when he was here on this earth (again, past time in a linear sense). However, in the Hebraic sense of time the Kingdom of God is also present *now*, at all times, in those who believe in God's son as we read in Romans.

> We have been buried with Him through baptism into death, so that as Christ was raised from the dead through the glory of the Father, so we too might walk in newness of life. (Rom 6:4)

When we walk in newness of life, we are walking in the Kingdom. Then we note that "the one who says he abides in Him ought himself to walk in the same manner as He walked" (1 John 2:6). Thus, it is possible to walk as Jesus Christ walked. When we do, we are walking in the Kingdom of God. We have brought the future into our present lives, and are living the past in more than memory.

Turning specifically to believers in Christ, we know that righteousness is in Christ, and Christ is in you who believe in him (Col 1:27). So, when you walk in the faith of Yeshua, you are walking in righteousness in the Kingdom of God. You have drawn near to Him. In fact, you are in His presence in righteousness. We might say that righteousness is available in part now, from time to time, whenever we walk in the faith of God's son.

We have now drawn two conclusions about the Hebraic sense of time. First, those who belong to God have righteousness in them because God is their Father and they are His sons. God has created them in His own image, which is righteous and holy. Second, God then calls them to walk in that righteousness. When they do, they are walking in the presence of God in His Kingdom. This understanding is essential to appropriate the powerful message of the parables. "The Kingdom of Heaven is like" instructs us how to walk in righteousness. When we do, we will be in God's presence in the His Kingdom. We must live our lives now in the eager expectation of complete and final righteousness that God will accomplish at some time in the future.

## Listening to the Text

Another key concept in our journey to penetrate a depth of meaning in the parables is the way people of the first century received the words of the Holy Writings. An interest has been growing in the academic community to "hear the parable as the original audience heard it."[19] This new awareness has been directed largely to the study of ancient sociological customs and to the linguistic patterns of Greek rhetoric.[20] The approach in this study, on the other hand, which identifies the connection to the Hebrew Scriptures that haggadic midrash employs, is a relatively new proposal. Nevertheless, much has been accomplished in academic circles to draw our attention to the oral nature of the transmission of text and its reception by the ancient audience, which reinforces the suggestion of the parables as haggadic midrash..

Today we typically read the Scriptures. However, in the ancient world we must remember that people did not have books. Instead they "heard" the Word of God. So, as we work to recreate first century methods of searching the Scriptures we must learn to "listen to the text." But let me forewarn you. You will not hear a simple exposition or narrative. Instead you will hear all kinds of pneumonic devices such as repetition, contrast, chiasm, and a word that may only be used once in Scripture.[21] You will begin to

---

[19] Amy-Jill Levine, "The Many Faces of the Good Samaritan-Most Wrong," *Biblical Archaeological Review* (January/February 2012): 24, 68.

[20] Rhetoric is the art of persuasive speaking or writing. The ancient Greeks promoted rules of rhetoric, and honored excellence in oral persuasion.

[21] "Pneumonic" refers to something the ear will hear. Chiasm is an ancient linguistic pattern that employs parallel lines to point to a chiastic center. A word only used once is called a *hapax legomena*.

hear these pneumonic devices as you train your ear to listen.

The biblical text is filled with nuances of meaning. English and Greek, on the other hand, tend to be more precise. In contrast to the well-defined nature of many other linguistic traditions of communication, I call Hebrew an artistic language. For example, Scripture frequently employs irony, which says one thing but really means another. Irony can take the form of sarcasm or ridicule. If received as meaningful instruction, irony can become wit or humor when we see ourselves in the irony. Irony was an acceptable method of dialogue and instruction in the ancient world.[22] In fact, irony is quite prevalent in the New Testament where Yeshua is often in heated dialogue with the Pharisees.

You may also find a play on words. For example, two words can mean the same thing, one word can have two meanings, or two words can sound the same but have different letters, hence different meanings. The biblical authors often "played" with words to convey a deeper sense of meaning.

Another artistic element, which is evident in the New Testament where we find the parables, is what Richard Hayes has called "echoes of Scripture."[23] These echoes are allusions to other parts of the Holy Writings. The ancient ear would have heard these allusions. For students of the New Testament today, that means we must be thoroughly absorbed in the Hebrew Scriptures just like the people of the first century who knew their Holy Writings by heart. We may not have memorized the Hebrew Scriptures, but we can still learn to hear the echoes.

Finally, in this brief discussion of listening to the text, we must acknowledge figures of speech, which also play with words and concepts by saying one thing on the surface but actually meaning something else. Examples include simile, metaphor,

---

[22] Sarcasm and ridicule is not acceptable in our modern world although it was in ancient Israel. For further information, see Edwin M. Goode, *Irony in the Old Testament* (London: SPCK, 1965).

[23] Richard Hayes, *Echoes of Scripture in the Letters of Paul* (New Haven: Yale), 1993.

hyperbole, and hypocatastasis.[24] Figures of speech were common in ancient Greek rhetoric and are also prevalent in the biblical text.

As we continue to discuss each parable, I will draw your attention to all these examples of listening to the text, and will explain their meaning as we proceed through the parables.

## I began with the Parable of the Prodigal Son

My understanding of the parables as haggadic midrash followed a slowly emerging process of discovery. I began by questioning certain traditional Christian interpretations of New Testament passages that seemed confusing or illogical. I was drawn in particular to verses that offered several possible interpretations. I was curious. For example, what did Paul mean by speaking allegorically and then contradicting the Hebrew Scriptures?[25] Is the law really a curse?[26] How will all Israel be saved?[27] What does the New Testament *really* tell us about divorce...and the law...and the power of the Holy Spirit....and so many other puzzling aspects of Christian interpretation?[28]

I slowly began to penetrate these questions as I pored over everything I could find about ancient methods of midrash. I started by discovering legal midrash (*halachah*) in Paul's letter to the

---

[24] A simile compares one thing to another using "like" or "as." A metaphor is an implied comparison between two things that are literally dissimilar but nevertheless have a subtle relationship. Hyperbole is extreme exaggeration. Hypocastasis is a metaphor by implication.

[25] Galatians 4:21-31.

[26] Galatians 3:13.

[27] Romans 12:26.

[28] I have concluded that the "divorce passage" in Matthew 19:3-11 is a carefully crafted construction of halachic midrash that employs three citations and one allusion from the Hebrew Scriptures. I presented a paper on this topic to the Society of Biblical Literature in 2006. You can find an in-depth analysis of this passage in a DVD presentation in the BibleInteract online store (www.bibleinteract.tv/store).

Galatians.[29] Then I began to explore the rich artistry of Paul's
language in the preceding passage in Galatians, which I recognized
as employing similar linguistic artistry to what I had discovered
when reading the Hebrew Scriptures in the original language.
Finally, I added parables to this process of discovery.

I was preparing to teach on the Parable of the Prodigal
Son, and by this time I was immersed in recovering likely first
century methods of searching the Scriptures. So, I was "listening
to the text" and I "heard" repetition and contrast. I "felt" a strong
emotional response, and I "saw" the horror of the pig sty, the
father's agony, and the fury of the firstborn son. I also began to
recognize an echo from the Hebrew Scriptures - the inheritance of
the birthright by the children of Israel, God's firstborn son, and
the loss of that special inheritance for unworthy behavior. After
all, in the context of the passage Yeshua was directing his parable
to Pharisees and scribes, who were righteous in their own eyes.
Were they worthy of this special inheritance?

My curiosity was certainly peaked at this point. Could the
parable of the prodigal son be some kind of haggadic midrash, I
wondered? If so, it would have to be an expansion and
commentary on a specific verse or passage in the Hebrew
Scriptures. So, I began to look for a connection to the Tanach,
which I suspected I would find in the Torah since I knew that the
Jewish sages considered the Torah the central core of the Hebrew
Scriptures.

I was aided in my search by repetition in the New
Testament parable as heart-breaking words began to ring in my
ears. When the prodigal son "came to his senses," he cried out,
"Father, I have sinned against heaven and in your sight; I am no
longer worthy to be called your son" (Luke 15:18-19). When the
father saw his returning son, he "felt compassion and ran and
embraced him and kissed him." I could see the son falling to his
knees in humble agony for his grievous sins. Then, in this
humbled position, the son repeated, "Father, I have sinned against
heaven and in your sight; I am no longer worthy to be called your
son."

---

[29] Galatians 3:6-13.

I recognized an echo in the Hebrew Scriptures through the repetition, "I am not worthy," which are the same words that Jacob cried out to God. Just like the prodigal son, Jacob had also sinned against his father, Isaac, by stealing the blessing of his brother, Esau, the firstborn son. Jacob had also left his father and gone to a foreign land in exile. He too returned with a heavy heart, expecting to face the fury of his brother Esau. However, Jacob turned to God with these words. "I am unworthy of all the lovingkindness and of all the faithfulness which you have shown to Your servant." Only after this act of submission did Jacob petition God, "Deliver me, I pray, from the hand of my brother" (Gen 32:10-11).

Since this first discovery of the Parable of the Prodigal Son as haggadic midrash, where the parable expands and comments on an account from the Hebrew Scriptures, I have been methodically proceeding through all the New Testament parables. It is not always easy, and it often takes considerable time, because my knowledge of the Hebrew Scriptures is not through memorization that internalizes the text. However, in every case I have found a connection to the Hebrew Scriptures. After thoroughly reviewing the context of the connecting passage from the Hebrew text, I return to the New Testament parable with anticipation and excitement that invariably leads to a deeper understanding, a more intimate relationship with God, and a profound impact on my life.

## Seven Steps to Uncovering Mysteries in the Parables

Scripture tells us that the simple story of the parables is for all of God's children. Yet, only those with a heart to go deeper will uncover the hidden mysteries.

> To you it has been granted to know the mysteries of the kingdom of heaven [Yeshua was talking to his disciples], but to them [pointing to the crowd of people who had come to listen to him teach] it has not been granted (Mat 13:11)

I truly believe that a hungry heart is the one and only requirement for us to uncover a hidden depth of meaning in the parables. Yet, it took me literally years of searching and working before I came to the place where I am today. So, I have developed a seven-step program for others to follow the same path that has led to my discoveries. To make it even easier, these seven steps fall logically into one cluster of three, and then a second cluster of three. The seventh and last step stands alone and is, therefore, the most important. As all haggadic midrash is designed to help us appropriate biblical principles in our daily lives, so I draw your attention to step #7, which is practical application.

> STORY
>> 1. Context of the setting
>> 2. Main characters in the setting
>> 3. Strange or puzzling
> CLUES
>> 4. Hebraic artistry of language
>> 5. Connection to the Hebrew Scriptures
>> 6. The ending
> HOW DO WE APPLY THIS MESSAGE
>> 7. Practical application in our lives today

The setting of the Parable of the Prodigal Son (#1 and 2) is not the parable itself but the context in which Yeshua presents the parable to those who are listening. We might ask, what has prompted Yeshua to speak this parable? For example, was he responding to the Pharisees? If so, what tradition or teaching of the Pharisees was he attempting to dispute?

As we begin to read the parable as an artistic narrative, another important element is to ask, "What in the parable is strange or puzzling" (#3)? The first century listeners would have heard any anomaly, that is, anything that did not fit what would have been expected. In his study of Hasidic parable traditions, Wiseman found frequent emphatic shifts to new and unexpected directions.[30] We will find the same thing in the New Testament parables. This strange or puzzling element will become a clue that can lead to deeper meaning.

---

[30] Aryeh Wineman, "Wedding-Feasts, Exiled Princes, and Hasidic Parable-Traditions," *Hebrew Studies* 40 (1999): 194.

So, we turn next to "clues." First we must listen to the text for all the artistry of language. Repetition, contrast, figures of speech, irony, and play on words are some of these clues (#4).

The connection to the Hebrew Scriptures (#5) is hard for a beginner to find. So, with each parable I will share with you the connection that I have found from searching the Hebrew Scriptures. However, the last step in Clues, the ending (#6), is something that you can do. There are three possible endings. A tragic ending is one that could have been prevented, but a bad decision led to the tragedy. A happy ending needs no explanation. However, the third ending is the most common. I call it open-ended. That is, we don't know how the story ends so we put ourselves into the parable and ask, what decision would I make in this situation?

Finally, we come to the most important step, appropriating the message in our own lives (#7). Don't pass over this one too quickly, but ponder the depth of its meaning. Remember, if you are a disciple and a follower of Yeshua with a heart that truly desires to grow closer to him, then the mystery of the parable will be opened to you. But first you must look deeply into yourself and consider how you might change in order to better serve your Lord and to grow closer to your God. In this way you will be walking in the Kingdom of God.

# Part One

## Parables about Inheritance of the Birthright

Chapter One

# Parable of the Sower and the Seed

Parables as haggadic midrash promote a depth of understanding from the Hebrew Scriptures that encourage us to walk in the ways of the Kingdom of God. As an introduction to the parables as haggadic midrash, we will begin with the parable of the sower and the seed. Start by reading the parable in Matthew 13:1-9.[31] For now we will not consider the "explanation" that follows, so simply "listen" to the parable in vv. 1-9 as the people of the first century would have "heard" the words of Yeshua.

Now consider a distinguishing element of this particular parable that follows. Yeshua had been speaking from a boat, and "great multitudes" were gathered on the beach to hear him. Later the disciples came to him and asked, "Why do you speak to them [referring to the great multitudes] in parables?" Of course the disciples had just been listening to these same parables as the crowd, so what we have is ironic humor. The disciples were really asking, "Why do you speak in parables to us, who are disciples, just like you are speaking to the common people in the crowd?" That is, "Why are you treating us like everyone else?"

Eventually Yeshua will give his disciples a simple explanation, which is part of the sarcastic irony because the details are so simple and do not penetrate a depth of meaning. The seed is simply "the word of the kingdom," and there are four ways to receive this instruction (Mat 13:18-23). However, consider what is sandwiched between the parable in vv. 1-9 and the explanation of the parable found in vv. 18-23. Yeshua cites Isaiah 6:9-10 with extensive commentary. We can perceive this construction visually.

1. Parable (vv. 3-9)
2. Citation and commentary (vv. 10-17)
3. Simple explanation of the parable (vv. 18-23)

---

[31] The parable of the sower and the seed also appears in Mark 4:3-9 and Luke 8:5-8. I have selected to work on this parable in Matthew because of its more extensive treatment there.

The citation and commentary in the middle delivers the meat of what Yeshua is trying to convey. Many will hear but not understand, and will see but not perceive, which leads us to ponder the reverse. Only some will hear and understand, and only some will see and perceive. Will those who understand be all the disciples of Yeshua? Or perhaps only some of the disciples will perceive the deeper meaning. Most important, will *we* understand and perceive?

I suggest that these words by Yeshua about understanding and perceiving do not refer to believing unto salvation, or unbelief leading to eternal condemnation, nor do they apply to "the crowd" as distinct and separate from the privileged disciples. Instead, Yeshua is telling all of us that the words he is speaking about the Kingdom of God are as deep and rich and infinite as God. Those who have ears to understand, eyes to perceive, and a heart that hungers for God will penetrate this depth of meaning.[32] That thought makes our efforts to uncover the mystery of the parable that much more intriguing and compelling.

My suggestion, that Yeshua is treating the disciples no differently than all those who have come to hear him speak, helps explain the startling words of Yeshua when he answered their question, "Why do you speak to them in parables?" Yeshua responded, "To you it has been granted to know the mysteries of the kingdom of heaven, but to them it has not been granted" (Mat 13:11). This language is a form of exhortation. "You can do it; you are my followers (disciples), so you have eyes to see and ears to perceive if that is what you want."

## Mysteries in Scripture

We need to pause and learn more about "mysteries" in Scripture. You will remember that people in ancient Israel believed that God had placed, in the infinite depth of His Word, everything that mankind would ever need to know. The plain or simple meaning (called the *p'shat* in Hebrew) is for all to see. However, there is also

---

[32] The heart is a metaphor for the innermost part of a person. For example, the metaphor "thoughts of the heart" captures this understanding (Gen 6:5).

a depth of meaning as infinite as God, which the people called "mysteries." There were methods of midrash to uncover these mysteries, and the parables are a form of haggadic midrash.

The Hebrew word "mystery" (רז, *raz*) appears only in the Book of Daniel.[33] However, Job uses a different word to convey the same concept, which has been translated into English with the word "mystery." "God reveals mysteries from the darkness, and brings the deep darkness into light" (Job 12:22). There is significant use of the word *raz* in the Second Temple Literature,[34] so it appears that the concept of mysteries in Scripture was a familiar feature at the time Yeshua was speaking the parables.

The Greek word that has been translated "mystery" is μυστήριον (*musterion*), which appears frequently in the New Testament. Paul talks repeatedly about uncovering these mysteries.[35] The biggest mystery of all was Yeshua the Messiah and, in particular, "Christ in you, the hope of glory" (Col 1:27). However, Paul and the other NT authors uncovered other mysteries as well."[36]

So, Yeshua told his disciples, "To you it has been granted to know the mysteries of the Kingdom of Heaven." What follows has often troubled Christian commentators because it excludes a large number of God's people from understanding these mysteries. Citing Isaiah Yeshua declares, "You will keep on hearing, but you will not understand; and you will keep on seeing, but will not perceive" (Is 6:9-10). David Juel observes, regarding this citation, that "the most difficult verses are the ones omitted in the lectionary," and comments, "the parable of the sower is

---

[33] Dan 2:18, 19, 27, 28, 29, 30, 47; 4:9.

[34] We have a significant number of extra-biblical texts dating from approximately 200 B.C to the destruction of the temple in 70 A.D. These writings are collectively called the Second Temple literature. One example is the Dead Sea Scrolls,

[35] Rom 11:25, 16:25; 1 Co 2:7; 4:1; 13:2; 14:2; 15:51.

[36] Eph 1:9; 3:3,4,9; 5:32; 6:19; Col 1:26, 27; 2:2; 4:3; 2 Th 2:7; 1 Tim 3:9,16; Rev 1:20; 10:7; 17:5,7.

problematic."[37] However, we learn that understanding the mysteries is available to the disciples of Yeshua, which includes all who have "ears to understand and eyes to perceive."

We will use the parable of the sower and the seed as a model paradigm to learn the method of instruction through haggadic midrash, which Yeshua is using in this and the other parables. It will take work on our part, which is characteristic of ancient Hebraic instruction. However, the result will be a deep and rich understanding that will sometimes be breathtaking and will always guide us in a path to God and the Kingdom to which He is leading us.

## Getting Started

Begin by observing the three parts of the parable. Now read once more the parable itself in Matthew 13:1-9. The sower is Yeshua, and the seed represents God's people.[38] Then continue reading Yeshua's commentary to his disciples in vv. 10-17, which is anything but straightforward. In fact, these verses are rich with a depth of meaning because of the exquisite connection to the Hebrew Scriptures. Following the parable and the citation with commentary is what many Bible versions have labeled an "explanation." However, this "explanation" in vv. 18-23 is quite simple, and does not seem compatible with the suggestion of uncovering mysteries. However, if you are curious you will find that there is an interesting connection to the Hebrew Scriptures that will lead you to a much deeper meaning.

---

[37] Donald H. Juel, "Encountering the Sower: Mark 4:1-20," *Interpretation* (July 2002): 272-83.

[38] Heil demonstrates, in the parallel account of the sower and the seed in Mark 4:3-20, that the sower is Yeshua. He argues that the sower *went out* to sow, an expression that Mark uses to introduce Yeshua's ministry work. See, for example, Mark 1:35, 38; 2:13. John Paul Heil, "Reader-Response and the Narrative Context of the Parables about Growing Seed in Mark 4:1-34, *Catholic Biblical Quarterly*, 54 (1992): 271-86. The seed representing the people of God is a common metaphor in the Hebrew Scriptures. See, for example, Is 5:1-7.

Are you surprised that there is a deeper meaning in the citation and commentary beyond what Yeshua "explained" to his disciples in the following verses? You shouldn't be. The Hebraic way of teaching does not present the meaning (in this case, the complete depth of meaning) but offers enough clues so those with a heart to hear, that is, the disciples or followers of Yeshua, will be able to search and uncover the mysteries.

## Parable of the Sower and the Seed

Let us turn now to the parable in Matthew 13:1-9 and put aside for a moment any explanation that follows. The first thing we see is repetition. "The sower went out to sow; and as he sowed..." Certainly this gives us a rhythm that is characteristic of the biblical language. However, we also ask, "Is this repetition a clue? Could it be alluding to a concept of sowing in the Hebrew Scriptures?" After all, we are trying to "hear" the ancient text the way the people of the first century would have heard it.

There is another repetition that is even more glaring. The conclusion of the parable states, "Others fell on the good soil, and yielded a crop, some a hundredfold, some sixty, and some thirty. He who has ears, let him hear" (Mat 13:8-9; repeated in Mat 13:23). Let us begin with the repetition of sowing.

The three-letter verbal root for sowing in Hebrew is זרע (zarah) from which various linguistic forms can be constructed including a verb (to sow) and a noun (what is sown, which is seed). The noun form is most common in Scripture, referring to seed of a woman that leads to offspring or descendants. For example, God told Abraham, "All the land that you see I will give to you and your offspring [seed] forever" (Gen 13:15). "Seed" or "offspring" is the noun form of זרע, to sow seed.

The first time זרע is used in its verbal construct is in Genesis 26:12. "Now Isaac sowed in that land and reaped in the same year a hundredfold. And the Lord blessed him." Stop! Do you hear something that echoes the Parable of the Sower? If not, return to the parable and "listen."

As you continue considering the parable in Matthew 13:1-9 you will see there are four categories of those who belong to God. Nevertheless, they live their lives in different ways. Before continuing, consider these four categories, which is an easy but essential exercise.

As you follow the four categories, you will find the heart of the parable in the second repetition. Those whose seed fell on good soil "yielded a crop, some a hundredfold, some sixty, and some thirty. He who has ears, let him hear" (Mat 13:8-9; repeated in Mat 13:23). This repetition is a clue that leads us to the Hebrew Scriptures. We have seen in Genesis 26:12 that Isaac sowed and reaped a hundredfold. In the parable, those who sowed on good soil yielded a crop (which is reaping a crop that the seed produces) that was a hundredfold. This startling connection to the Hebrew Scriptures is followed by Yeshua announcing, "He who has ears, let him hear," which is going to become significant in our understanding of the parable because, before Yeshua delivered the "explanation" to his disciples he cited a passage from Isaiah about "deaf ears" and "failing to hear." With this repetition of "deaf ears" and "failing to hear," Yeshua *wants* his disciples (and we are disciples if we have a heart to hear) to go deeper than the understanding of the crowd. Are we going to be part of the crowd, or are we going to penetrate the depth of what Yeshua is trying to tell us?

## More Connections to the Hebrew Scriptures

We have seen the connection of reaping a hundredfold in Genesis 26:12 where Isaac sowed an abundance described as a hundredfold. However, the parable continues. Those whose seed fell on the good soil "yielded a crop, some a hundredfold, some sixty, and some thirty" (Mat 13:8). So we ask, "Could there be a connection to the Hebrew Scriptures for sixty and thirty as well?" Before returning to the Hebrew Scriptures, what do *you* think, and how can *you* search the Scriptures?

A concordance will tell you where the numbers sixty and thirty appear in Scripture. I suggest you do your own work first before reading what I have discovered. You will need to scan through the various verses in a concordance that list where the Hebrew words sixty and thirty appear. Then select the two verses with שׁשׁים שׁנה and שׁלשׁים שׁנה that seem to relate to the story in the parable.

**Following the Seven Steps**

You should now be quite proficient in the first two steps of analyzing the story, the context of the setting in which Yeshua tells the parable and the characters or people in that setting. We have already seen the context. Yeshua delivered the parable from a boat to a multitude on the beach. Then his disciples took him aside and asked him what the parable meant. So, we have no Pharisees or scribes in this setting. Instead we have two groups of people, the crowd and the disciples.

The larger group came to hear Yeshua teach. They would likely have been Jews for whom the Hebrew Scriptures were part of their tradition. They apparently recognized Yeshua as a master who could unfold for them the deeper meaning of the Holy Writings. However, in the citation that follows this parable, Yeshua declares that Isaiah's prophecy was then occurring. "You will keep on hearing, but will not understand; and you will keep on seeing, but will not perceive." He is referring to the crowd on the beach because these people cannot perceive the mysterious depth of what he is teaching. Instead, they can only hear the plain or simple meaning.

The second group, on the other hand, was composed of a small number of disciples. Throughout much of Yeshua's ministry we tend to assume he had only twelve disciples. However, for all the numerous times that disciples are mentioned in the gospels, seldom does it refer to the inner circle of twelve, so there were likely other disciples as well. This is not unusual because it was expected in ancient Israel that skilled teachers, knowledgeable in the Law, would pass on their understanding to those who chose to follow the master, and these followers were called disciples. For example, John the Baptist had disciples (Mat 9:14; Luke 5:33). Furthermore, in Acts, after the death and extraordinary resurrection of Christ, we read that disciples were increasing in number.

The point I wish to make is this. You are a disciple if you are a follower of Christ, you desire to learn from him, and your heart yearns to grow closer to God the Father through His Son. You should be identifying with the second smaller group of disciples who came to Yeshua because they wanted to know the deeper meaning of the parable.

So, given the four categories of those who sowed seed, the first three are characteristic of the ones in the crowd who were not disciples or committed followers of Yeshua. Nevertheless, if you are a follower or disciple of Jesus, you are sowing seed on good soil. In fact, some of you are yielding a crop that is bearing a hundredfold, others sixty, and still others thirty. However, we cannot begin to draw conclusions about this seed on good soil without first examining the verses in the Hebrew Scriptures to which a hundredfold, sixty and thirty are pointing.

We have already identified Genesis 26:12 that talks about Isaac sowing and reaping a hundredfold. However, you still need to find verses about sixty and thirty. Have you used a concordance to find the two connecting verses about bearing seed sixty and thirtyfold? Have you read all three connecting verses (a hundredfold, sixty and thirty) in their context in the Hebrew Scriptures? (By context I mean the surrounding verses). If so, you are ready to consider what I have discovered.

## The Importance of Context

We will work together now on the verse about Isaac reaping an abundance of crops, described as a hundredfold, in order to follow an important principle. We must read our verse, Genesis 26:12, in its context. I suggest that you stop now and follow this principle of reading Genesis 26:12 in its context before continuing. Then ponder the following questions.

1.  What verses comprise the context of Genesis 26:12?
2.  Why did Isaac go to Gerar, to Abimelech king of the Philistines? How does this action by Isaac form a contrast to the abundance of his later reaping a hundredfold? Why is this contrast important to the inner sense of the story in Genesis?
3.  As you read through this account, what did Isaac do? That is, what were his actions that led to God's blessing him?
4.  What is the symbolism of three words that relate agricultural activities to godly ways of living - seed, sowing, reaping?

5. Why did Isaac tell Abimelech that Rebekah was his sister? What are several possible scenarios of what *might* have happened as a result of this seemingly deceitful act? What *actually* happened? How do you explain the outcome?
6. Why did God bless Isaac with such an extraordinary abundance of crops?
7. "A hundredfold" is likely an exaggeration for the purpose of emphasis, a linguistic device in the ancient world called hyperbole. What is hyperbole, and how is it functioning in this verse?

The general concept in this passage about Isaac bearing a hundredfold is that Isaac responded to a famine, which represents the trials and tribulations of the world, by obeying God who then blessed him with abundance. Relate this principal of responding to tribulation by obeying God to the second group in the parable, the disciples.

8. Now consider how the account of Isaac in Gerar helps us understand how to live as disciples of Yeshua.
9. What will be at least one of our rewards?

## Continuing to Search the Hebrew Scriptures

We turn now to the number sixty. As I searched in a concordance I followed the principle that would have been characteristic of first century thinking, that all major concepts in the Hebrew Scriptures appear first in the Torah and are therefore significant. The number sixty appears in only four passages in the Torah: Genesis 25:26; Leviticus 27:3,7; Numbers 7:88; Deuteronomy 3:4. I selected Genesis 25:26 as the most likely verse to which the parable is referring, which happens to be its first occurrence. There we learn that when Rebekah bore twin sons to Isaac (Esau and Jacob), "Isaac was sixty years old when she gave birth to them." Scripture does not identify the age of a person unless there is some significance. Furthermore, numbers in Scripture have symbolic meaning.

The classic work for explaining the symbolism of numbers is *Numbers in Scripture* by E. W. Bullinger. Published originally in

1898 it is now in the public domain, so you can find this book in its entirety online. Sixty is six multiplied ten times for emphasis, so six is the number we need to scrutinize.

Bullinger explains that the number six is generally related to the world. However, he also points out something I think is relevant to our parable. Explains Bullinger, "*Man* was created on the *sixth* day... Moreover, *six* days were appointed to him for his labour; while *one* day is associated in sovereignty with the Lord God, as His rest. *Six*, therefore, is the number of *labour* also, of man's labour as apart and distinct from God's rest [italics are Bullinger's]." Thus, a follower of the Lord Yeshua is called to be a servant to work for the Master, and labor (the work of service) is an important requirement for disciples. The parable is continuing to instruct us how to become disciples of the Lord Yeshua, so committed followers of Yeshua are expected to work for him. He is their Lord. This, I suggest, is the significance of bearing sixtyfold in the parable.

We turn now to the number thirty. I believe the verse with the strongest evidence for a connection to our parable is Genesis 41:46. "Joseph was thirty years old when he entered the service of Pharaoh, king of Egypt." The key concept again seems to be service. We have just learned that a disciple serves his master, so who was Joseph serving? Our answer lies in the symbolism of Joseph as a "type" of Christ, and the Pharaoh as the authority over Joseph, thus representing God the Father. So Joseph, who is a type of Christ, serves the Pharaoh, who symbolizes God the Father. This powerful imagery extends to disciples who serve their Lord and Master, Yeshua the Messiah, who then leads them to the higher authority of God the Father. So, this verse about Joseph seems to be an echo for our parable. Joseph was thirty years old when he entered the service of the Pharaoh. By the way, thirty in the ancient world was also considered to be the age of maturity.

So, our parable concludes that those whose seed falls on good soil "yield a crop, some a hundredfold, some sixty, and some thirty." Yeshua is encouraging us to be dedicated followers who labor in the service of our Master to bear fruit for God.

## Disciples of the Lord Yeshua

Following the parable in Matthew 13:1-9, we see two distinct sections. First is the citation from Isaiah 6:9-10 with accompanying commentary (Mat 13:10-17). We remember that we must compare the citation in the New Testament with what it cites in the Hebrew Scriptures. If there seems to be a significant difference, it may be for the purpose of conveying a deeper meaning. However, in this case, the citation spoken by Yeshua seems to have no significant difference when compared to the passage in Isaiah. If this is so, then the purpose of the citation is a "prooftext." That is, something prophesied in the Hebrew Scriptures was taking place in the time of Yeshua. In this case, many of God's people were unable to know the mysteries of the kingdom of heaven because they were not committed followers of the Master. Nevertheless there were some who were obedient in the same way that Isaac was obedient. They were working for God as the number sixty represents. They were serving in the service of God as Joseph was serving his master the Pharaoh.

God wants these disciples to uncover the mysteries of the kingdom of God. So, Yeshua concludes this citation of Isaiah with these encouraging words. "Blessed are your eyes because they see; and your ears because they hear. For truly I say to you that many prophets and righteous men desired to see what you see, and did not see *it;* and to hear what you hear, and did not hear *it.*" What were the disciples seeing and hearing? They were seeing and hearing the mysteries of the kingdom of heaven. What can you see and hear if you are a disciple or follower of your Lord Yeshua? You can also see the mysteries of the kingdom of heaven.

Yet, there is a second distinct section that follows the parable, which we find in Matthew 13:18-23. The title for this section in the New American Standard version declares, "The Sower Explained." However, the deeper meaning of the parable goes beyond what we read in Matthew 13:18-23. The enticing clue to the deeper meaning is the repetition of the powerful words about yielding a hundredfold, sixty and thirty in the concluding verse Matthew 13:23. "The one whose seed was sown on the good soil, this is the man who hears the word and understands it; who indeed bears fruit, and brings forth, some a hundredfold, some sixty, and some thirty" (Mat 13:23). If you compare this verse 23 with what it repeats in verses 8-9, you will see that something has been added. The ancient ear would have heard this expansion.

1.  Compare Matthew 13:8-9 and 13:23. What has been added?
2.  What is the difference between "hearing" the Word of God and hearing it with your heart?
3.  What are the requirements for you to "understand" the Word of God?
4.  What is the relationship between hearing and understanding?

There is also an expansion of the three categories that relate to the crowd on the beach, those who hear but do not understand and see but do not perceive. These people who came to hear Yeshua teach were not disciples. They were not obeying God and laboring in His service. They were not bearing fruit for God. Therefore, they were not capable of comprehending the mysteries of the kingdom of heaven as the disciples can do from the instruction of their master Yeshua.

## Mystery #1 in the Kingdom of God

You are a disciple of the Lord Yeshua *if* you obey and submit to your Master, and *if* you labor in order to bear fruit for God. As a disciple or follower of your Lord, you are entitled to know the mysteries of the kingdom of heaven. All of the parables lead you to these mysteries and to a depth of understanding that God has made available to those who serve Him.

The purpose of this book is to give you the skills you will need to penetrate these mysteries. Your success will require, first and foremost, a heart that hungers to grow closer to God. Second, you will need to work diligently by using the skills you will learn in this book.

Chapter Two

# Parable of the Prodigal Son

As you proceed through this and subsequent chapters, I will continue to follow a method of instruction that is compatible with the Hebraic way of approaching Scripture in the first century. I will combine my own commentary and explanation with periodic questions that I will ask you to consider carefully before you proceed to read my remarks. Sometimes I will offer my own understanding of the answer, but other times I will remain silent. In this way you will learn to ask your own questions in order to penetrate the depth of Scripture without my help.

This well-known parable of the prodigal son is found only in Luke 15:1-33. Start by reading the parable aloud and practice listening to the text. You can then respond to provocative questions that will start you on a journey that will penetrate a depth of meaning.

## Context

In our seven steps of scrutinizing the parable, we start with the context of the parable, which begins in Luke 15:1. Before you continue reading in this chapter, carefully answer the questions below.

1. How do you find the context of a passage in Scripture? Why is Luke 15:1 the beginning of the context of the Parable of the Prodigal Son?

2. List from memory the three steps under "Story."

3. What is the setting in which Yeshua spoke this parable?

4. Who are the main characters, not in the parable but in the setting? You will find them in Luke 15:1-2.

5. In Luke 15:3 it says that Yeshua told "them" the parable. In the context, to whom was Yeshua referring?

6. Now it is time to look for something strange and puzzling. Try to do this first before reading the commentary below.

As you look for something strange or puzzling, begin by re-reading the entire parable. How was the father's response to his son's request in Luke 15:12 strange and puzzling?

## The Birthright of Inheritance

There are two sons in this parable. The oldest son does not enter the story until Luke 15:25. However, the traditional inheritance of the oldest son is crucial to an understanding of the parable.

The oldest son was entitled to a special inheritance known as the birthright. All Israel has been born to this birthright, for in Exodus 4:22 God instructs Moses to tell the Pharaoh, "Israel is My son, My firstborn," referring to all the children of Israel. Deuteronomy 21:17 explains not only that the son born first was entitled to this special inheritance but also that the birthright included a double portion of his father's land and possessions. This special inheritance gave the firstborn son four additional benefits, which included a special blessing,[39] the office of high priest of his clan or tribe, a position of authority and leadership, and procreative vigor.[40]

These characteristics of the birthright are associated with responsibilities of leadership. Thus, the purpose of the birthright, which was bestowed on the firstborn son, was to create leaders of God's people who would submit to God in obedience, lead God's people in righteous ways, and ultimately command the army that

---

[39] Esau was born to the birthright but lost his special blessing (Gen 27:30-46).

[40] Gevirtz has conducted an interesting study of Reuben's blessings in Gen 49:3-4. He concludes, based on a semantic analysis, that "the beginning of my strength" refers to procreative power. Stanley Gevirtz, "The Reprimand of Reuben (Gen 49:3," *Journal of Near Eastern Studies*, 30 (April 1971): 09.

would defeat God's enemy. All the children of Israel have been born to this birthright. They are God's chosen people.[41]

Nevertheless, one born to the birthright could lose this special inheritance for unworthy behavior. Take, for example, Reuben, the firstborn son of Jacob. 1 Chronicles 5:1 tells us why he lost his birthright and who then received it.[42] From another perspective the firstborn had to demonstrate his worthiness and ability to lead in order to claim the inheritance to which he had been born.

Let us return now to the parable. The younger son asked for his inheritance and the father "divided his wealth between the sons." This is certainly strange and puzzling because the inheritance would never have been given to the sons before the death of the father. Furthermore, the division would not have been equal. The oldest son who was born to the birthright would have received a double portion, and the younger son a single portion.[43]

The younger son "spent everything," so none of his inheritance remained. Yet, after the younger son returned to his father in humility and repentance, the imagery of the parable suggests that the father bestowed the inheritance of the birthright on the younger son. That is, the father "brought out the best robe and put it on him [apparently a robe of royal color], and put a ring on his finger." The signet ring had the seal of the father embedded in it. When dipped in molten wax and used to seal a document, it

---

[41] "The LORD your God has chosen you to be a people for His own possession out of all the peoples who on the face of the earth" (Deut 7:6; 14:2). The Hebrew word translated "chosen" is the verbal root בחר from which the noun "birthright" is derived.

[42] Reuben "defiled his father's bed, his birthright was given to the sons of Joseph the son of Israel; so that he is not enrolled in the genealogy according to the birthright" (1Ch 5:1-2).

[43] We see this double portion of inheritance in Deut 21:17. There is also ample evidence from other Near Eastern documents that this practice of a double portion for the firstborn son was widespread in the ancient world. See Eryl W. Davies, "The Inheritance of the first-born in Israel and the Ancient Near East," *Journal of Semitic Studies* 38:2 (1993): 175-91.

carried the same authority as that of the father or king (or in the case of Joseph, the pharaoh; see Genesis 41:42).

Since the father had declared the younger son to be worthy of the birthright, the younger son was now entitled to the inheritance that the birthright bestowed. However, we perceive a problem. The younger son had already wasted his own single portion that was now gone. The story then implies that the double portion of the older son was divided equally between the two sons so each received a single portion. This is a familiar concept in Scripture since Joseph, who received a double portion as the one with the birthright, gave half of his inheritance to his firstborn son Manasseh, who did *not* inherit the birthright, and the other half to his son Ephraim who did. The two tribes that emerged from Joseph's two sons, the tribes of Manasseh and Ephraim, both inherited land in the Promised Land.

In the context of the parable, we see that Yeshua was directing ironic sarcasm (even to the extent of ridicule) against the Pharisees and scribes who were entitled to the birthright because, as children of Israel, they were God's firstborn son. They apparently thought they had demonstrated worthy behavior by knowing the Law. Yet, they were acting inappropriately as leaders of God's people because of their pride and arrogance. However, we remember that God is the One who determines worthy behavior, so carefully consider the following questions before continuing in this chapter.

1.  How did the younger son in the parable demonstrate worthy behavior?

2.  How does the context of the sinners and tax-gatherers relate to the younger son in the parable?

3.  Why did the Pharisees and scribes perceive the sinners and tax-gatherers as unworthy to inherit the birthright?

Note: tax-gatherers were typically Jews employed by the Romans to collect taxes. They were required to deliver to the Roman government a certain amount. Anything over that amount was theirs to keep as payment for their services. The amount of the surplus was not regulated carefully by the government so oppressive excesses were common.

4. In the context of the first century in general, and the setting of the parable in particular, why are the Pharisees and scribes unworthy to inherit the birthright?

## Asking Questions

The western tradition (direct, analytical and immediate) tends to view those credentials as elevated in the eyes of the world. The ones whom the world perceives today as leaders have attained a higher position of authority than those over whom they teach or preach. Truth and correct understanding appears to reside in the teacher or preacher, who stands above the audience (often in a literal way). These perceived leaders in our western tradition teach others their version of truth and correct interpretation.

The first century Hebraic way, on the other hand, is quite different (indirect, artistic and slowly emerging). We remember that everyone can listen to the simple story of the parable, but only those with a heart to submit and obey will penetrate the mysteries that lie behind the plain and simple meaning.

So, in the Hebraic tradition the master (in this case Yeshua) would not explain the mysteries. By contrast, the western teacher delivers truths while students take notes and demonstrate understanding in a final exam. However, the Hebraic tradition stimulates curiosity that leads disciples (followers of the master) to ask questions. As they ponder answers, they are penetrating a deeper meaning. If the followers of the master ask *him* a question, he will likely resist a direct response, but will compose his answer in a way that stimulates further curiosity and more penetrating questions. So, how does the disciple demonstrate an understanding of the master's teaching? Not with words, but with godly behavior. Each day he becomes more and more like his master.

This Hebraic tradition of teaching is why I periodically list questions for you to consider. If you are passing quickly over these questions, then you are still in the Greco-Roman western mode of deferring to the knowledge of the teacher. You need to respond to the questions in the manner of the first century disciples.

**Clues**

We are ready to examine the clues. Here it is essential that you struggle with the questions. In the first century the disciples were paired in twos so they could direct questions to each other, and then ponder answers through dialogue and discussion.[44]

Therefore, I encourage you to find a study partner with whom you can study and dialogue.

1. Who would be your best study partner? Why?

2. Reread the Parable of the Prodigal Son and make a list of all repetitions and contrasts. How does each one act as a clue?

3. We have seen the imagery of the robe and the signet ring, and have realized that the imagery is symbolic. An image gives us a vivid visual picture whereas a symbol represents something else. Yet images and symbols seem to be related in this parable. What other significant imagery do you see in the parable? Is the distant country symbolic? How about the pig sty? What other images and symbols do you see? What does each image and symbol signify?

Perhaps the most important clue is the one that will lead us to a verse in the Hebrew Scriptures. After all, as haggadic midrash the parable is commenting on a verse or passage in the Hebrew Scriptures (for the people of the first century their Holy Writings would have been what we call the Old Testament and what I prefer to call the Hebrew Scriptures). The parable retells the earlier account through a creative and imaginative story in order to encourage us to walk as disciples. So, it is essential to recognize the verse in the Hebrew Scriptures on which the parable is built.

---

[44] The gospels may capture this tradition of studying in pairs.. "He [Yeshua] summoned the twelve and began to send them out in pairs, and gave them authority over the unclean spirits; (Mar 6:7; cf. Lk 10:1).

In the Introduction of this book you read about this particular connection to the Hebrew Scriptures. Carefully review that explanation again.

> When the prodigal son "came to his senses" he cried out, "Father, I have sinned against heaven and in your sight; I am no longer worthy to be called your son" (Luke 15:19). When the father saw his returning son, he "felt compassion and ran and embraced him and kissed him." Then the son repeated, "Father, I have sinned against heaven and in your sight; I am no longer worthy to be called your son" (Luke 15:21).

You will remember that I discovered this echo in the Hebrew Scriptures through the repetition, "I am not worthy." These are the same words that Jacob had cried to God. Jacob had also sinned against his father, Isaac, by stealing the blessing of his brother, Esau, the firstborn son. Jacob also left his father and went to a foreign land in exile. He too returned with a heavy heart, expecting to face the fury of his brother Esau. However, Jacob turned to God with these words: "I am unworthy of all the lovingkindness and of all the faithfulness which you have shown to Your servant." Only after this act of submission did Jacob petition God, "Deliver me, I pray, from the hand of my brother" (Genesis 32:10-11).

4. Carefully read the account of Jacob in Genesis 25:19-33:17. What are the following parallels between the Jacob story and the Parable of the Prodigal Son?

   - The son's sin (both Jacob and the prodigal son)
   - Consequences of the sin
   - Their desire to return from exile
   - Demonstration of worthy behavior upon returning
   - Indications that the younger son will receive the birthright
   - Do you see any other parallels?

5. How is the Parable of the Prodigal Son haggadic midrash on the story of Jacob? That is, how is the parable a retelling of the Jacob story with application to the lives of all the characters in the setting of the parable as well as to our lives today?

## Imagery and Symbolism of the Older Son

The parable is seemingly divided into two parts. The first part is about the younger prodigal son, and the second concentrates on the older son. Luke 15:25 begins the distinction between the two portions: "Now the older son was in the field, and when he came and approached the house he heard music and dancing."

We must stop here and reflect again on the inheritance of the birthright by the firstborn. In our Parable of the Prodigal Son the older son was born to the birthright and the younger son was not. The birthright would have given the older son not only a double portion of inheritance when his father died but also a role of leadership over his brothers while his father was still living. So, we have something strange and puzzling. When the younger son demanded of his father "the share of the estate that falls to me," why didn't his older brother speak up in his elevated position as the firstborn? However, in the parable the older brother is strangely silent.

We turn now to the second portion of the parable about the older son. Here you must begin by asking, "What are the key words?" I can share with you some of the key words I have seen, but you may see some that did not catch my attention. I truly believe that the Holy Spirit will guide you, as a believer in Christ, to become curious about certain words. So, begin by letting yourself be curious and ask, "What are the key words in Luke 15:25-32?"

1. Make a list of what seem to be key words in this passage.
2. Which key word in your list seems to be the most significant?
3. For your significant key word, use a concordance to look up the Greek word that has been translated into English.

4. Peruse other verses in the New Testament that use this same Greek word. Read each in its context to gather a deeper understanding about how this word is used in Scripture.

5. What are the various English translations for this one Greek word? Do the English translations give you a sense of the nuance of meaning?

I was drawn to the older brother, who summoned one of the servants and "inquired" what these things might mean (Luke 15:26). I can't explain what drew me; I was just curious. The Greek word is πυνθάνομαι (*punthanomai*), which has been translated in various ways as *ask, inquire* and *learn*. However, as I examined other verses in the New Testament that use this same Greek word (*punthanomai*), I began to see an interesting nuance of meaning.[45] The Greek word does not simply mean to ask, but to deliver a barrage of questions as in a court of inquiry. When we perceive this shade of meaning and return to the parable, we see that the older son was outraged by his father's decision to honor the prodigal son with his signet ring. In essence, the older son was demanding a judicial verdict that he thought would reverse his father's decision and favor him as the son born to the birthright.

Now we turn to examine the older son's evidence that he presents to support his case. "Look! For so many years I have been serving you, and I have never neglected a command of yours; and *yet* you have never given me a kid, that I might be merry with my friends" (Luke 15:29). What is the strength of his evidence? What is the weakness of his argument?

## Chiasm Points to the Central Focus

Chiasm is a common linguistic device in ancient literature, and the Holy Writings of Judaism and Christianity are no exception. Chiasm employs repetition in the form of parallel lines that point to a significant central feature. Chiasmus is a Greek word that

---

[45] To sense the nuance of meaning, examine other passages that contain this Greek word: Mat 2:4; Luke 15:26; 18:36; Acts 4:7; 10:18, 29; 21:33; 23:19, 20.

means a crossing or intersection of two elements (the parallel lines), thus forming the letter X with a central point at the intersection. The elements on one side of the central point are related to parallel elements on the other side. These parallel elements and their relationships are pointing to the central idea at the intersection.

The parable of the prodigal son employs two chiastic structures. The first is a simple ABA construction.

> 18-19: I have sinned; no longer worthy; make me a servant
>> 20: Father saw, had compassion, ran, embraced, kissed
> 21: I have sinned; no longer worthy; OMISSION

The two parallel lines are verses 18-19 in parallel with verse 21. They are connected by repetition: "I have sinned; I am no longer worthy.". However, the second parallel line omits "make me a servant," which the ancient ear would have "heard." In the chiastic center (verse 20), the father has shown compassion and is going to welcome the prodigal back as his son. Thus, the chiastic center focuses on the forgiving action of the father, and leads us to an understanding that the prodigal son is ready and willing to submit as a humble and obedient servant, the requirement of the son with the birthright.

The second chiasm is an exquisite structure with a powerful central focus. The numbers below are verse numbers that display the chiasm.

22: Inheritance of the younger son (birthright)
  23: Fattened calf at banquet of celebration
    24: Dead now alive; lost now found (evidence)
      25-26: Older son inquiring (seeking fair judgment)
        27: Father killed fattened calf; received him back
      28: Father began pleading with the older son
    29: Older son's evidence (served and obeyed)
  30: Fattened calf is older son's complaint
31: Inheritance of the older son (all that is mine is yours)
  32: Repetition of dead now alive; lost now found; celebration

As you look at this chiastic structure, start by noting the parallel
lines. Verse 22 is parallel with verse 31; verse 23 is parallel with
verse 30; and so on. Then carefully consider the chiastic center in
verse 27 to which the parallel lines are pointing. Verse 32 is a
repetition of verse 24 and seems to stand alone for emphasis.

We will now examine the relationship between the parallel
lines.

> 22: The father said to his slaves, "Quickly bring out
>     the best robe and put it on him, and put a ring
>     on his hand and sandals on his feet."
> 31: "Son, you have always been with me, and all
>     that is mine is yours."

These two parallel lines are both about what the sons will inherit.
The younger son receives the signet ring and the royal robe, and
will apparently inherit the birthright. The older son still belongs to
the father and will inherit, but he will apparently not inherit the
birthright. There is a relationship between these two parallel lines,
which is the inheritance of each son.

Now it is your turn to examine relationships between the
parallel lines.

1. What is the relationship between verses 23 and 30?
   What are the similarities that make them parallel?
   However, there is a subtle distinction between them.
   What is this subtle distinction?
2. What is the relationship between verses 24 and 29?
   What are the similarities that make them parallel? Do
   you see a subtle distinction between them? Explain.

We will now focus on the verses that immediately
surround the chiastic center. By their proximity to the central idea
of the chiasm, they become especially important.

> 25-26: Now his older son was in the field, and
>        when he came and approached the house, he
>        heard music and dancing. And he summoned
>        one of the servants and began **inquiring** what
>        these things could be.

28: But he became angry and was not willing to go
in; and his father came out and began
**pleading** with him.

Verses 25-26 and 28 provoke for me the vivid imagery of a
courtroom drama. We have seen with the word "inquiring" that
the older son is demanding a different decision. The father, on the
other hand, knows that the verdict of awarding the inheritance of
the birthright to the younger son is just and righteous. Yet, the
older son is still his son, and the father's heart is filled with
compassion. The father is now "pleading" with his son. The Greek
word is παρακαλέω (*parakaleo*), which is often translated as
"comfort," and conveys the sense of calling someone to your side.

Finally we come to the chiastic center. The father held a
victory banquet for his younger son and received him back. The
verdict is just and righteous. The younger son is worthy to inherit
the birthright because of his repentance (repent means to change)
and his humility ("I am no longer worthy to be your son").

## Ending of the Parable

We can now consider the ending of the parable. We remember
there are three possibilities - tragic, happy and open-ended.
Nicholas Lunn suggests that the parable is open-ended, and I
agree. "Following the father's appeal to the elder son, the parable
ends. No response of the son is given."[46] You will likely find one
ending for the younger son, another ending for the older son, a
third ending that applies to the Pharisees and scribes in the setting,
a fourth ending that relates to the sinners and tax collectors in the
setting, and a fifth ending that will apply to you. Stop and consider
each of these five endings.

1. Younger son
2. Older son
3. Pharisees and scribes
4. Sinners and tax collectors
5. You

---

[46] Nicholas Lunn, "Parables of the Lost? Rhetorical Structure and the
Section Headings of Luke 15," *Bible Translator* 60/3 (2009): 164.

You are now ready for the last and most important step. Ponder your answers very carefully and reply truthfully from your heart.

1.   What is a specific meaning of the parable that I can incorporate into my life?

2.   What are the sequential steps that I must take activate this commandment?

3.   What changes must I make to appropriate the meaning of the parable to my life?

4.   What blessings might God bestow on me as a result of my actions?

After three months have elapsed, answer these four questions once more. Are the blessings you have received different from what you expected?

---

## *Mystery #2 in the Kingdom of God*

The mystery will continue to be mysterious if you have not carefully considered the questions. However, if you have, you are beginning to perceive that God is selecting from among His people those whose hearts are committed to obey and follow Him. He continues to love all His children, who still belong to Him. However, some are becoming leaders, both in this life and in a future role that will defeat God's enemy. What, then, have we seen as characteristics of these leaders?

▶ Responding to sufferings of this life by turning to God

▶ Seeking forgiveness with a heart that truly desires to change

▶ Humility in the presence of God that encourages obedience

These are the true leaders of God's people.

## Chapter Three

# Parable of the Lost Sheep

If any man has a hundred sheep, and one of them has gone astray, does he not leave the ninety-nine on the mountains and go and search for the one that is straying? (Mat 18:12)

"What man among you, if he has a hundred sheep and has lost one of them, does not leave the ninety-nine in the open pasture, and go after the one which is lost, until he finds it?" (Luke 15:4).

This parable appears in two of the gospels, Matthew and Luke. It is so frequently used in sermons and Bible teachings that I was a bit concerned I would be unable to perceive a greater depth of meaning than what is often delivered from the pulpit. I should not have worried. I followed my own principles of using first century methods of searching the Scriptures, and there it was right in front of me. However, I do not want to jump ahead and share my discovery too soon. Instead I would like to take you with me on my journey as I searched for a penetrating understanding. Only in this way will you learn how to uncover mysteries in your own right.

Of course I looked first at the context of the story where we see Yeshua responding to the Pharisees and scribes who were grumbling and saying, "This man receives sinners and eats with them." So, I suspected that the parable was responding to their grumbling. Then, looking at the story of the parable itself, I could see there was only one main character, the kind shepherd. But what were the linguistic devices that act as clues to a deeper meaning? And what is it about this parable that is strange and puzzling?

## Symbolism of Numbers

Certainly leaving 99 sheep alone and unattended sounded a bit startling, but was that really the main clue? So, I considered next the symbolism of the numbers 99 plus 1, which equals 100, because the biblical language often applies symbolic meaning to numbers. The number 1, of course, represents the unity and primacy of God, and the number 100 is an exaltation of God. Certainly the shepherd had brought the lost sheep to the one true God. However, what about the number 99, which is the number 9 expanded for serious emphasis? E. W. Bullinger explains that the number 9 stands for God's wrath and judgment, and offers numerous examples in Scripture. [47]

We can see one example in the story of Deborah, the judge who helped rescue Israel from the Canaanite enemy in the walled city of Hazor. The Canaanites had 900 iron chariots with razor-sharp spikes on their wheels, and these 900 chariots carried powerful soldiers who could wield flashing swords. The Israelites, by contrast, were on foot with crude weapons. However, with wonderful ironic humor God arranged for the battle site to take place in a dry river bed, which suddenly became filled with water from a cloudburst in the hills above, thus turning the battle field to a mire of mud where the 900 chariots became stuck. The brave Israelites could then attack and destroy the enemy. The humor continues as Sisera, the enemy commander, left his chariot and escaped on foot. Sisera came to the tent of Jael, the Kennite woman who gave him warm milk that put the exhausted enemy soldier to sleep. Then she drove a tent peg through his head. So much for the enemy of Israel who had 900 iron chariots but whom God judged in His wrath.

Another example is King Hoshea, who ruled the northern kingdom of Israel from its capital Samaria for nine years. During these nine years we learn that Hoshea "did evil in the sight of the Lord" (2 Kings 17:2). However, the story does not end there. As the brutal enemy warriors of the Assyrian empire approached, Hoshea allowed himself to become a "servant" of the Assyrian king and paid him tribute. That is, Hoshea submitted to the humiliating role as a hostage to the enemy. "But the king of Assyria found conspiracy in Hoshea, who had sent messengers to the king of Egypt," so the king of Assyria turned his terrifying army against Samaria, which had to bear the hideous consequences

---

[47] E. W. Bullinger, *Number in Scripture* (Kregel, 2003 [1894]). This book can also be found on the web in its entirety. I suggest www.levendwater.org.

of three years of siege before the city finally fell. The people in the northern kingdom were then led into captivity with hooks in their noses and nooses around their necks. Now, that is an awesome example of the Lord's wrath and judgment against King Hoshea, who reigned for nine years, and against those who do evil in His sight.

So, what do we perceive from the 99 sheep that the shepherd left in "the open pasture?" Perhaps the 99 sheep represent those who are unworthy in God's eyes to inherit the leadership role that the birthright will bestow. Thus, the 99 have earned God's judgment and wrath, which can be perceived as strict encouragement by those who receive the God's actions as instruction. However, before we can address this possibility, we must turn to the phrase "open pasture." That intriguing description is what caught my attention, and it is the question that the pulpit seems to have missed.

## Imagery of Biblical Words

I don't know about you, but as I read the Scriptures my curiosity invariably draws me to certain words. Perhaps that is the Holy Spirit guiding me. In any case, I think of myself as the humorous monkey, Curious George of childhood fame. His curiosity always gets him in trouble with the world around him, but his compassionate owner, the man with the red hat, understands and applauds his amusing learning experiences. My own curiosity is often unorthodox, but invariably results in exciting discoveries.

We have seen that the Parable of the Lost Sheep is found in two of the gospels. In Matthew, the English translation in the New American Standard Bible says the shepherd "leaves the ninety-nine on the mountains and goes to search for the one that is straying." However, Luke declares, he "left the ninety-nine in the open pasture." These translations are from the NASB which I use because it translates as closely as possible to the original text. So, what do we have here with the two translations, "the mountains" and "the open field?"

The original Greek text in Matthew clearly means "mountains" (ὄρη). So let us imagine the "mountains" of Israel's hill country and what they represent. In ancient Israel this area was wild and hostile. Remember Samson who killed a lion (lions lived in the thick undergrowth of the Jordan Valley and would forage in the higher hills nearby). Furthermore, David was skilled with a slingshot and killed a bear. So, we have the 99 sheep that are left alone in the hostile and frightening mountains and perhaps are bearing the wrath of God's judgment. In wonderful biblical fashion God is not the One who brings pain and suffering upon His children, but allows them to bear their own consequences of ungodly behavior. Could Yeshua be referring to the Pharisees and the scribes as the 99 sheep who were righteous in their own eyes, I wondered? After all, "pride *goes* before destruction, and a haughty spirit before stumbling," we read in Proverbs 16:18.

So, let us look now at the version in Luke, which uses another word that the NASB has translated "open field." You will see a note in the middle margin of the NASB that offers an alternate translation of "wilderness." Of course that stimulated my curiosity. So I turned to the Greek text to find the original word, which is ἔρημος (eremos) meaning solitary or desolate, hence a wilderness. It is time now for you to ponder some provocative questions.

1.  Wilderness is a recurring biblical concept. What is the importance of the wilderness in the Exodus account? That is, what is this wilderness account teaching us?
2.  How many years were the Jews in the wilderness after the Exodus from Egypt? Is there a relationship between the symbolic meaning of the number forty and the wilderness wandering?
3.  Who was prepared to enter the Promised Land to defeat the enemy and claim the inheritance after the forty years of wilderness wandering? Why were they selected? How is the land an inheritance?
4.  When was Yeshua in the wilderness? How long was he there? What happened when he was in the wilderness?
5.  What do you think is the underlying meaning of the account of Yeshua in the wilderness?

I am certain that you are following me in this adventure of discovery because we all know that Yeshua was in the wilderness for forty days and forty nights. There he was tempted by the devil, which is an "echo" of the forty years of wilderness wandering after the Exodus from Egypt. The children of Israel had left Egypt, which represents the world, but then they had to learn how to replace their worldly thoughts and actions with the ways of God.

So, God had a purpose for the forty days Yeshua was in the wilderness and the forty years of wandering by the children of Israel after the Exodus. Bullinger suggests that the number forty represents chastisement for instruction and preparation for service. In the wilderness wandering after the Exodus, God was instructing His children in two ways. First, He gave them His Torah through His prophet Moses at Mount Sinai (Torah means "guidance" or "instruction"). Second, God used a method called "testing," which allowed worldly consequences to come upon His children when they did not obey Him. This is a form of chastisement for the purpose of instruction.

## Instruction by Testing

We learn about "testing" during this account of the wilderness wandering. After the miraculous rescue from being forced to return to bondage in Egypt, when God destroyed Pharaoh and all his army at the Sea of Reeds, the children of Israel "went three days in the wilderness and found no water" (Ex 15:22). Three days without water will cause death, so the Israelites were on the verge of dying. We can then imagine what must have appeared to them as a mirage, and then remarkably became a real oasis as they drew closer to a pool of water in the wilderness. Yet we learn that they "could not drink the waters of Marah for they were bitter."[48] So the people grumbled at Moses saying, "What shall we drink"? We remember that Moses cried out to the Lord, and God showed him a tree and told him to throw it into the waters. The bitter water in the oasis then turned sweet, and the people were able to drink. "There God made for them a statute and regulation, and there He tested them" (Ex 15:25). Then the account goes on to explain this process of testing.

---

[48] The word *marah* is derived from a Hebrew word meaning "bitterness." So the name of the place describes the undrinkable water of the oasis.

If you will give earnest heed to the voice of the
Lord your God, and

- do what is right in His sight, and
- give ear to His commandments, and
- keep all His statutes,

I will put none of the diseases on you which I have
put on the Egyptians; for I, the Lord, am your
healer. (Ex 15:26)

I have purposely placed the list of requirements in a format
that will catch your attention. First God gives us His words of
instruction so we can "do what is right," "give ear to His
commandments," and "keep all His statutes." Then God blesses
us with "wholeness," that is, healing of worldly pain and suffering
when we do as Moses did and cry out to the Lord.

I call this method of testing a "process" because we grow
gradually in our confidence and obedience to the Lord through
our hard-knock experiences.[49] The wilderness account teaches us
this lesson. After the miracle that turned water from brackish to
sweet, the children of Israel came close to starvation from a lack
of food. Again they began to "grumble against Moses and Aaron
in the wilderness," and they cried out, not to the Lord, but to
Moses, saying,

Would that we had died by the Lord's hand in the
land of Egypt, when we sat by the pots of meat, when
we ate bread to the full; for you have brought us out
into this wilderness to kill this whole assembly with
hunger.
(Ex 16:3)

The Israelites perceived the comforts of the world as
preferable to trusting God in a wilderness, which can often be a
challenge in the midst of worldly deceit. So, God responded by
raining a gift of bread from heaven. However, He also gave

---

[49] The Hebrew word is נָסָה (nasah), which means to test by going through
some kind of a trial. My use of the word "process" refers to a continuing
growth process that testing promotes.

explicit instructions that required obedience in order to prevent further worldly consequences.

> Behold, I will rain bread from heaven for you; and the people shall go out and gather a day's portion every day, that I may test them, whether or not they will walk in My instruction. (Ex 16:4)

Of course some did not listen, but hoarded what was left over after the evening meal had ended. Therefore, the next morning the leftover mannah had bred worms and become foul. Thus, God was teaching His people to trust in Him through this process of testing, and He placed them in a wilderness in order to instruct them to trust and obey Him.

Although these accounts of God testing His children in the wilderness occurred many centuries ago, they are nevertheless for our instruction today. Consider the following questions.

1. What is an example of a dramatic testing event in your own life? How did you respond? If you had it to do over again, how *would* you respond?
2. What is an example of a small testing event that happened recently in your life? How did you respond? If you had it to do over again, how *would* you respond?
3. How would you explain to another person the concept of testing, and how would that become a blessing in one's life?

## Wilderness Preparation for Entering the Land

The purpose of God's instruction in His Torah, and His further instruction through the process of testing, was to prepare His people to enter the Promised Land. It took forty years for that preparation. God declared that He would give the land to the descendants of Abraham, Isaac and Jacob as an inheritance forever (Ex 32:13). However, this inheritance required that God's people defeat those already living there, the pagan Canaanites who worshipped other gods and were therefore enemies of the True God. "Hence I have said to you," said God, that "you are to possess their land, and I Myself will give it to you to possess it, a land flowing with milk and honey" (Lev 20:24). "Possess" is the

Hebrew word יַרַשׁ (*yarash*), which means seizing and dispossessing those who are already there.

Possessing the land in order to claim an inheritance is prophetic of a future battle when God's people will finally defeat Satan and his minions as we will see later in Chapter Sixteen. So, through this story of forty years of wilderness wandering we perceive that God was preparing His people to defeat the enemy. However, only those who had submitted to God in humble obedience would be ready to participate in the battle. Only those who "do what is right in His sight, and give ear to His commandments, and keep all His statutes" will be equipped to overcome the enemy both in this life now and also to participate in the future battle on behalf of God.[50]

In Chapter Two we encountered the special inheritance known as the birthright to which all the firstborn sons were entitled. I am suggesting that those who are worthy of this special inheritance will be the ones prepared to defeat the enemy in a future battle. So, let us stop for a moment and spend more time on the inheritance of the birthright.

In the Exodus narrative, before the final devastating plague when all the firstborn sons of Egypt died, God instructed Moses:

> Then you shall say to Pharaoh, "Thus says the Lord, Israel is My son, My first-born."
> So I said to you, "Let My son go, that he may serve Me." But you have refused to let him go. Behold, I will kill your son, your first-born." (Ex 4:22-23)

The firstborn son, of course, was entitled to the birthright. However, this passage in Exodus stimulates an important question. Does Israel refer here to Jacob, whose name God

---

[50] I caution you not to conclude that only those who have successfully passed through the 40 years of wilderness wandering are entitled to eternal life. As you proceed through the parables in this book, I will address the concept of a remnant, who are those children of God who are prepared to fight in this battle.

changed to Israel? Or does it mean all the children of Israel? In Chapter Four I will demonstrate that this passage refers to all the children of Israel whom God calls His firstborn son.[51]

The biblical narrative explains that, just because a son was born first, he would not inherit the birthright unless God declared him worthy of this leadership role. We read repeatedly of firstborn sons who lost their birthright including Ishmael (birthright given to Isaac), Esau (he sold his birthright to Jacob), Reuben (1 Chronicles 5:1-2 tells us that Reuben defiled his father's bed so the birthright was given to Joseph), and Manasseh (Jacob gave the birthright to Ephraim by placing his right hand of blessing on the head of Ephraim). So, all the children of Israel have been born to a special inheritance known as the birthright, but only those who pass successfully through the wilderness wandering to overcome the temptations of the world will be entitled to this special inheritance.

As we return to the forty years of wilderness wandering by the children of Israel, God's firstborn son, we learn that only some were declared worthy to enter the Promised Land to defeat the enemy and possess their inheritance.

> None of the men who came up from Egypt, from twenty years old and upward, shall see the land which I swore to Abraham, to Isaac and to Jacob; for they did not follow Me fully, Except Caleb the son of Jephunneh the Kenizzite and Joshua the son of Nun, for they have followed the LORD fully.   (Num 32:11-12)

The younger ones, those who were less than 20 years old, did not have the ways of the world engrained in them, but had been successfully instructed and tested by God. Of the remaining Israelites, only Joshua and Caleb had proven their total confidence in God when they returned from spying out the land unafraid of the giants and the walled cities they had seen there.

---

[51] See also Anne Kimball Davis, *The Law is not a Curse: Paul's Midrash in Galatians* (published by BibleInteract, 2012).

With this perspective of Israel's inheritance of the birthright as God's firstborn son, with the real possibility of individuals being declared unworthy of that birthright, we can now return to the parable and scrutinize the Pharisees and scribes who were complaining with hostile condemnation that Yeshua was "receiving sinners and eating with them." These leaders of God's people, the Pharisees and the scribes, had been born to the birthright along with all the children of Israel.

1. What do you think Yeshua was saying to the Pharisees and scribes through this parable of 99 sheep that the shepherd left in the wilderness?

2. Are the 99 sheep wandering in the wilderness because they are not yet prepared to enter the Promised Land to defeat God's enemy? Is their pride causing them to stumble?

3. Do you know leaders of God's people today who are not walking in the ways of God? Consider some examples.

4. Think of one person who displays godly characteristics of humility and obedience. Do you think this person is a true leader of God's people? Has this person been called to a position of leadership? Are you respecting this person as a leader?

## Imagery of the Pharisees as Shepherds

We turn back now to our parable. It appears that the 99 sheep in the wilderness represent the Pharisees and scribes who are not worthy to lead the people of Israel because they are still "in the wilderness." They are not yet obedient servants who are prepared to serve God and fight for Him.

The relationship of these self-appointed leaders to the biblical text is easy to see. Shepherds are a common biblical symbol for the leaders who tend God's flock, and Scripture often judges against those who do not lead in a way that God considers worthy.

My people have become lost sheep; their shepherds have led them astray. They have made them turn aside *on* the mountains; they have gone along from mountain to hill and have forgotten their resting place. (Jer 50:6)

This verse in Jeremiah is a likely candidate as the connection to the Hebrew Scriptures because Matthew says they were left on the mountains. It is certainly possible to regard these sheep as God's people who have been led astray by the false leaders. However, I do not think so. Jeremiah's shepherd has led the sheep astray, whereas the shepherd in the parable is a leader whom God would certainly declare to be worthy. This shepherd undoubtedly represents Yeshua, who has rescued the one lost sheep and has brought him to God. The 99 sheep are still lost, apparently representing the self-righteous Pharisees and scribes who were grumbling about Yeshua. It is only the one sheep that is ready to be "found" by the good shepherd. The 99 still have their hearts hardened, and are not yielding to God in humble submission. They are still in need of testing in the mojuntains where the threat of ravenous animals represents the destructive ways of the world. Luke calls this place a wilderness, and we have seen how the wilderness represents a training field that instructs us to be humble and obedient to God.

## Conclusion

I was drawn to this parable by asking questions. The teaching that we often hear in the pulpit tends to draw our attention to the one lost sheep that was found (there is certainly a message in being found). However, I was puzzled by the remaining 99, and my curiosity led me to ponder the meaning of those left alone on the mountain (Matthew) and in the wilderness (Luke). Relating the parable to its context, the grumbling and condemning words by the Pharisees and scribes are certainly a clue. Returning to the Hebrew Scriptures to identify the passages on which the story was based was indeed a big help. The Pharisees and scribes are the shepherds, who have led God's people astray and have made them turn aside on the mountains. They have left God's people in the wilderness of the world instead of leading them to God.

Yet, God's Word is positive, not negative, so we must not leave the parable with the condemnation of Pharisees and scribes. We must remember that the purpose of the parables, which comment on some passage or narrative in the Hebrew Scriptures, is to teach us how to walk in the ways of God. When we walk in harmony with God, we are entering the Kingdom in our lives today. This understanding alone is an exciting and rewarding blessing, but there is more.

God has placed us in the wilderness of the world to prepare and select those who are ready to participate with Him. He is drawing His children to Him in righteousness through a refinement process that enabling some of His children to defeat the enemy and the enemy's weapon, which is sin. At the end of this process of refinement there will be a final battle where those who are prepared will participate. When we begin to perceive this prophetic future, our desire to be part of the remnant grows, and causes us to stand today. Perhaps God will consider us worthy to inherit the birthright, and to participate with our Lord in the future battle that will defeat God's enemy. Even now we may be participating in that ongoing battle by our humble obedience and service to our Lord Yeshua.

# Mystery #3 in the Kingdom of God

After reconsidering this parable of the lost sheep, are you still being led astray on the mountain and in the wilderness by the ways of the world and the teachings of false prophets? Or, have you repented of your worldly ways, turned to the Holy Writings for instruction, and responded faithfully to testing experiences in your life?

Have you submitted to the kind Shepherd, your Lord Yeshua, and made Him the center of your life? If so, you are the one lost sheep, formerly wandering on the mountain and in the wilderness as a child of God, but now strengthened and prepared to meet the challenges of the world and the attacks of the enemy.

More likely, you are in the *process* of being strengthened and prepared. You are learning to search the Scriptures for deeper meaning, and you are applying the Word of God to testing experiences. You have before you a growing excitement for the future battle that will ultimately destroy God's enemy, and your desire to participate is building as you commit to service under the lordship of Yeshua the Messiah.

Chapter Four
# Inheritance of the Birthright
This chapter is a revised version of an article published in
*Chafer Theological Seminary Journal*, 13/1 (2008).

## Summary

The birthright was a special inheritance to which the firstborn son was entitled. The Hebrew Scriptures portray the birthright as bestowing not only a double portion of the father's land and possessions but also a special blessing, priestly office, position and authority of lordship, and procreative power that produces an abundance of righteous seed. However, inheritance of the birthright, which is distinct from the inheritance bestowed on other members of the family, requires obedience to the Mosaic Law and faithful service to God as preparation for the responsibility of leadership. The narrative portrays individuals losing the birthright for failure to uphold these requirements. Yet, the one who loses the birthright does not lose his status as a son and still receives an inheritance, although not the inheritance of the birthright.

## "Israel is my Firstborn Son" means All the Children of Israel

In the Exodus narrative, before the final devastating plague when all the firstborn sons of Egypt died, God instructed Moses:

> Then you shall say to Pharaoh, "Thus says the Lord, Israel is My son, My first-born."
> So I said to you, "Let My son go, that he may serve Me; but you have refused to let him go. Behold, I will kill your son, your first-born." (Ex 4:22-23)

This passage stimulates an important question. Does Israel refer here to Jacob, whose name God changed to Israel, or does it refer to the children of Israel? I have concluded that Israel in this passage refers to all the children of Israel, whom God has called His firstborn son, based on the biblical text. For example, in the Exodus narrative God told Pharaoh, "I will kill your firstborn son" (Ex 4:23). In the context of this passage, "son" represents more than Pharaoh's one son because all the firstborn of Egypt died in the last plague, both people and animals. Furthermore, the narrative contrasts the firstborn son of Pharaoh (implying many) with the firstborn son of God, that is, Israel, which also suggests many.

A second literary device employs a contrast that helps clarify the meaning. Following God's declaration, "Israel is my firstborn son," the text continues, "I said to you, Let my *son* go that *he* may worship me" (italics added for emphasis in this and the following quotations). However, the continuing narrative shifts from singular (son/he) to plural (people/they). So, after Exodus 4:22-23 God repeatedly says, "Let my *people* go so *they* may worship me" (Ex 7:16; 8:1, 20; 9:1, 13). In other citations the Lord declares, "Let the *people* go" (Ex 7:14; 9:17), and three times the narrative identifies the people as the Israelites (Ex 6:11; 7:2; 9:35). However, never again, after Exodus 4:23, does God declare, "Let my *son* go so *he* may worship me." Thus, the Hebrew text conveys a startling parallel construction by contrasting terms that nevertheless mean the same thing, My son/he and My people/they.

We can now draw a conclusion from the context of the Exodus narrative together with the linguistic marker of son/people and he/they. The simple meaning of "Israel is My son, My firstborn" in Exodus 4:22 refers to all the children of Israel.

Jewish interpretation recognizes the importance of both the plain meaning and a midrashic interpretation that suggests deeper understanding. However, this tradition has typically followed Rashi's explanation (Rashi was born in 1040 A.D.). According to Rashi, "firstborn son" in Exodus 4:22-23 denotes "an expression of greatness," and its deeper spiritual meaning is Jacob whose name God changed to Israel. Thus, Rashi understands "Israel My firstborn son" as God honoring Jacob with the birthright to which Esau had been born.[52] However, Bonchak observes, "Ironically, Rashi's midrashic explanation [Jacob is God's firstborn son, who is entitled to inherit the birthright] takes the word 'firstborn' literally, while his p'shat

[52] Rabbi Yisrael Isser Zvi Herczeg, ed., *Rashi: Commentary on the Torah*, 4th ed. vol. 2 (New York: Mesorah Publications, 1999), 38.

explanation [the simple meaning, an expression of greatness] takes the word allegorically."[53] Therefore, Rashi's reversal of understanding (the plain meaning is allegorical; the deeper meaning is liberal) intentionally invites further consideration, especially since Jewish commentary earlier than Rashi acknowledges the simple meaning as the people and nation of Israel.[54]

Nevertheless, Jewish tradition continues to recognize the importance of both the simple meaning as well as the midrashic interpretation.[55] Therefore, this study concludes that "Israel is My son, My firstborn" refers to all the children of Israel in its plain meaning, and the reference to both Jacob and an expression of greatness are midrashic interpretations. We will proceed with the simple meaning that God's firstborn son means all the children of Israel.

## The birthright: Double portion of inheritance

If all the children of Israel have been born to the birthright we must now ask, how does the Hebrew narrative portray the nature of that inheritance? In particular, why did certain individuals lose the inheritance of the birthright?

The birthright belonged to the firstborn son simply by the position of his birth. For example, in Genesis 43:33 the brothers of Joseph sat before him from the eldest to the youngest, with the eldest described as "the firstborn according to his birthright." Furthermore, in the case of twins, the first to emerge from his mother's womb was the firstborn. This is evident with Esau, the

---

[53] Avigdor Bonchek, *What's Bothering Rashi? A Guide to In-Depth Analysis of His Torah Commentary: Shemos*, vol. 2 (Jerusalem: Feldheim Publishers: 1999), 38.

[54] I. Epstein, ed., *Babylonian Talmud* (London: Soncino, 1935): *Seder Mo'ed: Shabbath*, vol. 1, p. 426, tr. 89b; *Seder Nezikin: Abodah Zarah*, vol. 4, p. 6, tr. 3a.

[55] W. G. Braude, *Midrash as Deep Peshat*, in *Studies in Judaica, Karaitica and Islamica*, Sheldon Brunswick, ed. (Jerusalem: Bar-Ilan University, 1982): 31-38.

first of twins born to Isaac and Rebekah (Gen 25:24-26), and also
with Zerah, the first of twins born to Judah and Tamar (Gen
38:27-30; cf. Gen 46:12).

The birthright entitled the firstborn to inherit a greater
share of his father's land and possessions than the remaining heirs.
The most common understanding of this greater part in the Jewish
literature is a double portion, which is twice the amount that each
of the other sons received.[56] Some theologians have criticized this
interpretation of a double portion,[57] but the most common
understanding is twice the amount that the other sons received.

For the purpose of this study, we will view the inheritance
of the firstborn son as double that of each of the other sons. Not
only is it the most common interpretation in Jewish literature, but
Eryl Davies' extensive search of Babylonian and Assyrian records
suggests that the firstborn received an amount larger than that of
his brothers, often indicating this amount as a double portion.[58] As
this study will demonstrate, the greater portion of inheritance
assisted the son with the birthright to perform his responsibility of
leadership.

---

[56] Rabbi Adin Steinsaltz, *A Reference Guide to the Steinsaltz Edition of the
Talmud*, trans. Rabbi Israel V. Berman (New York: Random, 1989), 170;
Louis Ginzberg, *Legends of the Jews*, vol. 3 (Philadelphia: Jewish
Publication Society, 1966), 211.

[57] For example, Hiers notes that this notion of a double portion depends
largely on Dt 21:15-17, which contemplates only two sons. Richard H.
Hiers, "Transfer of Property by Inheritance and Bequest in Biblical Law
and Tradition," *Journal of Law and Religion* 10:1 (1993-94): 143. However,
other subtle references in Scripture refer to a double portion of
inheritance. See, for example, 2 Kings 2:9; Is 61:7.

[58] Eryl W. Davies, "The Inheritance of the first-born in Israel and the
Ancient Near East," *Journal of Semitic Studies* 38:2 (1993): 175-91. Davies
has searched in documents of ancient Near Eastern cultures for evidence
of the birthright and finds that the inheritance of the firstborn son was
treated in a preferential manner. He concludes that the exact portion of
the inheritance lacks sufficient data for a definitive ratio, but adds that a
double portion is evident in the texts he examined. Davies concludes
that we should retain the traditional understanding of a double portion.

## Redemption of the firstborn son

The concept of the birthright in Scripture is similar in many ways to legal practices affecting firstborn sons in surrounding cultures. However, the Hebrew Bible develops one aspect of this inheritance that is different from that of Israel's neighbors. It originates in the Exodus event. The Hebrew text highlights God's rescue of the children of Israel, His firstborn son, from death and destruction that fell upon all the other firstborn in Egypt, both people and animals.[59]

The Hebrew narrative further explains and develops the importance of the firstborn in three ways. First, the text notes the special status of all firstborn sons by consecration, which sets apart the firstborn as sacred and holy. Sanctification of firstborn animals was also an essential element in the custom of sacrifice. We will soon see that sanctification of the firstborn children of Israel was for service to God which is a "living" sacrifice.

> Consecrate to Me all the first-born, the first offspring of every womb among the sons of Israel, both of man and beast; it belongs to Me. Ex 13:2
>
> The first-born of an ox or the first-born of a sheep or the first-born of a goat, you shall not redeem; they are holy. You shall sprinkle their blood on the altar and shall offer up their fat in smoke as an offering by fire, for a soothing aroma to the Lord. (Num 18:17)

Second, after God redeemed the children of Israel from death in Egypt, the Hebrew Scriptures portray an ongoing need for redemption of the firstborn son. The redemption in Egypt had taken place after the placement of blood from a sacrificed animal on the doorpost. Continuing redemption of the children of Israel

---

[59] Ex 6:6; cf. Ps 103:4; Is 44:22-23; 63:9.

also involved animal sacrifice. The sacrificial system substituted an unblemished animal as a gift to God. [60]

The first redemption from death in Egypt, and the ongoing need for redemption, implies a continuing redemption from death.[61] The text explains this need for ongoing redemption.

> When in the future your child asks you, "What does this mean?" you shall answer, "By strength of hand the Lord brought us out of Egypt, from the house of slavery."
> "When Pharaoh stubbornly refused to let us go, the Lord killed all the firstborn in the land of Egypt, from human firstborn to the firstborn of animals. Therefore I sacrifice to the Lord every male that first opens the womb, but every firstborn of my sons I redeem." (Ex 13:14-15)

Third, the Hebrew narrative explains that the firstborn's consecration (setting apart as holy) initiates a different kind of sacrifice. Paul will later call this a "living sacrifice," which he defines as a "spiritual service of worship" (Rom 12:1). Paul's exhortation is compatible with the Hebrew Scriptures because, in the Exodus account, God repeatedly commands, "Let my people go that they may worship me." The Hebrew word that is translated "worship" is עבד (avad) from which the word for servant is constructed (eved). In Hebrew, humble service acknowledges the

---

[60] The most noted example in the Hebrew Scriptures is the substitution of a lamb for Abraham's near sacrifice of Isaac. The New Testament further develops this concept of substitution. For example, I Co 5:7 explains that "Christ our Passover also has been sacrificed."

[61] It was customary in the ancient Near Eastern world to sacrifice a firstborn son to the gods. That the Hebrew Scriptures strictly forbade this practice suggests an occasional tendency in Israel to follow this custom. The practice of sacrificing the firstborn son may have been the nature of the death that prompted God's ongoing redemption by substituting the sacrifice of an animal.

one true God through proper worship.[62] This study will demonstrate that the relationship between consecration and service to God is characteristic of the birthright, and requires the firstborn son to be holy as God's servant and the designated leader of God's people.

Thus, the Hebrew narrative develops the importance of the firstborn in three ways. First, it assigns a special holy status to all firstborn sons. Next, it requires an ongoing need for redemption by substitution of sacrificial animals. Finally, it sets the firstborn sons aside for the sacrifice of worship through service.

## The Birthright: Benefits and Responsibilities

The firstborn received four additional benefits and responsibilities in addition to a double portion of his father's estate: a special blessing, the office of high priest of his clan or tribe, a position of authority and leadership, and procreative vigor. These attributes are associated with responsibilities of leadership.

First, the special blessing acknowledged both current and future benefits.[63] That all the other sons received lesser blessings is apparent from the Jacob narrative. There are numerous examples. Esau received a blessing even after he sold his birthright to Jacob (Gen 27:39-40). Jacob bestowed Manasseh's birthright on Ephraim but gave Manasseh a blessing (Gen 48:19). Furthermore, all the sons of Jacob, including those who did not inherit the birthright, received blessings (Gen 49:3-27). Even Reuben, the firstborn son of Jacob whose birthright was transferred to Joseph, received a blessing (1 Ch 5:1). However, a special blessing was reserved for the son with the birthright as Esau declared when he cried to his father, "He [Jacob] took away my birthright and look,

---

[62] For the connection between freedom from slavery in Egypt and serving/worshipping God, see Ex 7:16; 8:1, 20; 9:1, 13; 10:3, 7.

[63] Jacob Neussner, ed., *Dictionary of Judaism*, ed. Jacob Neussner (Peabody: Hendriksen, 1999), 98.

now he has taken away my blessing," meaning the special blessing that accompanied the birthright (Gen 27:36). [64]

Second, in addition to a special blessing and a double portion of land and possessions, the firstborn served as the high priest of his clan. [65] Regarding this priestly office, the sages later commented on Exodus 24:5, understanding "young men of the people of Israel" to be firstborn sons, leaders of their clans and tribes. "He [Moses] sent young men of the people of Israel [na'arei b'nei Yisrael], who offered burnt offerings and sacrificed oxen as offerings of well-being to the Lord" (Ex 24:5). The sages concluded that "the young men of the people of Israel" were firstborn sons who performed sacrificial service until the construction of the tabernacle and the substitution of the Levites as the priestly class. [66]

The firstborn sons of Israel apparently lost this right and privilege to offer sacrifices to the Lord because of the incident with the golden calf. Ancient commentators asked, "Who caused the firstborn to forfeit all this glory?" They gave as an explanation the worship of the golden calf, and concluded that the firstborn sons "are found in fetters" because they are prohibited from offering to the Lord anything prepared by fire, undoubtedly

---

[64] Note the distinctive characteristics of the birthright in Joseph's blessing. (Gen 49:22-26) Joseph will be victorious in battle, receive blessings beyond imagination, produce abundant offspring, and he is "set apart from his brothers." Although the Hebrew text acknowledges Judah's prophetic status as a leader, with certain characteristics of the birthright, it assigns the inheritance of the firstborn's birthright to Joseph (I Chr 5:1-2).

[65] The firstborn's right to the priestly office preceded the assignment of that role to the Levites. The later position of High Priest in the temple should also be distinguished from this earlier period. The earliest priestly responsibility of the firstborn sons is recognized both in the Jewish and non-Jewish literature. See, for example, *Midrash Rabbah: Exodus*, eds. H. Freedman and Maurice Simon, trans. S. M. Lehrman, 3rd edition (London: Soncino, 1983), Numbers I, 101; cf. Numbers 72-73. See also Ginzberg, *Legends*, 211; Beitzel, "Right of the Firstborn," 180.

[66] *Midrash Rabbah*, Numbers I, 101.

meaning sacrifices to the Lord.[67] Ginzberg comments on the firstborn's loss of the priestly office.

> God elevates no man to an office unless He has tried him and found him worthy of his calling. He did not say, "and the Levites shall be Mine," before He had tried this tribe, and found them worthy. In Egypt none but the tribe of Levi observed the Torah and clung to the token of the Abrahamic covenant, while the other tribes, abandoning both Torah and token of covenant, like the Egyptians, practiced idolatry. In the desert, also, it was this tribe alone that did not take part in the worship of the Golden Calf. Justly, therefore, did God's choice fall upon this godly tribe, who on this day were consecrated as the servants of God and His sanctuary.[68]

Thus, the firstborn sons of Israel lost their priestly position and functions, and the Levites assumed the firstborn responsibility of offering sacrifices to the Lord on behalf of others (Num 3:44-45). Because the firstborn sons had lost this priestly responsibility bestowed by the birthright, the Lord instructed that a ceremony of redemption be performed when the firstborn child was thirty days old, which consisted primarily in the payment of five shekels to a priest by the child's father for his firstborn son.[69] This payment signified redemption for the firstborn's lost responsibility of the priestly office, which had required him to be holy and consecrated for service to God on behalf of others.

Third, in addition to a double portion as well as a special blessing and the priestly office, the firstborn received a position of

---

[67] *Midrash Rabbah*, Numbers, 161. The midrash does not explain "anything prepared by fire," but offerings were frequently burned and identified as "offerings by fire." See, for example, Lev 1:9, 13; 2:2, 16; 3:3, 9, 11; Num 15:3, 10; 28:3, 19.

[68] Ginzberg, *Legends*, v. III, 211.

[69] Numb 3:47; 18:16; cf. *Midrash Rabbah*, Numb 73, f. 1. Many Jews still practice this ceremony of redemption today. See Isaac Klein, *A Guide to Jewish Religious Practices* (NY: Jewish Theological Seminary, 1979), 431-32.

authority and leadership. During his father's lifetime, the eldest son apparently exercised authority over his brothers as the narrative of Reuben conveys. When the other brothers wanted to kill Joseph, Reuben's decision for life was decisive (Gen 37:21-22). Furthermore, upon the death of his father the firstborn became the next leader of his clan or tribe, which made his elevation to this authoritative position part of his inheritance. Beitzel explains.

> The purpose of primogeniture then was the systematic and orderly transference of social, legal, and religious authority within the family structure. The firstborn male was made the principal heir and was given a sizeable portion of the estate because it was he who was to perpetuate the family name and lineage and who was to bear the chief burden for the continuance and welfare of the family....[70]

The Hebrew narrative portrays this concept of responsibility and lordship. For example, when Joseph became viceroy of Egypt he fulfilled a prophecy. Joseph had dreamt that his sheaf of grain was standing upright while those of his brothers were bowing down to his sheaf. His brothers responded with indignation. "Are you indeed to have dominion over us?" (Gen 37:5-8). The rhetorical answer, of course, is "yes!"

Another example is Jacob, who inherited the blessing of the birthright and the position of authority even though he was the younger son. This understanding of leadership becomes clear through Isaac's words to his firstborn son, Esau, when Isaac described Jacob's special blessing. "I have already made him [Jacob] your lord, and have given him all his brothers as servants" (Gen 27:37a). Leadership is a position of authority, which would lead Esau and his descendants to become servants of Jacob after Isaac's death.

Finally, in this position of leadership and authority, the firstborn son increased the strength of his tribe through procreation so that he could claim his inheritance by conquering

---

[70] Beitzel, "Right of the Firstborn," 180.

the land that had been promised to him.[71] Jacob's blessing of Reuben, who was born to the birthright which he subsequently lost, includes this attribute of the birthright: "my might and the first fruits of my vigor [*ohn*]" (Gen 49:3; cf. Dt 21:17). Fohrer notes that *ohn* conveys primarily the vigor that results from a man's procreative power, and further explains, "The man with such strength is able to acquire 'property' as the result or consequence of forceful action."[72] This strength of procreative power for the purpose of conquest is a meaningful concept in Scripture, apparently related to the blessing of abundant seed given to those patriarchs who inherit the birthright: Abraham, Isaac, and Jacob (Gen 15:5; 26:4; 28:14).[73]

To summarize, the firstborn son was entitled to his birthright by virtue of the position of his birth, which bestowed on him a double portion of his father's land and possessions. The birthright included four additional benefits and responsibilities. First was a special blessing that was greater than the blessings of his brothers. Second was the office of high priest to his family, clan or tribe. Third was a leadership position of authority over his clan. Finally, the son with the birthright was endowed with procreative power to strengthen his clan or tribe for the purpose of conquest. These birthright benefits are attributes of leadership. In the prophetic passages they point to a future role of service to God and His people.

---

[71] *Yarash* is often translated "inherit." However, the word also conveys the concept of inheritance by "taking possession" of land and "dispossessing" those who live in that land. Francis Brown et al., eds., *Brown-Driver-Briggs Hebrew and English Lexicon* (Peabody: Hendrikson, 1997), 439.

[72] Goerg Fohrer, "Twofold aspects of Hebrew Words," in *Words and Meanings*, eds. P. R. Ackroyd and B. Lindars (Cambridge: Cambridge University, 1968), 99.

[73] Related to abundant offspring is the promise that nations will come from the one receiving the birthright (Gen 17:4-6; 26:4; 35:11). The plural, nations (*goyim*), conveys a great abundance of many distinct peoples.

However, as we shall see in Part Two of this parable study, the firstborn son could lose his inheritance for unworthy behavior. In order to inherit the birthright the son was required to demonstrate leadership qualities. Only then would God select him to be worthy of this special inheritance of the birthright.

---

## *Mystery #4 in the Kingdom of God*

There is a special inheritance called the birthright to which the firstborn son was entitled. All the children of Israel have been born to this birthright, which is a position of leadership. However, the firstborn son had to prove that he was worthy of this special inheritance or God would select another son.

Because the New Testament parables exhort God's people to walk with Him in His Kingdom, they make frequent reference to the inheritance of birthright, and offer instruction for becoming worthy in the eyes of God.

---

Part Two

# Parables of Selection

Chapter Five

# Parable of the Pharisee and the Tax-Collector

This parable appears only in the Gospel of Luke. Before continuing, read Luke 18:9-14. Then practice going through the seven steps on your own before reading the thoughts and suggestions that follow.

There is imagery in this parable about Jewish tax-collectors, who worked for the Roman government. So, we will look briefly at this historical administrative position.

## Setting

Yeshua spoke this parable to "certain ones who trusted in themselves that they were righteous and viewed others with contempt" (Lk 18:9). In the context of the other parables these would likely have been leaders of the people such as Pharisees, scribes and elders. The story takes place on the temple grounds, so we will stop briefly and visualize the temple complex in Jerusalem at the time of Yeshua.

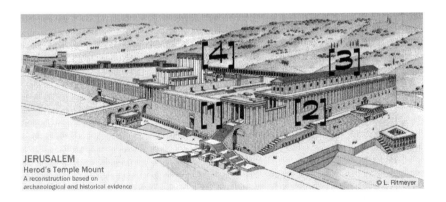

JERUSALEM
Herod's Temple Mount
A reconstruction based on
archaeological and historical evidence
© L. Ritmeyer

There were two separate entrances, one for the religious leaders [1] and the other for the common people [2]. The religious leaders would have spent much of their time in the large building known as the Treasury [3] where the religious administrative work of Judaism took place. As only two examples, the money from tithing was kept in the Treasury, and the Sanhedrin, the high court of Judaism, met there.

In front of the Treasury was a long covered porch or portal known as Solomon's Porch. Here the people would gather in the shade of the porch to hear the teachings of such masters as Yeshua. The Temple itself was a building that only the priests could enter, and then only at prescribed times for specific purposes. However, much of the activities related to the Temple would have occurred in the two open courtyards that were in front of the temple building [4].

As one entered this Temple complex, the first and largest courtyard was for the people (in the first century women sat in a second story balcony that overlooked the open courtyard). The smaller courtyard, directly in front of the temple, was where the altar of sacrifice was located, and only the priests could enter here.

The parable narrates that a Pharisee and a tax-gatherer "went up into the Temple to pray." This opening line is certainly startling. Freidrichsen observes, following Crossan's original ironic comment, that "a proposed modern rendition would be for today's hearers: Two people went up to St. Peter's Basilica to pray, one a pope, the other a pimp."[74] The tax-collector would have climbed up to the Temple Mount through the entrance for commoners, which passed under the Treasury and emerged in front it. The Pharisee, on the other hand, was privileged to use the special entrance for religious leaders that led into the interior of the Treasury. Both would have then proceeded across the Temple Mount to the first courtyard of the Temple to pray. Yet, we hear that the tax-collector stood some distance away from the Pharisee because he felt unworthy to be in the presence of this learned and powerful leader of God's people.

---

[74] Timothy A. Friedrichsen, "The Temple, A Pharisee, A Tax Collector, and the Kingdom of God: Rereading a Jesus Parable (Luke 18:10-14A)," *Journal of Biblical Literature* 124/1 (2005): 89. See also John Dominic Crossan, *In Parables: The Challenge of the Historical Jesus* (San Francisco: Harper & Row, 1973), 68-69.

## Tax Collectors in the Roman Empire

At the time of Yeshua, the Romans had so expanded their empire that Roman citizens in Italy no longer had to pay taxes but relied on taxation in the provinces to fund all of the administrative functions of the Roman government. The tax rate under normal circumstances was 1% throughout the provinces, but sometimes would climb as high as 3% in times of war. Roman taxes were levied against land, homes and other real estate, as well as slaves, animals, personal items and monetary wealth. A proper accounting of taxes was based on the periodic taking of a census.

This tax levy by the Romans was a modest amount when compared to the 10 percent tithe paid to the Jewish authorities in the Treasury. However, the Roman tax would often be much higher because of the Roman method of collection, and the subsequent opportunity for corruption. Tax collectors, known as *publicani*, were local provincials who knew the people in their provinces. They had the responsibility of converting properties and goods they collected into coinage. The *publicani* would keep anything in excess of what they owed the Roman government, which often became a very large sum that entered the pockets of these tax-collectors.

The publicans also used tax proceeds to act as money-lenders, charging high interest for the use of the excess funds they collected from the people. We have historical accounts of publicans who purchased large wholesale quantities of grain at low cost, then held this food in reserve until times of shortage when they sold it for high prices. The tax collectors were hated by the people, and the land of Israel was no exception.

Just because a tax-collector was a publican working for the Romans did not necessarily mean he acted corruptly. However, he was likely Jew who had to live among his people with the public perception of corruption. So, the people in Israel disliked, often to the point of animosity and loathing, these wealthy Jewish tax-collectors who worked for the Roman government.

We must now consider another aspect of the parable that is startling because of its contrast to the expected corrupt behavior of a tax-collector. We learn that the tax-collector in the parable "was even unwilling to lift up his eyes to heaven, but was beating his breast [an expression of extreme grief] saying, 'God, be merciful to me, the sinner!'" We recognize his cry of repentance, which God honors as righteous behavior. However, there is another aspect to this account. Perhaps the tax-collector saw himself as unrighteous simply as a reflection of the contempt of others. Those few who were learned in the Scriptures, and were recognized leaders of God's people, were inadvertently condemning others by seeing themselves as pure and righteous. In fact, look at the prayer of the Pharisee. "God, I thank you that I am not like other people: swindlers, unjust, adulterers, or even like this tax-gatherer." The parable handles the language artistically to portray worldly condemnation of a tax collector, who was nevertheless humble and righteous in God's eyes, and godly condemnation of the pride of knowledge and position that the world elevates.

## Connection to the Hebrew Scriptures

I could find no direct citation that leads us to the Hebrew Scriptures. However, there is a glaring repetition that would have caught the attention of the first century listener and that acts as a clue for modern readers. "Everyone who exalts himself shall be humbled, but he who humbles himself shall be exalted" (Mat 23:12). Knowing that the parables are *haggadic midrash*, which comment on some passage or narrative in the Hebrew Scriptures, our curiosity is drawn to this puzzling repetition. The clue is in the word "exalted," and the connection, I suggest, is in the Cain and Abel story. Here God speaks to Cain after he killed his brother Abel.

> Why are you angry? And why has your countenance fallen? If you do well, will not *your countenance* be lifted up [*se'et;* exalted]? And if you do not do well, sin is crouching at the door; and its desire is for you, but you must master it. (Gen 4:6-7)

Now we will see that there is more in this account of Cain and Abel that gives meaning to our verse in the parable about the Pharisee and the tax-collector.

## Cain and Abel

We remember that Cain and Abel were the sons of Adam and

Eve. Both brought offerings to God, but God only accepted Abel's offering. We will read what follows in English, but even in the English translation we can observe a common Hebraic play on words. Then we will use a concordance to further examine a significant Hebrew word.

> NASB TRANSLATION: The LORD said to Cain, "Why are you angry? And why has your countenance fallen? If you do well, will not *your countenance* be lifted up?"

> MY TRANSLATION: The LORD said to Cain, "Why are you angry? And why has your countenance fallen? If you do well, will you not be exalted?"

Italics in the NASB translation indicate words that the translators have added to clarify the meaning. In this case they inserted *your countenance* and translated *se'et* as "lifted up." This is a good translation for the plain meaning of the text. We are drawn to the juxtaposition of Cain's face having "fallen," which is shown in contrast to his face being "lifted up." However, there is also, in this verse, a play on words that conveys a deeper meaning.

When we delete the second countenance, which is not in the original text, we are left with "will you not be lifted up?" Our omission of the italicized countenance, which the translators added because the word is implied, makes perfect sense in light of the Hebrew word. Using a concordance we discover that the word is שאת (*se'et*), which means to be lifted up in a way that is exalted. When will Cain be exalted? When Cain (and this applies to us also) "does well." "Does well" is a translation of the verbal form of a Hebrew word you may recognize, which is טוב (*tov*), meaning "good", that is, "doing something well." In the very first usage of the word *tov* we read, "God saw that the light was *good*; and God separated the light from the darkness" (Gen 1:4). Thus, if we are pleasing in God's eyes (represented by light in Gen 1:4), then we are walking in His ways in humble obedience with love in our hearts. Thus, God is holding out to Cain a potential blessing. If he "does well" he will be "exalted." (Unfortunately Cain did not accept this offer).

Now let us go back to our verse in its context in the Cain and Abel story because there is more that is significant.

> "If you do well, will you not be lifted up [exalted]?
> And if you do not do well, sin is crouching at the
> door; and its desire is for you, but you must master
> it." (Gen 4:7)

The concept of "mastering sin" is conveyed by the Hebrew word משל (*mashal*), which means to rule, have dominion over, or be lord over. Now our curiosity is drawn to "sin is crouching at the door." We must practice responding to this vivid imagery, not with our twenty-first century minds but with an ancient mind that knew the Hebrew Scriptures intimately and heard these echoes.

Let me stop for a moment and point out something about the life of people in Israel during the time of Yeshua (and even earlier for that matter). The Jordan River valley was so dense with undergrowth that lions could live there. In fact, the Romans captured lions from the Jordan River Valley and brought them to Rome where they amused the people by feeding undesirables to the lions. So, for the people of ancient Israel something crouching at your door could easily have been a lion. What makes this suggestion likely is the echo of Samson who killed a lion. Metaphorically speaking, Samson was killing the enemy, which is sin, in order that he could rise up to become a prophet of God.

So, Cain's face has fallen because he has committed a grievous sin, which means he has brought himself low and must bear the consequences. Yet, God extends the hope of reversing the penalty. If Cain can have dominion over sin in his life, God will exalt him.

### Returning to the Parable

The early listeners to this parable would likely have heard the echo of "exalt" and "humble." We can now apply it to the repeated refrain in our parable: "Everyone who exalts himself shall be humbled, but he who humbles himself shall be exalted." That is, if one "does well" by mastering sin he will be exalted. However, if he "does not do well," his face (and much more) will fall. What does it mean to "do well?" We must humble ourselves before the Lord our God in loving worship and serving obedience.

Yeshua is using irony when he applies the Cain and Abel story to both the Pharisee and the tax collector in the parable.

Irony is a linguistic device that conveys a figurative sense, which is the exact opposite of its literal meaning.

Before Yeshua delivers his cutting and sarcastic words as a form of ironic instruction, the Pharisee would have identified with Abel whose unblemished sacrifice was a sweet aroma that ascended to God. Certainly the Pharisee saw himself as an acceptable sacrifice to God. However, the parable twists what the Pharisee expected to become the opposite of the expectation. The Pharisee was actually like Cain whose offering was *not* accepted by God.

At this point we must turn to the reason that Abel's sacrifice was pleasing to God and Cain's was not. Again we have a translation problem that struggles to convey the nuance of the Hebrew text. Nevertheless, you do not have to be fluent in Hebrew to see it. Let your curiosity be drawn to the key word "firstling" of his flock (NASB, KJV), also translated "firstborn" of his flock (NIV). The Hebrew is בכור (*bechor*), meaning the firstborn animals, the best and most choice animals that were given to God in sacrifice. The Hebrew language is formed from three-letter verbal roots. In this case בכר (*bachar*) means to be chosen or selected. From this verbal root various related words are formed including the birthright (בכרה; *b'chorah*) and firstfruits (בכורים; *b'chorim*). That is, Abel gave his best to God, the first fruit of his flock, and by this sacrifice of love he was worthy to inherit the birthright.

The relationship of Abel's acceptable sacrifice to our parable is poignant. God asks all His children to offer themselves as an unblemished, that is, a righteous sacrifice (fortunately God only sees the heart). Yet, "pride *goes* before destruction, and a haughty spirit before stumbling" (Pro 16:18). We can imagine the Pharisee's face falling as he began to perceive the message of the parable.

Where is the tax collector in this story? He had climbed to the temple mount through the commoner's entrance. He was working for the hated Roman government by collecting taxes from the people. He saw himself as a grievous sinner. "God, be merciful to me, the sinner!" In his humility he must not have expected the twist in the parable message. God was simply telling him to "do well" and to "master sin." If he did this, God would see him as an acceptable sacrifice and would accept his prayer. Perhaps he had been overcharging the people so he could become wealthy. However, in the parable he displays humility.

1. How do you think the tax collector responded to the message of the parable?
2. How do you think the Pharisee responded to the message of the parable?
3. Do you put yourself in the position of the Pharisee or the tax collector?
4. How do you respond to the message of this parable?

## The Ending

We have been identifying with the tax-collector, who was a sinner as we are. To be justified in the eyes of God the sinner simply prayed, "God, be merciful to me, the sinner!"

We have probably been gloating over God's judgment of those who "trusted in themselves that they were righteous, and viewed others with contempt." After all, we are not self-righteous... are we?

This conclusion is open-ended. I suggest that we have elements of *both* the sinner *and* the self-righteous Pharisee in us. The parable urges intense self-examination of who we are and who we want to become.

## Mystery #5 in the Kingdom of God

Our hearts desire to "do well" and to please God. We can look at Abel who gave God his very best, which the first fruits of his flock represents. When we give God our best we are exalted in His eyes. The best that the sinner had to give in the parable was a prayer from his heart, not from his head or his lips. "God, be merciful to me, the sinner."

If we "do not do well," we will be like Cain who was cast out of God's presence. We will be left to the whims of the world and will suffer the consequences of our worldly actions. Yet, we must remember that even Cain, who killed his brother, did not earn the penalty of death. We read that "the Lord appointed a sign for Cain, lest anyone finding him should slay him" (Gen 4:15). God has given His children the gift of life, but then He exhorts them to a living walk that draws them near to Him.

Thus, when we "do not do well" we are separating ourselves from God. But when we "do well" by humbling ourselves before God, we are exalted in His eyes.

## Chapter Six

# Parable of the Mustard Seed

We all know the parable of the mustard seed that appears in all three of the synoptic gospels.[75] I remember hearing this story as a young child in Sunday School, although I don't remember the moral lesson, but I'm sure there was one. What teacher or pastor can overlook an opportunity to explain that we may feel small, but when we have God in our lives we are giants.

This traditional Christian understanding is known in Hebrew as the *p'shat*, the simple or plain meaning. The Hebrew tradition acknowledges the *p'shat* and considers it important because God placed it there. However, we must remember Yeshua's words, that these parables also contain mysteries about the Kingdom of God. This deeper meaning can be uncovered by those with hearts that yearn to grow closer to our heavenly Father through their Lord Yeshua. The Jewish tradition calls this deeper meaning "midrash."

When I finally uncovered the mystery of the mustard seed, I was thrilled to perceive something quite different from my Sunday school lesson. That does not negate the moral instruction about the perception of size. However, the mystery penetrated such a depth of understanding that I felt awed and humbled in the presence of a God who would reveal such wonders to me. I will not tell you right now what I discovered. That would be the Greco-Roman approach. Instead, I will try to lead you with me on a path of discovery.

Although this parable appears in three of the gospels, my own preference is not to conflate the three accounts by attempting to make them one unified parable, but to select one. In this case, I have chosen Matthew 13:31-32.

---

[75] Matthew 13:31; Mark 4:31; Luke 13:18.

## Setting

We start, of course, with the setting. I suggest we have to go all the way back to Matthew 13:1-2 to see the beginning of the setting. However, we must also give careful consideration to Matthew 13:10. Yeshua was speaking to great multitudes who had come to hear him speak.

The setting of this parable is significant because it does not continue what we have seen in the last two parables. The former parables portrayed a stark contrast between the religious leaders of the day, who were self-righteous in their own eyes, and the humble, who came to God with a heart seeking His forgiveness. However, here in Matthew 13 Yeshua is talking only to those who want to hear him speak so there is a different kind of distinction. On one hand we have "great multitudes," and on the other we have a small group of disciples or followers.[76] The same is true today. Among Christians, only some are dedicated followers of the Lord Jesus Christ although there are many who believe in him.

So, Yeshua was teaching in parables, and we must identify with the disciples, those who were committed to following their Lord in humble obedience. To these disciples "it has been granted to know the mysteries of the kingdom of heaven."

## Kingdom of God or Kingdom of Heaven

Let me stop here for a moment to comment on two terms, Kingdom of God and Kingdom of Heaven. Students sometimes ask if they are the same, or are they different. If a student is learning how to search the Scriptures using first century methods, he or she sometimes requests this as a topic for a class project. If you conduct this same study by searching the Scriptures to find where these terms appear, you will likely conclude that the two

---

[76] The Greek word that is translated "disciple" is μαθητή ς (*mathetes*). In the first century tradition, the teacher was a master and disciples were his students who followed him, learned from him, and desired to be like him. When Yeshua said to Peter and Andrew, "Follow me,." he was conveying a request for them to become his disciples as followers of their Lord and master.

terms seem to be synonymous. At least that is my conclusion and tends to be the conclusion of my students. However, you will probably also discover something rather startling. The term, Kingdom of Heaven, is only used in the Gospel of Matthew whereas Kingdom of God is quite prevalent in the other three gospels and also the letters of Paul.

I suggest there may be a simple explanation. The Gospel of Matthew is quite Hebraic in its language, imagery, and its relationship to the Tanach.[77] It was undoubtedly composed by a Jew, perhaps originally for an audience of Jewish believers. Today in Orthodox Judaism the name of God is not spoken aloud. Instead, we may hear *Adonai* (My Lord) or *HaShem* (the name) or in English, The Holy One. The same may have been true in the first century. So, the author of Mathew may have substituted, for Kingdom of God, the Kingdom of the Holy One or Kingdom of our Lord or Kingdom of *HaShem*. But perhaps instead he substituted Heaven for God, thus Kingdom of Heaven.

I tend to use these terms interchangeably. So, hopefully this explanation will prevent confusion.

## Bible Versions

Our parable occupies only two verses so there is not much in the way of imagery and artistic language. However, what jumps out immediately in my Bible version is the citation from the Hebrew Scriptures, which you can identify in a Bible version that puts these citations in small capital letters. So, this is a good time for me to explain the Bible versions.

We read the New Testament in some kind of English version, but of course the Bible was not written in English. The Hebrew Scriptures were composed predominantly in Hebrew, although there are small passages in Aramaic. However, the New

---

[77] Tanach is an acronym that refers to the Hebrew Scriptures (the Old Testament). Tanach stands for Torah (first five books of Moses), Nevi'im (the Prophets) and Ketuvim (the Writings).

Testament was originally written in an ancient Greek dialect called Koine.[78] But let me insert a word of caution.

Every English Bible is a translation from the original Greek, Hebrew and Aramaic. A "version" refers to a particular translation. The King James Version, for example, was a translation completed in 1611. Most other versions are more recent. However, the versions are different depending on the specific purpose of the translation. The New American Standard Version, which I prefer to use, stays as close to the original text as possible. The New International Version, on the other hand, is a translation that sounds more like the English that we speak today, but it takes liberties with the translation to achieve this goal.

I recommend to my students the New American Standard Bible Reference Edition for several reasons. First, we have already noted that the NASB attempts to translate as close to the original Hebrew and Greek as possible, even if the translation sounds somewhat stilted. Second, if the translators felt they needed to add a word to make the translation more understandable, they marked the addition in italics. Third, what is helpful to our work on the parables is the identification of citations with small capital letters. Fourth, in the middle margin you will find the location of each citation in the Hebrew Scriptures. Finally, the NASB uses red letters for words spoken by Yeshua, so it is easy to locate the setting as separate from the parable.

Now we are ready to look at the citation in the New American Standard Version.

---

[78] In the first century, Hebrew was the language of the Holy Writings just as Latin is the language of the Catholic Bible today (known as the Vulgate Version). Aramaic was the common dialect of the people in Israel, which they had brought back with them from their period of captivity in Babylon (Aramaic was also the lingua franca of the Fertile Crescent). After the Greeks conquered much of the ancient world, a dialect of Greek known as Koine became the common language of trade. After the Romans conquered the Greek empire, Latin emerged as the language of government and administration.

> He presented another parable to them, saying,
> "The kingdom of heaven is like a mustard seed,
> which a man took and sowed in his field;
>
> and this is smaller than all *other* seeds, but when it
> is full grown, it is larger than the garden plants and
> becomes a tree, so that THE BIRDS OF THE AIR come
> and NEST IN ITS BRANCHES." (Mat 13:32)

You can see the citation. THE BIRDS OF THE AIR...NEST IN ITS
BRANCHES. The middle margin of the NASB tells us to go to
Ezekiel 17:23. However, before we do that, I must explain how
the people of the first century would have responded to this
citation.

## What to do with a Citation from the Hebrew Scriptures

We remember that people in ancient Israel did not have books,
but had memorized the Holy Writings from the time they were
small children. Boys may have learned to read later in the
synagogue, but even in the synagogue much of the instruction was
oral. Furthermore, they did not memorize verse-by-verse but in
blocks or portions of Scripture. So, when they read a small citation
like this one in the Parable of the Mustard Seed, it would have
stimulated the entire memorized passage in their minds. That is
why we must turn to the Hebrew Scriptures and learn how to
identify the context of the cited verse. Context means the
surrounding verses that complete one unified thought.

Turn now to Ezekiel 17:23 but keep your finger in
Matthew 13:32. You will be flipping back and forth between the
two, but we will start in Mathew.

1. The citation in the NT is not exactly the same as the
   verse in Ezekiel. Why do you think the translators
   selected Ez 17:23 as the likely verse in the Hebrew
   Scriptures that the parable was citing?

2. If Scripture was memorized in blocks, then we must
   identify that block in Ezekiel. We will never know for
   certain, but at the very least we must ask, "What is the
   context in which Ez 17:23 is located?" That is, what

verses do you think constitute the context? In the
following questions I will call this context "the block."

3. We often make a distinction between the immediate
   context and the larger context. The larger context
   would be the memorized block. The immediate
   context is a smaller portion that contains a smaller
   sub-idea within the larger context. The immediate
   context can also assist in understanding how the
   citation functions in the NT passage. Do you agree
   with me that the immediate context is Ez 17:22-24,
   and the greater context probably begins in Ez 17:11?
   However, for our purposes, we will work now with
   the immediate context of Ez 17:22-24. Read these
   three verses carefully, almost to the point of
   memorization.

4. The cedars of Lebanon portray an image of being large
   and majestic. Note that the translators have added the
   word *sprig*. Without this additional word we probably
   have a more accurate meaning. God has taken from
   the lofty top of this majestic tree. The verbal root for
   the Hebrew word "top" is רום (*rum*), which means
   exalted. So, God is selecting only a small portion of
   the majestic tree, the new life at the topc, and these
   few branches are exalted.

5. Before we can continue, we need to "hear" Ez 17:22 in
   its poetic rhythm. My translation follows.

   I will take from the exalted top of the cedar,
   And I will give [as an offering] from the tender
       head branches,
   And I will transplant it to a high and towering
       mountain.

If you read this verse aloud, you will hear the rhythm that evokes
emotion. However, you also need to capture the visual imagery.
The topmost branches are new, light green, and tender. They are
being transplanted from the mountains of Lebanon to Mount
Zion in Jerusalem. As for symbols, the towering cedar tree

represents Israel,[79] but only the tender head branches are being selected and transplanted to Mount Zion.

There are also some astonishing words in our passage in Ezekiel that you may not see in an English version. We have already identified my translation from the Hebrew as "exalted top of the cedar." Various English versions have translated "highest branch of the high cedar" (KJ), "the very top of a cedar" (NIV), or "the lofty top of the cedar" (NASB). However, I suggest that "exalted" in this passage refers to people, that is, some of God's people whom God has exalted. Why have I drawn this conclusion? In part because the Hebrew word that has been translated "top," "high" or "lofty" is ראש (rosh), which is Hebrew for "head," that is, head branches. Rosh in the Exodus account refers to the leaders or heads of the clans and tribes of Israel,[80] who are undoubtedly the ones who will inherit the birthright that we saw in the Parable of the Prodigal Son.

With the exalted top branches we also see a selection from the cedar tree. Since the cedar tree represents Israel, God is making a selection from Israel. I suggest that we can extend this concept to include a selection from all God's people including Gentile believers in His son. One thing is certain. Only the exalted ones at the top of the majestic tree are worthy in God's eyes. These are the ones who are leaders of God's people, who are worthy to inherit the birthright, and whom God will bring to Mount Zion.

Let us look now at the next verse, Ezekiel 17:23.

1. In the first half of the verse, what is the key word? Actually it is two words that convey one concept.

2. Who bears fruit for God?

---

[79] Wood from the cedar tree was considered a holy and cleansing element (Lev 14:1-7, 48-57). Cedar was used in the building of the temple (1Kings 5:5-10). The lofty cedar tree that grew in the mountains of Lebanon became the symbol for a righteous man (92:12). Zech 11:2 uses the cedar figuratively of fallen Israel.

[80] Ex 6:25, 18:25; Deut 1:15; Joshua 14:1.

3. Why are those who bear fruit for God exalted by Him?

4. What is the relationship between the words "exalted" and "head" as they relate to the inheritance of the birthright?

Now it is time to turn back to the NT, but keep your finger in Ezekiel. Look again at the citation in the NT parable that we have just seen in the second half of Ez 17: 23. You will note that the citation in the NT is not exactly the same as the verse it is citing. The ancient ear would have heard the difference, and in the intentional difference you will discover an exciting meaning.

The birds of the air come and nest in its branches.
(Mat 13:32)

Birds of every kind will nest under it;
They will nest in the shade of its branches.
(Ez 17:23b)

I believe the ancient listener would have been startled because there is a striking difference between nesting *in* the branches, which I suggest represents the completion of God's work when His people are at rest, and nesting *under* the branches in shade. Nesting under the branches seems to represent loving protection so we ask, "When do we need loving protection?" We need it in our loves today. If we place ourselves in the loving protection of God, we are walking in His ways and serving Him.

5. So now we ask, "When do we need loving protection?" We need it in our loves today. If we place ourselves in the loving protection of God, we are walking in His ways and serving Him.

6. Our next question must be, "Who do the birds represent?" First consider the two physical objects. In Ezekiel we have already seen the topmost branches of the lofty cedar tree that God transplanted to Mount Zion. Now we have birds that are nesting in the shade of the branches. Who do the birds represent?

7. Do you think the meaning of the parable in Matthew is related to "in the branches" or "under the shade of the branches" or could it be both? Explain your answer

8. Who do the branches represent? How do they provide shade and/or make a place for the birds?

9. In Ezekiel 17:24 God has brought down the high tree ("high" represents pride) and has exalted the low tree ("low" represents humility). Who are the high and who are the low?

I suggest that nesting in the shade of its branches (Ezekiel) represents the end of God's work when all His children will be at rest in God's loving and comforting presence. The different words of the parable would have startled the ancient listeners by the distinct difference from what they had memorized in Ezekiel. Given the imagery of God selecting those who are worthy of leadership and transplanting them to Mount Zion, it seems that nesting in the branches could signify the role of the remnant, those who serve God by leading His people. The multitude or the crowd (all of God's people) are in need of the protecting shade that God provides through His remnant, not only now by the leadership role that guides God's people in righteousness but also in the future when the remnant will be prepared to possess the inheritance by defeating the enemy.

## Returning to the Parable

It is time now to return to our parable in Matthew. Let me point out something else that is especially startling. The mustard plant in the parable is not a large and lofty tree like the cedar in Ezekiel. True, it has a small seed, but the plant is anything but lofty. The mustard plant is not a tree. It is a bushy and straggly plant that grows like a weed in Israel. You can find photos of it on the web if you choose.

So, what we seem to have again, as we are learning about how to walk in the Kingdom of God, is that the Heavenly Father is making a selection of the tender tops of the cedar tree (Israel) whom He has exalted. God's choice is not for the purpose of who will be saved and who will not be saved, but He is selecting those who come to Him in humble obedience as they are being trained as leaders of God's people. They appear as a small, bushy, straggly plant to the world, but they are, in fact, humble and obedient before the power of God. They are towering and majestic trees in God's eyes.

## Mystery #6 in the Kingdom of God

I suggest that those whom the world sees as bushy, straggly and not that large may be, in God's eyes, worthy of the inheritance of the birthright. These tiny mustard seeds may have hearts that truly love God by humbly submitting in obedience to Him. If the cedar tree represents all of God's children, then these tiny mustard seeds are the humble ones who are submitting in obedience to God. They are becoming a new creation with new life, and are bearing fruit for Him. At some time in the future God will exalt them and make them "head" (that is, leaders) over His people, and He will place them on Mount Zion in His presence. But now, God is exalting, in His eyes, those who are humble and bearing fruit. These are the true leaders of God's people today.

Viewing this parable through the Hebraic sense of time we can see exalted ones among us now, not necessarily those whom the world has exalted but those whom God sees as worthy to serve Him as obedient servants and leaders of His people.

## Chapter Seven

# Parable of the Lowest Seat

As always, you should start by carefully reading the parable, which you will find in Luke 14:7-14. By now you should be able to follow the seven steps before considering my thoughts and suggestions.

1. Describe the setting in which Yeshua is speaking this parable.
2. Who are the main characters in the setting? Is the parable responding in any way to the setting and the main characters?
3. What is it about the parable that is strange and puzzling? Are you asking yourself questions that may lead you to the puzzling aspect of the parable? You may not know the answers to your questions yet, but at least you should be asking questions.
4. There is a lot of repetition in this parable. What repetition do you hear? Do you recognize a central verse? What makes it central? What is on either side of this central verse?
5. Finding the connection to the Hebrew Scriptures can be a challenge, but go ahead and try. Here is a hint. I focused on "the last place" which is in contrast to the place of honor that would be "the first place."
6. Is the ending tragic, happy, or open-ended?
7. Leave the practical application of the parable until after you have worked it and penetrated its deeper meaning.

## Hebraic Artistry of Language

The parable is written in Greek, but the linguistic artistry is characteristic of biblical Hebrew, which makes perfect sense because early listeners knew the Hebrew Scriptures intimately and undoubtedly spoke Aramaic, which is related to Hebrew. For example, let me draw your attention to the pivotal verse and why I drew this conclusion. "Everyone who exalts himself shall be humbled, and he who humbles himself shall be exalted" (Luke 14:11). The entire parable rotates around this pivotal focus. Now look above this central idea and all three verses are about being invited to some kind of banquet or special meal (verse 8 calls it a wedding feast).

> [8]**When you are invited** by someone to a wedding feast, do not take the place of honor, for someone more distinguished than you may have been invited by him,
>
> [9]**And he who invited you** both will come and say to you, 'Give your place to this man,' and then in disgrace you proceed to occupy the last place.
>
> [10]**When you are invited**, go and recline at the last place, so that when the one who has invited you comes, he may say to you, 'Friend, move up higher'; then you will have honor in the sight of all who are at the table with you.

1.  How are verses 8 and 10 similar (in addition to the beginning words)?
2.  How has verse 10 been expanded with an addition? The ancient "ear" would have heard this addition. What makes the addition significant to the meaning of the parable?
3.  Verse 9 is central and therefore highlighted and significant. Who is the person in verse 9? Who does he likely represent? What is the word of authority that he declares? What is the importance of his words to the meaning of the first three verses?

The invitation to a special meal is evident. However, do you see the repetition of "when you are invited?" This repetition seems to be bracketing a chiastic center in verse 9, which shifts our attention away from the person who is invited (apparently a disciple or one desiring to be a disciple) to the one making the invitation (the disciple's master). Furthermore, there is an expanding relationship between the two parallel verses 8 and 10. In the first (verse 8), the instruction is simply not to take the place of honor. In the parallel line (verse 10), the instruction is specifically where to sit and the reason for this particular seating. The master seems to be instructing his disciple.

Now look below the central focus and the verses are no longer about being invited to a banquet but about *giving* a banquet.

> [12]**When you give a luncheon or a dinner**, do not invite your friends or your brothers or your relatives or rich neighbors, otherwise they may also invite you in return and that will be your repayment.
> [13]**When you give a reception**, invite *the* poor, *the* crippled, *the* lame.

1. In these two verses, consider the examples of *how* we can be exalted by humbling ourselves.
2. Who is doing the talking?
3. How are these words a form of instruction?
4. Do you agree with me that the one who is giving the banquet in verses 12 and 13 is apparently a disciple who has become a master and is now inviting others to become *his* disciples?
5. In verse 12, did you notice the negative criticism (do not invite friends or brothers or relatives)?
6. In verse 13, did you hear the sudden shift from the negative to the positive command (invite the poor, crippled, lame and blind)?

There is irony in this invitation because the master's choice of disciples is the poor, the crippled and the lame, not those who already know the Law and consider themselves exalted by this knowledge.

Now let us return to the pivotal verse, Luke 14:11. The one who exalts himself will be humbled and the one who humbles himself will be exalted. Above the pivotal verse the person is learning the importance of "humbling." This person is a disciple, or one who desires to be a disciple. Below the central verse the person has matured to the point where he (or she) is teaching by "doing." This person is a former disciple who has become a master and is now teaching other disciples by his (or her) godly walk and actions. In the middle pivot, the instruction is expressed with irony. When we think we are exalted, we will be humbled. When we humble ourselves before God, He will exalt us.

Luke 14:14 is a conclusion to verses 12 and 13. However, the conclusion also has a relationship to the focal verse 11 by explaining the positive consequence or result of humbling yourself before God as a disciple, who will eventually become a master of other disciples. Yes, the one who humbles himself will be exalted. However, the conclusion tells us that the disciple will also be blessed with some kind of reward at the time of the resurrection of the righteous.

> Focal verse of the parable: "Everyone who exalts himself will be humbled, and he who humbles himself will be exalted."
> Conclusion to verses 12-13: "You will be blessed, since they [the poor, the crippled and the lame] do not have *the means* to repay you; for you will be repaid at the resurrection of the righteous."[81]

## Curiosity and Questions

Very often repetition is the clue in a parable that will lead you to the Hebrew Scriptures. There is repetition in this parable, but not with the same words. Instead it seems to be a repetition of concepts.

> [8] "Do not take the place of honor...."
> [10] "Recline at the last place...."

We remember that the first three verses are clustered together by inviting the disciple to a banquet. The master who is extending the invitation declares, "When you are invited, go and recline at the last place...."

I was drawn to the phrase, "last place." The parable tells us that the one who occupies the last place is actually humbling himself and will be exalted to "the first place." That is, the one

---

[81] *The means* has been italicized by the editors of the NASB translation because it is not in the original text, but has been added for clarification.

who is last will be first, and the first will be last.[82] So, we have in the parable a contrast between the "first place" and the "last place," as well as irony that the first is in fact the last, and the last will be first.

What is there in the Hebrew Scriptures that echoes these thoughts about the last being first, and the one in the last place going to the place of honor? Take some time to consider this question before continuing.

## Connection to the Hebrew Scriptures: Esau and Jacob

In the narrative in Genesis, we see two sets of twins. In both cases, the one born first became last in position by losing his birthright of inheritance, which was given to the younger brother. We remember that a son had to be "worthy" in order to inherit the birthright. Apparently the older brother, who considered himself worthy because he was born to a position (or seat) of honor, did not, in the end, deserve that seat. However, the important question is this. How and why did the younger brother earn the seat of honor? Let us look at the two accounts.

| Parents | Twins | Verses |
|---|---|---|
| Isaac and Rebecca | Esau and Jacob | Gen 25:19-34; 27:1-46 |
| Judah and Tamar | Perez and Zerah | Gen 38:27-30 |

Rebecca was the wife of Isaac. When she became pregnant "the children struggled together within her." Even in the womb there was a skirmish between the contenders for the leadership role that the birthright bestowed. From this struggle would emerge the one who was prepared and worthy to fulfill this position. The Hebrew word for struggle (רצץ *ratsats*) conveys a sense of confrontation that is so intense that one party will be crushed. Therefore, to be worthy of the birthright is not an easy path to

---

[82] The phrase, "first will be last, and last will be first", appears elsewhere in the gospels (Mat 19:30; cf. Mark 10:31). Although this exact phrase does not occur in the Parable of the Lowest Seat, the concept is the same.

follow. One must contend in a way that will result in struggle and battle to the point of crushing, not one's brother or sister, but Gods enemy.

Before continuing, read about Esau and Jacob in Genesis 25:19-34; 27:1-46. Then consider the following questions.

1. In the prophetic words that God spoke to Rebekah, what will be the two nations/peoples?
2. What does it mean that "one people shall be stronger than the other, and the older shall serve the younger?"
3. How did Jacob acquire the birthright?
4. We need to ask, "What in the narrative of Jacob's purchasing the birthright from his brother helps us understand that Esau was unworthy to inherit the birthright?" Keep in mind the requirement of obedience, even unto death.
5. How did Jacob acquire the blessing that accompanied the birthright?
6. What was Rebekah's participation in this deceit? What were the consequences that she had to bear?
7. Jacob also had to bear consequences for his actions. What were these consequences? How did Jacob emerge from the consequences of his testing experiences a stronger and more worthy candidate than his brother Esau? Why was Jacob worthy to inherit the birthright?

## Connection to the Hebrew Scriptures: Perez and Zerah

The account of the birth of Perez and Zerah occurs in Genesis 38:27-30. However, to fully appreciate this story you must read these four verses in their context, which is all of Genesis 38. Before continuing, read Genesis 38.

1. Which twin does Scripture tell us "came out first?"
2. The other twin would have been "last." But what happened at the time of his birth?

We need to look at Hebrew words and names which are rich with meaning. We will start with the scarlet thread that the midwife tied on the hand of the one who "came out first." There is one other account of a scarlet thread, when Rahab helped the

Israeli spies escape from Jericho (Joshua 2:28). So, the color scarlet
(שָׁנִי shani) apparently has powerful symbolic meaning. We gain an
understanding of this symbolism from God's careful instructions
for building the tabernacle, which included fabric woven from
scarlet thread for the two veils, one veil placed before a priest
entered the first portion of the tabernacle, and the other before the
high priest entered the innermost part known as the Holy of
Holies. So, the color scarlet is related to entering the holy presence
of God. Thus, the one born first, who was entitled to the
birthright, nevertheless had to prove he was worthy of that
inheritance. As God's representative he would be acting as leader
of his tribe, serving as high priest, and commanding the army in
battle. These are positions of authority and require a close
relationship with God that the color scarlet signifies.

However Zerah, the one who came out first, drew back
the hand on which the scarlet thread had been tied. Then his twin
brother, Perez, emerged from the birth canal. Perez was the
younger and second-born. "What a breach you have made for
yourself," declared the midwife. "So he was named Perez." The
word "breach" and the name Perez are constructed from the same
verbal root פרץ (parats), which is a significant word in Scripture. It
means a bursting forth or breakthrough, conveying a prophetic
image of something future and a significant part of God's great
plan for mankind. So, let us examine in greater depth this word
parats.

We first see parats in God's words to Jacob. "Your
descendants will be like the dust of the earth, and you will spread
out [פרץ, burst forth or break through] to the west and to the east
and to the north and to the south" (Gen 28:14). This concept of a
multitude beyond imagination appears again in another passage of
prophecy. "Your barns will be filled with plenty and your vats will
overflow [פרץ] with new wine" (Pro 3:10). What is significant is
this concept of abundant descendants and overflowing vats of
wine, which is characteristic of the son who will inherit the
birthright with an abundance that the double portion represents.

In his position of leadership and authority, the firstborn
son must increase the strength of his tribe in order to claim his

inheritance by conquering the land that the Lord has bequethed to him.[83] He will bear abundant seed, which is righteous because he is righteous. Jacob's blessing to his firstborn, Reuben, who was born to the birthright which he subsequently lost, includes this attribute of the birthright. "My might and the first fruits of my vigor [ohn]," declared Jacob (Gen 49:3; cf. Deut 21:17). Fohrer notes that *ohn* conveys the vigor that results from a man's procreative power, and further explains, "The man with such strength is able to acquire 'property' as the result or consequence of forceful action."[84]

However, the words of prophecy about Reuben continue. "Checked like water you may not lead." Reuben lost his ability to bear abundant seed after his kind, which must be humble, obedient and righteous, because Reuben was declared unworthy to inherit the birthright. Instead, this leadership role was given to Joseph. God has given this strength of procreative power, which will lead to conquest and overcoming the enemy, to those patriarchs who were worthy in His eyes – Abraham, Isaac, Jacob and Joseph (Gen 15:5; 26:4; 28:14).[85] These patriarchs will be blessed with abundant seed like the stars in the sky and the sand on the seashore.[86]

---

[83] *Yarash* is often translated "inherit." However, the word also conveys the concept of inheritance by "taking possession" of land and "dispossessing" those who live in that land. Francis Brown et al., eds., *Brown-Driver-Briggs Hebrew and English Lexicon* (Peabody: Hendrikson, 1997), 439.

[84] Goerg Fohrer, "Twofold aspects of Hebrew Words," in *Words and Meanings*, ed. P. R. Ackroyd and B. Lindars (Cambridge: Cambridge University, 1968), 99.

[85] Related to abundant offspring is the promise that nations will come from the one receiving the birthright (Gen. 17:4-6; 26:4; 35:11). The plural "nations" (*goyim*) conveys a great abundance of many distinct peoples.

[86] Genesis 15:5; 22:17; 26:4.

## Returning to the Parable

The parable declares, "When you are invited...." The invitation is to participate in a banquet, which symbolizes a future celebration of victory after defeating God's enemy. Who will be prepared and worthy to fight this battle? They are the ones who are humble in the presence of God by their submission and obedience.

By their humility they seat themselves in the lowest seat, which is where God can begin to work with them. You have read the account of Jacob. He may have purchased the birthright from his brother and received by deceit the blessing that accompanied the birthright, but God did not declare him worthy until after he had spent twenty years in exile in Padan Aram. During that time God was working with Jacob to instruct him how to walk and act in godly ways. It was not until after Jacob had wrestled with an angel, when he was returning to the Promised Land, that God changed his name from Jacob to Israel. At this point God deemed him worthy to inherit the birthright that he had originally purchased (Gen 32:24-32).

## Practical Application

The ending of this parable depends on the way each individual receives its message. If you are prideful about your perceived position in the eyes of God, the ending will be tragic. You will not be invited to the victory banquet. If you are humble and submit to instruction from God, the outcome may be a happy one. If God deems you worthy to be part of the future remnant that will defeat God's enemy, you will be present during the banquet and will share in the celebration. However most of us are in a stage of our lives that presents the parable as open-ended. We are not in the prideful camp of self-righteousness, nor are we walking in righteousness with a humble heart that allows God to work with us in a truly meaningful way.

Thus, the practical application of this parable is especially strong. We must start by putting ourselves in the lowest seat. As we allow God to help us shed our worldly ways and grow in holiness, we become responsible for all that God has taught us. Then we invite others to share in the bounty of our blessings – the poor, the crippled, the lame and the blind. God will bless us and repay our service of work at the resurrection of the righteous. I suspect this is the resurrection of a remnant that will be prepared to defeat God's enemy.

We can only grow in our knowledge of God by meeting Him in His Word and making His son Lord in our lives. This humble submission as a servant of our Lord brings us into God's presence. As we grow in righteousness in the eyes of our Heavenly Father, we become stewards of this knowledge and understanding. We then instruct others by our godly lives, as well as by words of instruction. We share the abundance of joy that we have in our lives with others who are hungry to know and grow closer to God.

# *Mystery #7 in the Kingdom of God*

Learning and practicing humility can be a slow and painful process. The world teaches two extremes that are contrary to God. First, we are encouraged to excel in school, in sports, as parents, as participants in our work place. Yet, we often fail to meet this expectation, which can lead to a low self-image, the opposite of self-pride. However, now we have learned from this parable that a humble personality is required in order to be exalted in God's eyes, humble, that is, to submit and obey.

The emphasis of the parable is not on failure but on success. The one who succeeds in humility will be declared worthy of the birthright. He or she has been elevated in God's eyes and will bear abundant and righteous seed for a strong and faithful army. These humble ones, now exalted by God as true leaders of His people, will ultimately defeat the enemy and possess the land of their inheritance.

## Chapter Eight
# Selection of a Remnant
This chapter is a revised version of an article published in
*Chafer Theological Seminary Journal*, 13/1 (2008).

Many of the parables point to God making a selection. God seems to be in the process of determining who, from those born to the birthright, are worthy to inherit this special leadership role. This includes all the children of Israel as God's firstborn.

What, we now ask, are the requirements to be declared worthy? Scripture answers this question largely through the narrative. Repeatedly we see a son born to the birthright who lost this inheritance, which God then bestowed on another son. The Hebrew text records this transfer of inheritance throughout the patriarchal period. We see, for example, Ishmael's inheritance given to Isaac; Esau to Jacob; Reuben to Joseph; and Manasseh to Ephraim.[87] The transfer of inheritance includes all the attributes of the birthright: property, special blessing, priestly office, position of authority and leadership, and procreative power.

Ishmael was the firstborn son of Abraham. That he was entitled to an inheritance is apparent from Sarah's vehement demand that Abraham disinherit Ishmael: "The son of this slave

---

[87] The Hebrew text describes a firstborn's loss of his elevated position even in the time before Abraham. Cain was the firstborn son of Adam, but God placed him under a curse for killing his brother, Abel, and drove him from the land. Seth then assumed the elevated position that Cain had lost. Another example is Japheth, the firstborn son of Noah (Gen 10:21). Because Shem ascended to the elevated position normally reserved for the firstborn son, the order of the names is inverted in the Hebrew narrative to Shem, Ham, and Japheth (Gen 5:32; 6:10; 9:18; 10:1). Cf. E. W. Bullinger, ed., *The Companion Bible* (Grand Rapids: Kregel, 1990), 16, n. 21. Furthermore, the text identifies Ham as Noah's youngest son (Gen 9:24). Yet Ham is listed before the fallen firstborn, who was Japheth. It is also possible that Abram was the youngest son of Terah, and Haran the oldest (ibid., 17, n. 27), but the narrative is unclear. As for Isaac and Jacob, the narrative is not only clear but also quite detailed.

woman shall not inherit along with my son Isaac" (Gen 21:10; cf. Gal 4:30). The text narrates that Abraham "gave all he had to Isaac" (Gen 25:5). Thus, Ishmael apparently lost an inheritance to which he would have been entitled as the firstborn son of Abraham.

Esau was the firstborn son of Isaac (Gen 25:14-15). However, God's prophecy to Rebekah declared, "Two nations are in your womb, and two peoples born of you shall be divided; the one shall be stronger than the other, the elder shall serve the younger" (Gen 25:23). It is apparent from the narrative that the stronger brother was Jacob, the younger of the two. Jacob and his descendants would have authority over Esau and his descendants. The narrative includes a detailed account of Esau, who sold his birthright to his younger twin brother Jacob (Gen 25:29-34). Esau also lost the special blessing reserved for the son with the birthright (Gen 27:36).

From the numerous examples of younger sons who acquired the birthright, one might conclude that this was the norm rather than the exception. Some scholars suggest that ultimogeniture (inheritance by the youngest son) may have been a customary practice among the ancient Israelites. However, de Vaux dismisses this claim, as does Greenspahn.[88] Moreover, it is important to note that the genealogical lists typically record the order of the sons from the eldest (identified occasionally as the firstborn) to the youngest. The list of Ishmael's sons is an example.[89]

Even when there were unusual circumstances surrounding the birth, a son was entitled to his inheritance. The Hebrew text gives two interesting examples. One was Jephthah, the son of a

---

[88] Roland de Vaux, *The Early History of Israel to the Exodus and Covenant of Sinai* (London: Darton, Longman & Todd, 1978), 235. Frederick E. Greenspahn, "Primogeniture in Ancient Israel," in *Go to the Land I Will Show You: Studies in Honor of Dwight W. Young*, ed. J. E. Coleson and V. H. Matthews (Winona Lake: Eisenbrauns, 1996), 70.

[89] "These are the names of the sons of Ishmael, by their names, in the order of their birth" (Gen 25:13-15).

harlot. The expectation is that such a son might not be entitled to inherit, and certainly not to inherit the birthright as the firstborn son. Thus, Greenspahn notes that the expulsion of Jephthah from his household (Jdg 11:12) suggests that he was entitled to a part of the inheritance. Otherwise there would have been no need to expel him. Another example is the sons of a slave woman. However, Greenspahn again notes the text's assumption that Ishmael was entitled to receive some kind of inheritance because of Sarah's desire that Hagar be expelled (Gen 21:10).[90] Furthermore, Jacob's four sons by the slave women, Bilhah and Zilpah (Gen 35:25-26), inherited equally with the other sons. Dan and Naphtali, sons of Rachel's maidservant Bilhah, as well as Gad and Asher, sons of Leah's maidservant Zilpah, not only received blessings from Jacob (Gen 49:16-21) but their descendants also became four of the twelve tribes of Israel that received an inheritance in the Promised Land.

This study is particularly interested in the relationship between slavery/freedom and its connection with how and why the firstborn could lose his birthright. The study focuses on accounts of several patriarchal figures: Ishmael/Isaac, Esau/Jacob, Reuben/Joseph, and Manasseh/Ephraim. We will conclude that individuals lost the birthright to which they were born by failing to develop and exhibit commitment and service to God that are characteristic of priestly service and leadership in battle.

## Ishmael Lost the Birthright

Ishmael was the son of a slave woman, Hagar. The loss of his inheritance is especially interesting because Paul refers to this event in Gal 4:21-5:1. It is clear from the narrative that Ishmael did not receive the birthright since Abraham "gave all he had to Isaac" (Gen 25:5), which raises several questions. Did Ishmael, in fact, even have the birthright? If so, why did he lose it? Did he receive any kind of inheritance? Although the answers in the Hebrew text may not be conclusive, several aspects of the

---

[90] Greenspahn, "Primogeniture," 75.

narrative shed light on these questions. Furthermore, the more detailed accounts of Esau and Reuben fill in some of the gaps.

Ishmael was the firstborn son of Abraham. As noted earlier, the Hebrew text conveys the concept that the son born first was entitled to receive the birthright, which Sarah's demand to Abraham conveys. Even though Ishmael was the son of a slave woman, Hagar, it seems that he was entitled to an inheritance. By further example, the sons of the slave women, Zilpah, Bilhah and Keturah, were entitled to an inheritance. So apparently was Jephthah.

It should be noted that Abraham did not disinherit Ishmael by his own decision or because Sarah told him to do so. It was only after God instructed him to follow Sarah's advice that Abraham expelled his firstborn son, Ishmael.

> "The matter was very distressing to Abraham on account of his son. But God said to him, 'Do not be distressed because of the boy and because of your slave woman; whatever Sarah tells to you, do as she tells you, for it is through Isaac that offspring will be named for you. I will make a nation of him also, because he is your offspring'."
> (Gen 21:11-13)

One notes in this passage a characteristic of the birthright when God told Abraham, "It is through Isaac that offspring will be named for you." The recipient of the birthright was responsible for perpetuating the family name and lineage and was "the firstfruits" as well as the "firstborn" of his father's procreative vigor.[91] The text implies that Abraham expected his offspring to be named through Ishmael until God intervened and selected Isaac.

Moreover, although the text comments that Abraham "gave all he had to Isaac" (Gen 25:5), it provides a further

---

[91] In Hebrew, the text uses the same verbal root for firstborn (*b'chor*), for firstfruits (*bikkur*), and also for the verbal concept of selection (*bachar*).

explanation. "To the sons of his concubines ['concubines' is plural, meaning Hagar and Keturah] Abraham gave gifts, while he was still living, and he sent them away from his son Isaac, eastward to the east country" (Gen 25:6). Hiers notes the distinction between a bequest that a father could transfer during his lifetime by specific instructions and an inheritance that a son received upon his father's death as regulated by custom.[92] Ishmael apparently received a bequest from his father, as did the sons of Keturah.[93]

Abraham continued, nevertheless, to regard Ishmael as his son because the Hebrew text records the descendants of Ishmael in Abraham's genealogy (Gen 25:12-18). Furthermore, the text narrates that God acknowledged the status of Ishmael as Abraham's son when God told Abraham, "I will make a nation of him [Ishmael] also, because he is your offspring" (Gen 21:13). Finally, Ishmael must have continued to associate with his brother Isaac after Abraham cast Hagar out of his camp because both Ishmael and Isaac buried Abraham in the cave of Machpelah (Gen 25:9).[94]

In summary, it appears from the narrative that Ishmael, the firstborn son of Abraham, lost the inheritance to which his birthright entitled him. Logically, then, the birthright passed to Isaac, the younger son, through whom Abraham's "offspring will be named." Carrying the name is a concept that suggests the birthright. The Hebrew text does not terminate Ishmael's status as Abraham's son since Abraham's genealogical record includes

---

[92] Hiers, "Transfer," 122.

[93] Davies, "Inheritance," 180. Davies finds evidence in Babylonian records that "the father retained the right during his lifetime of making a special provision for a favorite son by granting him a gift," which is apparently what Abraham did with Ishmael and the sons of Keturah.

[94] Ginzberg notes two dissenting haggadic views regarding the reason that Abraham cast out Hagar and Ishmael from his camp. According to one, "Sarah noticed that Ishmael caught locusts and sacrificed them to the idols (that is to say, he was imitating adults, his locusts being 'toy sacrifices'; . . . according to another view Ishmael even committed adultery and murder." Ginzberg, *Legends*, 246 n. 211.

Ishmael. Nor does the biblical record disinherit Ishmael, to whom Abraham gave a bequest in lieu of his earlier expectation of an inheritance as Abraham's firstborn son...

## Reuben Lost the Birthright

The account of Reuben's loss of the birthright is more detailed and helps explain *how* the firstborn son could lose this inheritance. The Hebrew text narrates that Reuben lost the birthright. Reuben was "the firstborn, but because he defiled his father's bed his birthright was given to the sons of Joseph son of Israel" (1 Ch 5:1-2). Jacob apparently transferred the birthright from Reuben to Joseph when he adopted Joseph's two sons (Gen 48:5, 16). At this time Jacob shifted the double portion of inheritance in the land of Canaan from Reuben to Joseph by placing Joseph's two eldest sons in a position to inherit land. Ephraim and Manasseh were each entitled to inherit half of their father's double portion of inheritance, which gave each the equivalent of a single portion.[95]

So, why did Reuben lose the birthright? The text explains that he "defiled his father's marriage bed" (1 Chr 5:1) and mentions this event at the time that Jacob blessed his sons (Gen 49:3-4). Gevirtz has conducted an extensive linguistic study of Reuben's blessing and translates these verses as follows:

> Reuben, my first-born,
> you are my strength
> and the beginning of my vigor:
> pre-eminent in authority
> and pre-eminent in power.
> But, checked like water,
> you may not lead!

---

[95] Considering Jacob's adoption of Joseph's two sons, Mendelsohn has examined Babylonian adoption formulas. He finds a striking similarity between these adoption formulas and the words that Jacob used to claim Manasseh and Ephraim as his own. Isaac Mendelsohn, "An Ugaritic Parallel to the Adoption of Ephraim and Manasseh (Gen 48:5)," *Israel Exploration Journal* 9, no. 3 (1959): 180-83.

When you ascended your father's bed,
then you fouled the suckler's couch. (Gen 49:3-4)[96]

Gevirtz' rendering of *sh'et* as "authority" helps clarify Reuben's loss of leadership that the birthright conveyed. So does his understanding of *pa'chaz ka'mayim al-totar* as "checked like water, you may not lead!"

The reason for Reuben's loss of the birthright was an incident of filial impiety, a behavior that reflected on the nature of his character. In the blessing that Reuben received from his father Jacob, two contrasting lists of characteristics describe Jacob's firstborn son. The first list acknowledges Reuben's position as the son born to the birthright. Reuben was Jacob's "strength" and the beginning of Jacob's procreative "vigor." He was also, by his birthright, "pre-eminent in authority and pre-eminent in power." However, the passage then proclaims a contrasting list of attributes that highlights Reuben's loss of the birthright. Reuben was no longer "pre-eminent in power." He had conducted his life in such a way that he had to be "checked like water." He bore the consequences of his actions. Jacob told him, "You may not lead."

It is important to note, however, that Reuben did not lose his inheritance as a son, but only his inheritance of the birthright as the firstborn son. The tribe of Reuben received a portion of land, as all of Jacob's sons received an inheritance of land including Ephraim and Manasseh, each of whom received half of Joseph's double portion. Reuben also received a lesser blessing than the son with the birthright. So did all of the other sons of Jacob whose inheritance was not the birthright.[97]

---

[96] Translation by Stanley S. Gevirtz, "The Reprimand of Reuben (Gen 49:3)," *Journal of Near Eastern Studies* 30 (April 1971): 98.

[97] It is interesting to note that Judah's blessing also contains characteristics of the birthright (Gen 49:8-12). For example, "your father's sons shall bow down before you" and "the scepter shall not depart from Judah." However, Scripture assigns the birthright to Joseph (1 Chr 5:1-2). Apparently not one, but two of Jacob's sons, Joseph and Judah, were worthy of the leadership role that the birthright bestowed.

## Esau Lost the Birthright and the Special Blessing

The circumstances surrounding Esau's loss of the birthright explain that Esau initiated forfeiture by a deliberate decision to sell his birthright. When this occurred he was hungry to the point of death, and he acted contrary to the way of God by relying on a worldly solution rather than trusting the Lord to supply his needs. When he demanded that his brother give him food Jacob responded, "'First sell me your birthright.' Esau said, 'I am about to die; of what use is the birthright to me?' Jacob said, 'Swear to me first.' So he swore [an oath] to him, and sold his birthright to Jacob'" (Gen 25:31-33). Thus, Esau did not make a rash decision, but committed in his heart to deny his birthright, which the oath that he swore to Jacob demonstrates.[98]

The narrative discloses that the right of the firstborn son to a double portion of the inheritance also required a commitment to submit to godly authority for the purpose of leading God's people. In the culture and time of the patriarchs, members of the tribe gave obedience to their leader because he served as their priest with a direct relationship to God. Furthermore, the son with the birthright was responsible for perpetuating the family name and lineage in order for the tribe to defeat the enemy and conquer the Promised Land.

Esau lost not only his birthright (and its double portion of inheritance) but also his special blessing. "Esau said, 'Is he not rightly named Jacob for he has supplanted me these two times. He took my birthright; and look, now he has taken away my blessing.' Then Esau added, 'Have you not reserved a blessing for me?'" (Gen 27:36). What Esau lost was the blessing reserved for the firstborn son in addition to, and certainly connected with, the

---

[98] The New Testament later describes Esau as *pornos*, an immoral person, and *bebeilos*, vile, godless, and irreligious (Heb. 12:16), citing him as an example of behavior that defiles a person and causes him to fall from the grace of God. This paper suggests that "falling from the grace of God" is not necessarily equated with "losing one's eternal life" but may involve the nature of the inheritance.

inheritance of possessions. The firstborn son received I a double portion, apparently to complement his position of leadership and authority.

Two things help explain Esau's loss of the blessing to which the firstborn son was entitled. First is the deceit which Rebekah committed and in which Jacob participated. This deceit was contrary to the ways of God, and Jacob expressed concern to his mother: "Perhaps my father will feel me and I shall seem to be mocking him, and bring a curse on myself and not a blessing" (Gen 27:12). So, Jacob hesitated to deceive his father as his mother had instructed because he apparently knew what was right with God, and he understood that all people receive consequences of their actions. However, his mother said to him, "Let your curse be on me, my son, only obey my word" (Gen 27:13). Rebekah did indeed bring upon herself the consequences of her ungodly action, for she never again saw her son after Jacob left for Padan-Aram. Jacob also had to bear the consequence of twenty years of difficult exile before God allowed him to return to the Promised Land. Thus, the text suggests that Rebekah precipitated Esau's loss of the greater blessing by her deceit. Esau also brought consequences upon himself by despising his birthright (Gen 25:34) and failing to act in a manner expected of a firstborn son.

There is a second reason Esau lost the birthright and the greater blessing. Esau had taken two Hittite women as wives, and "they made life bitter for Isaac and Rebekah" (Gen 26:35). Later, when Rebekah convinced Isaac to send Jacob to Padan-Aram to find a wife, Rebekah said to Isaac, "I am weary of my life because of the Hittite women. If Jacob marries one of the women such as these, one of the women of the land, what good will my life be to me?" (Gen 27:46). Apparently Esau perceived Isaac's displeasure and responded by taking a third wife, who was a daughter of Ishmael (Gen 28:6-9). He may have known the words of Abraham, who had instructed his chief servant regarding Isaac. "I will make you to swear by the Lord, the God of heaven and earth, that you will not get a wife for my son from the daughters of the Canaanites, among whom I am living" (Gen 24:3).

Therefore, before leaving for Padan-Aram, Jacob received from Isaac the greater blessing, which Isaac described to Esau. "I have already made him [Jacob] your lord, and have given him all his brothers as servants, and with grain and wine I have sustained him" (Gen 27:37). Only the son with the birthright could have received this blessing. Not only would Jacob receive an abundance of the earth's richness in grain and wine, which signifies the double portion, but he would also be the lord of his tribe.

## Manasseh Lost the Birthright and the Special Blessing

A similar situation appears again in Jacob's greater blessing to Ephraim, the younger of Joseph's two sons. The younger son received the birthright as well as the special blessing normally reserved for the firstborn. When Jacob started to bless Ephraim (the younger son) with his right hand, Joseph tried to correct him:

> "Not so, my father! Since this one [Manasseh] is the firstborn, put your right hand on his head." But Jacob refused and explained, "I know, my son, I know; he also shall become a people [a nation], and he also shall be great. Nevertheless his younger brother [Ephraim] shall be greater than he, and his offspring [the descendants of Ephraim] shall become a multitude of nations." (Gen 48:17-19)

The key prophetic concept is an abundance of offspring that reflects the firstborn's strength and procreative vigor. Although Manasseh was to become a people or nation, Ephraim's offspring were to become plentiful enough for many nations. The distinction between one nation and many nations echoes the prophecies for Ishmael, the son of Abraham who lost the birthright ("I will make him a great nation," declared God; Genesis 17:20b). However, to Abraham, who would inherit the birthright, God said, "I will make you exceedingly fruitful; I will make nations of you" Gen 17:6).

## Conclusion

The birthright was the inheritance to which the firstborn son was entitled simply because he was born first. God declared Israel, meaning all of the children of Israel, to be His firstborn son, and then redeemed them from the last plague in Egypt. After redeeming His children from death in Egypt, God then offered continuing redemption by the substitution of a qualified sacrificial animal.

The inheritance of the birthright is more than a double portion of the father's possessions. The firstborn also received a special blessing, the office of high priest, a position of leadership and authority, and procreative power—all apparently for the role of leading God's people. However, the son born to the birthright could lose this special inheritance by failing to develop and exhibit a commitment to serve to God, which are characteristics of the priestly office and leadership in battle. When the firstborn sons lost their birthright (Ishmael, Esau, Reuben and Manasseh), this special inheritance passed on to another son considered worthy of assuming a leadership role and procreative power for righteous descendants (Isaac, Jacob, Joseph and Ephraim).

---

## *Mystery #8 in the Kingdom of God*

Perhaps it is human nature to be drawn to the dramatic narrative of those who were unworthy to inherit the birthright, and who subsequently lost this privileged position. However, the message is not so much the cause of loss (negative) but the reason for God's choice (positive). So we ask, what must we do to be worthy of this special inheritance?

One of our best models is Jacob, who spent 20 years in exile. This time in Padan Aram is an echo of the 40 years of wilderness wandering when God was instructing His people with the Law and with experiences of testing. When Jacob returned to the Promised Land he successfully wrestled with an angel, whereupon God changed his name from Jacob to Israel. Jacob then named the place Peniel, "for *he said*, 'I have seen God face to face'" (Gen 32:30).

We are also in the wilderness of the world where God is instructing us with His Word and with experiences of testing. We are wrestling with the ways of the world, and are learning to turn to God in humble obedience.

Part Three

**Parables about a Remnant**

# Chapter Nine

## Parable of the Talents

Before beginning to read this chapter, please carefully consider Matthew 25:14-30. Practice asking yourself questions as you read.

I must admit I have always been troubled by the Parable of the Talents. Why are the consequences so severe to the servant who protected the king's money by hiding it instead of investing it? The punishment seems greater than the sin of hiding the money. The servant is then cast into outer darkness, which I always thought represented death. I now think it is something other than death (read on). So, we must first ask, "Why would hiding money be a sin?" And we ponder, "The servant's sin must have been extraordinarily evil to warrant such a punishment."

We must again practice listening to the text as people of the first century would have heard it. I suggest they would have been asking the same questions that we are asking. However, the difference between then and now is that people of ancient Israel would have known what to do next. Well, you are in the process of learning what to do next, which I call the seven steps of penetrating a parable. So, review in your mind the first three steps that I call "The Story." You should be able to follow these steps on your own, or perhaps with the help of your study partner. I suggest you do not continue reading in this chapter until you have completed this task of following the first three steps.

### Hebraic Artistry of Language

We will turn now to the Hebraic artistry of the language in this parable, which begins in verse 14. We start by asking, "What are the key words in this verse that catch our attention?" What do you think are the key words and why?

The man going on a journey represents an authority figure such as a king or lord, who is a symbol for God. My Bible version then translates those under him as "slaves," which conveys people in bondage. I prefer the alternate translation of "servants" because servants represent those who are (or think they are) humble and submissive in service to their Lord.

In the next verse 15, the lord gives money to his servants in different quantities, "each according to his own ability." What catches our attention here is certainly the concept of ability. God's servants have varying abilities, which I find comforting because God is going to work with me for who I am. He does not expect me to be a "super person," which I clearly am not.

So, what do we do with the word "ability"? First I suggest you need to practice identifying key words. Certainly repetition can point to something important, which we have seen with "servant." However, simple curiosity and probing questions can also lead to other key words. So we ask, "What exactly do different people have in different quantities?" Then, if you look up the original word in a concordance or interlinear translation you will find that "ability" is a translation of the Greek word δύναμις (*dunamis*), which means "power." In our parable this ability is specifically the power to do God's will. Yet, we know that this power is latent, waiting for us to activate it by our love of God and faith in Christ. So, next we will turn to the repetitive word, "servant," and consider its relationship to an ability to operate this power of God.

**Word Study on "Servant"**

At this point I think we need to stop and consider again the thinking of people in the first century, which was characterized by memorization of the Hebrew Scriptures. Don't jump too quickly over the concept of a servant. If you do, you will be relying on your own twenty-first century experiences and understanding. So, take time now to carefully consider the following verses that contain the word "servant." You should read each in its context in the Hebrew Scriptures, that is, within the surrounding verses that convey a full meaning of the word "servant."

1.  For each passage below, carefully consider what it means to be a servant of God. Then ask, "What is the resulting relationship that God has with His servants?"
    Genesis 18:3, 5
    Genesis 26:24
    Genesis 32:10
    Genesis 50:17, 18

2. Why do you think Scripture calls Moses a servant of God? Respond to this question in four steps.

    (a) First, answer the question from your own perspective and understanding (don't skip this step; it is an important one).

    (b) Second, read Numbers 12:7 in its context.

    (c) Third, consider and compare your original answer from your tradition in (a) with what you have discovered in Numbers 12:7 (b).

    (d) Finally, after completing your comparison, how might you change your original answer in (a)?

3. The Exodus account offers a stark contrast between bondage to the ways of Satan and the world (represented by Pharaoh and Egypt) and humble service to God. Read the following verses in their context. Then describe the contrast between the two types of servitude.

    Exodus 13:3, 14

    Exodus 14:12

    Exodus 16:3

    Exodus 17:3

    Exodus 20:2

## Investing God's Money: More Artistic Language

Now that you have a good understanding of what it means to be a servant of God, we will return to the parable and to the symbolism of investing God's money.

Perhaps my initial confusion about this parable stems from my modern perspective of investing in the stock market. I leave that task to my husband, so the stock market seems vague and somewhat threatening to me. If I had to invest God's money in the stock market, I would probably fail as a servant. Nevertheless, let us practice asking questions. So, how would you answer the following?

4. Symbolically, what is God asking us to invest?

5. What does the growth of money represent?

6. If there is no growth of money, what are the symbolic consequences?

I trust you will wrestle with these questions (as Jacob wrestled with God's angel) before considering my thoughts that follow.

I suggest that God is asking His servants to invest themselves. This is a concept that would have been familiar to Jews at the time of Yeshua. A disciple desired to be like his master, and the master taught by his godly actions, that is, by who he had become through his study of the Torah, the Prophets and the Writings. The words that the master spoke simply reflected what was in his heart. So, what better investment for the master than raising up disciples, who were servants of God, and who then became masters themselves to gather and raise up their own disciples? What, then, do disciples do? They are servants who are learning how to care for God's people. God, who is the ultimate Master, invests His own people, who are His disciples. In this way He is nourishing all of His children so they may grow closer to Him.

What, we now ask, is the reward that God bestows on those whom He calls His good and faithful servants? The parable answers our question by the repetition of "faithful" for emphasis.

> Well done, good and faithful servant. You were
> faithful with a few things, I will put you in charge
> of many things. Enter into the joy of your master.
> (Mat 25:21)

For those who are faithful we see not one, but two rewards. The first is a position of responsibility. "I will put you in charge of many things," declares God. In the Hebraic sense of time that role of leadership refers, both to our present life now and also to a role that we may play at some time in the future. Yet, there is a second reward. The faithful servant will enter into the joy of God. What a magnificent reward for service!

## Irony and Hyperbole

You may think you are now ready to consider the servant described as "wicked and lazy." However, first let me explain two common characteristics of the biblical language. Both are figures of speech that say one thing on the surface but mean something quite different. I am referring to irony and hyperbole. Let us take irony first.

Irony says one thing but actually means the opposite. It is an expression of sarcasm which, in its extreme form can become ridicule. Irony was a common method of instruction in the ancient world, although ridicule is certainly not acceptable in our modern society.

In order to better understand the irony in this parable, let us review the setting, which takes us all the way back to Mat 24:3. Yeshua was speaking privately to his disciples. In this particular parable he was instructing his disciples about the godly role of leadership. Therefore, in the context of the setting I suggest that the "wicked and lazy servant" refers to any self-professed leader of God's people who does not walk in the ways of his master (in the context, master means his Lord Yeshua). The irony is in the dichotomy between those who perceive themselves with pride as leaders when they are not, and others who are truly humble in a simple faith of love and obedience. Thus, humble servants demonstrate quiet leadership by actions rather than prideful words. Yet, not only does the world fail to respect these humble servants, but the true leaders of God's people often do not even perceive themselves as leaders. It is ironic that worldly perception is often the opposite of God, who elevates simple servants instead of popular charismatic leaders.

Now let us turn to hyperbole, which is extreme exaggeration that far exceeds a normal and literal meaning. In his famous study of the parables, Jeremias pointed out that they often contain "an element of unexpectedness" and that this element "was intended to indicate where the meaning was to be found."[99] I have called these literary devices "something strange and puzzling" as well as "clues." Thus, we understand that the "wicked and lazy servant" is extreme language when applied to one of God's servants or, in this example, to one who considers himself a serving disciple when he is not acting like one. After all, hyperbole was an acceptable form of instruction in the ancient world, and this extreme description of a "wicked and lazy servant" may shake a disciple to return to humble godly behavior.

---

[99] Joachim Jeremias, *The Parables of Jesus,* 2nd rev. ed. (NY: Scribner's, 1972), 30.

In fact, hyperbole is quite common in prophetic language as well. Prophetic language refers to something future for the express purpose of encouraging obedience today. Our parable certainly has aspects of future prophecy. Note here, not only the prophetic future but also the extreme exaggeration.

> Throw out the worthless slave into the outer darkness. In that place there will be weeping and gnashing of teeth. (Mat 25:30).

Weeping and gnashing of teeth is a vivid image of a privileged person who suddenly realizes that expected privileges have suddenly been removed. The person is cast into outer darkness, which represents separation from God. In this case, I suggest that the lost privilege is the special inheritance of the birthright.

Thus, hyperbole uses extreme language to express a penetrating principle. The principle in this case involves the nature of the inheritance by God's people. Some will not inherit what they have been expecting. However, don't jump to the conclusion that this loss of inheritance means "eternal life." So, to fully appreciate this message of failure to inherit, we must turn next to step number five in our list that penetrates the parable.

## Connection to the Hebrew Scriptures

What is the connection to the Hebrew Scriptures? We remember that haggadic midrash comments on a story, verse or passage from the Hebrew Scriptures in order to teach us how to walk in godly ways. When we walk in righteousness, we are walking with God in His Kingdom. What is the connection to the Hebrew Scriptures?

I began my own search by focusing on the servant who *lost* his inheritance. This is human nature. We want to know the bad consequences first so we can avoid them. I already knew that "servants" in the Hebrew Scriptures were righteous ones. This remnant will inherit the birthright to which all Israel has been born as God's firstborn son. However, I also knew that only those children of Israel who were "worthy" would inherit this birthright. Scripture repeatedly narrates about individuals who were born to the birthright as the firstborn son but lost this special inheritance.

Ishmael (birthright given to Isaac)
Esau (birthright given to Jacob)
Reuben (birthright given to Joseph)
Manasseh (birthright given to Ephraim)
Possibly also Nachor (birthright given to his brother
    Abraham)

Silly me. I should have been focusing on the positive. Who
*did* receive the birthright and why? I returned to the parable and
considered again the faithful servants and the abundance they
received for their service, which was a double portion of what they
had originally received. I remembered that the son who was in line
to inherit the birthright received a double portion of inheritance.
Apparently the servant who failed to invest did not earn the
double portion of his birthright. Thus, he was unworthy to inherit
the birthright

I think, at this point, that to fully appreciate the message of
our parable we should consider the story of Jacob, who tried to
acquire the birthright by purchase and deceit. However, it was not
until God considered him worthy of this inheritance, after twenty
years in the "wilderness" of Padan Aram, that God finally
considered Jacob to be worthy and changed his name to Israel.

## Jacob, A Servant of God

You will remember that Jacob purchased the birthright from his
brother, Esau, for a bowl of porridge. That is, Esau was not willing
to serve unto death. So, we perceive that Esau was not worthy of
this leadership role which requires service even unto death. Then
Jacob proceeded to steal Esau's special blessing that accompanied
the birthright. In this deceitful act he was aided by his mother
Rebecca. However, these two events, purchase of the birthright
and stealing the blessing, certainly did not make Jacob worthy.
Only God could bestow the birthright on a son whom He deemed
worthy of this inheritance.

So, to learn more about Jacob who ultimately became
worthy in the eyes of God, read these two passages in their
context: Genesis 28:10-22 and Genesis 35:1-15. Then answer the
following.

1. In these two accounts, what is the progression that displays Jacob's growth, making him worthy of the birthright?

2. In the first account Jacob "places a stone at his head" (which is the literal translation of the Hebrew). What symbolism do you think "stone" and "head" might represent?

3. How is the dream of Jacob's ladder prophetic of Jacob eventually receiving the birthright?

4. Despite the prophecy of Jacob's ladder, Jacob was still not worthy to inherit the birthright. How does Genesis 28:20-22 convey this concept?

5. What does the name Bethel mean (*Beit-El* in Hebrew)? How does this name relate to both accounts, one in Genesis 28 and the other in Genesis 35?

6. Compare the account in Genesis 35:1-7 with Genesis 28:18-19 by considering that, in both, Jacob builds an altar. However, in the second account, how does Jacob demonstrate that he is now worthy to inherit the birthright?

After you have finished "wrestling" with these questions, you may consider my thoughts which I will now express.

I was drawn to Jacob's using a rock for a pillow. You might ask, what drew me to the key word "stone"? I can only explain that those who are believers in Christ have the gift of the Holy Spirit in them, and this gift can be a guide. So, I was guided by curiosity (and the Holy Spirit) to Jacob's using a rock for a pillow. In similar fashion, in your own search, you must take the first step to let yourself be curious and ask your own questions.

I was puzzled that Jacob would use a rock for a pillow. Even in the ancient world I did not think this would be a common practice. So, I noticed a marginal note in my reference Bible that the translation "put it under his head" could be literally translated, "put it at his head-place." That caught my attention because "stone" or "rock" is a common biblical concept for God. Take, for example, the following passages in Deuteronomy.

> The Rock! His work is perfect, for all His ways are just; A God of faithfulness and without injustice, Righteous and upright is He. (Deut 32:4)

> You neglected the Rock who begot you, and forgot the God who gave you birth. (Deut 32:18)

However, there is more to our passage in Genesis 28. The Hebrew ראש (*rosh*), meaning "head," can refer not only to the head of a body but also to a leader who is a servant of God. So, the possibility of Jacob putting a rock at his head-place intrigued me. Then Jacob turns the stone into an anointed pillar to pay homage to God. So, I began to see significant symbolism in the rock at Jacob's head.

Furthermore, the words of the Lord in Jacob's dream of the ladder that reached to heaven are certainly prophetic because Jacob will ultimately receive the inheritance of the birthright. The same promises that God had bestowed on Abraham and Isaac would pass to Jacob. However, Jacob's dream of the ladder and the words that God spoke were still prophetic of something future because Jacob was not yet worthy of this inheritance. He had not yet fully submitted to God by trusting Him as we see in the passage. Note Jacob's first word "if."

> Jacob made a vow, saying, "If God will be with me and will keep me on this journey that I take, and will give me food to eat and garments to wear, and I return to my father's house in safety, then the LORD will be my God." (Gen 28:21)

When we turn next to the passage in Genesis 35, we see a different Jacob who has matured after his twenty years in Padan Aram. I suggest that when God changed Jacob's name to Israel in Genesis 35:10, He was signifying that Jacob was finally worthy to inherit the birthright. This second passage offers interesting evidence to support this suggestion.

When God told Jacob to travel to Bethel, after returning to the Promised Land from Padan Aram, Jacob not only purified himself, but he also commanded all those with him to purify themselves and to put away their foreign idols.

What happens next is an echo of the end of forty years of wilderness wandering after the Exodus from Egypt, when the children of Israel were ready to enter the Promised Land to defeat God's enemy and possess their inheritance. God had helped them mature during the forty years of their wilderness experience. Only then were they ready to possess their inheritance. ow did they accomplish this? God caused the walls of the mighty city of Jericho to fall, which led to fear and trembling by the enemy. When we return to Jacob and to those whom he led after his name had been changed to Israel, we hear an echo from the battle of Jericho. "As they journeyed [Jacob and those with him], there was a great terror upon the cities which were around them, and they did not pursue the sons of Jacob" (Gen 35:5).

Finally, we see characteristics of the birthright in God's blessing of Jacob, whose name had now been changed to Israel. Not only a nation (that is, a people) would come from Jacob/Israel, but also *many* nations would also come from him. Furthermore, God will give Jacob the land. [100]

## Conclusion

Since you are reading this book, you undoubtedly belong to God already. You may have taken the next step, which is a longing to grow closer to God through understanding His Word and having a close relationship with Him. If your heart has submitted in humble obedience, then you are a follower or disciple of your Lord Yeshua.

This parable is directed today, as it was in the first century at the time of Yeshua, to those who are already disciples of the Lord Yeshua, or those who desire to become disciples. These committed followers of their Lord and Master are the children of God who want to be like their Master. They are growing in an intimate relationship with Him, and they are open to His guidance

---

[100] God first gave the promise of land and a multitude of nations to Abraham (Gen 12:7; 17:4), which then passed to Jacob (Gen 35:11-12).

and will obey as He directs. They are not only serving God's people today but God is also preparing them for a future role that will ultimately defeat God's enemy as we will see in later chapters.

This parable brings not only encouraging instruction to the Lord's disciples but also words of caution. What are we at risk of losing? Not our eternal life with God but a role of leadership in His Kingdom. I suggest that the servant who returned only what he had been given did not receive a double portion of inheritance that signifies the birthright. He had not invested himself to serve God's people. So, when others were rewarded with this special inheritance, which gave them a double portion and brought them into the presence of God, the servant was denied this reward.

Why, then, was there wailing and gnashing of teeth? At the time of Yeshua many leaders of God's people thought they were worthy of the inheritance of the birthright, but their self-righteousness disqualified them. The parable suggests that God has selected others and has found them unworthy of the double portion of inheritance. We can hear them wailing and gnashing their teeth at this rejection. Nothing has changed. There will be wailing and gnashing of teeth among God's people today.

## Mystery #9 in the Kingdom of God

What motivates us to stand firm in times of intense trouble and tribulation? We are encouraged by a positive reward of joy in God's presence. Yet, there is also an awareness of a potential loss of the inheritance of the birthright. When God announces who will be worthy to inherit a leadership role, do you want to be there? Or will you be cast into outer darkness, away from God's presence with wailing and gnashing of teeth, waiting for the righteous remnant to serve in whatever role God asks of them?

Chapter Ten

# Parable of Hidden Treasure

> The kingdom of heaven is like a treasure hidden in the
> field, which a man found and hid *again*; and from joy
> over it he goes and sells all that he has and buys that field
> (Mat 13:44).

This parable occupies only one verse, which makes it quite a
challenge. We can see the context; Yeshua is talking to his disciples
(see Mat 13:36, 51). However, there are no main characters, and
what are our clues? Nothing seems to be strange or puzzling, and
there are no linguistic devices like irony or contrast. However,
there is one key word that will lead us to a passage in the Hebrew
Scriptures.

A treasure has been hidden which a man has found, but
after he found it he hid it again until he could buy the field. We
have two key words by their repetition, "hide" and "find." I was
drawn to "hide." What is hidden? A treasure has been hidden just
waiting for the man to find it. In the repetition of the key word
"hide," which leads to "treasure," we hear an echo from the
Joseph story.[101]

When Joseph's brothers came to Egypt to buy food
because there was a famine in the land of Canaan, Joseph first hid
money in all of their sacks and later hid a silver cup in the sack of
Benjamin. As we explore this story in Genesis, we will find three
main principles. First, Joseph is acting as a type of Messiah.
Second, Joseph tests his brothers three times as a form of

---

[101] The dissertation of Dr. Tak Vui Lee proposes another conclusion
which I have find intriguing. The man is the Messiah and the field is the
world. The treasure is a righteous disciple whom God finds worthy to
enter His presence. Dr. Lee suggests that the parable is referring to the
story of Ruth and Boaz. Ruth is a treasure that must be purchased with a
bride price. *The Parables from a Hebraic Perspective* (dissertation), Trinity
Southwest University, 2013.

instruction and a method of judgment. Finally, during the third test Judah emerges as a righteous leader.

As we proceed to work through the Joseph story, we discover what will become our guiding words in Genesis 45:5, 7.

God sent me ahead of you to preserve life. (Gen 45:5)

God sent me before you to preserve for you a remnant in all the earth. (Gen 45:7)

With these guiding words in mind we will begin with Joseph as a type of Messiah. But first, carefully read Genesis 41:38-46.

## Joseph is a Type of Messiah

We remember that our parable in Matthew is haggadic midrash, which means it comments and expands on something in the Hebrew Scriptures for the purpose of practical application in our lives today. We also note the opening phrase, "The Kingdom of Heaven is like...." which means we will be learning a principle about righteous living so we can walk with God in His Kingdom. As God instructed Abraham, so Yeshua also seems to be exhorting us. God said to Abraham, "Walk before me and be תמים [tamim]," that is, holy, righteous, unblemished, and without sin.

We will now see Joseph through the eyes of the Pharaoh, and Joseph will emerge with characteristics of the Messiah. For example, Joseph has a divine spirit in him, and he is discerning and wise (Gen 41:38-39). So Pharaoh gives Joseph a position of the highest authority. "You shall be over my house, and according to your command all my people shall do homage" (Gen 41:40).

Next we see Joseph receiving objects of authority that were well known in the ancient Near Eastern culture. Pharaoh gives Joseph his signet ring, which had Pharaoh's seal on its face that could be dipped in liquid wax and pressed on a document to signify its authenticity from the Pharaoh. Furthermore, Joseph will wear a royal robe and necklace. Therefore, Joseph can act as Pharaoh, speak as Pharaoh, and rule on behalf of Pharaoh. The narrative tells us that Pharaoh had Joseph "ride in his second chariot; and they [the people of Egypt] proclaimed before him, 'Bow the knee!' And he [Pharaoh] set him [Joseph] over all the land of Egypt" (Gen 41:43). Joseph became to Pharaoh what

Yeshua is to God, His Father. "Only in the throne I will be greater than you," declared the Pharaoh of Egypt (Gen 41:40).

Regarding this position of authority the Apostle Paul tells us about Yeshua. "When all things are subjected to Him, then the Son Himself also will be subjected to the One who subjected all things to Him, so that God may be all in all" (1Co 15:28). Thus, Joseph and Yeshua are doing the work of those they represent, the Pharaoh who is symbolic of God and God Himself. They are guiding and leading the people who have been placed in their care.

So, as Yeshua is Lord over God's people, who are commanded to submit and obey to their lord Yeshua, so Joseph becomes lord over the Egyptians. "Moreover, Pharaoh said to Joseph, '*Though* I am Pharaoh, yet without your permission no one shall raise his hand or foot in all the land of Egypt'" (Gen 41:44).

How does this story in Genesis relate to our parable about hidden treasure? We are about to learn that Joseph, who represents the Messiah, has hidden money in the sacks of his brothers for the purpose of testing them. However, before returning to the Joseph story about hidden treasure, we must first understand the biblical concept of testing.

## Instruction through Testing

The classic story about testing is in the wilderness account, after God rescued the children of Israel from bondage in Egypt. Therefore, you should stop now and read these verses in Exodus 15:22-16:21 before answering the following questions.

1. Can you find the three times in this passage that the word for "testing" appears?

2. What are the three examples of "testing" in these verses?

3. The Hebrew word for "testing" is נסה (*nasah*). Can you find its meaning in a Bible dictionary or a concordance?

4. The first usage of *nasah* appears in Gen 22:1. Read this verse carefully in its context. Then explain in your own

words how God offers instruction to His people
through testing.

I often encounter Christians who have an understanding
of "testing" that troubles me because their emphasis is on negative
consequences rather than positive rewards. However, upon
reflection, the negative is as biblical as the positive. On the other
hand, the purpose of the negative is to lead us to a positive
understanding. So, on the negative side God gives us a free choice
and allows us to walk in worldly ways that bring about painful
worldly results. I tend to think of these negative consequences
with a visual image. I see myself stumbling and falling and
scratching my knee, or even breaking a bone. However, on the
positive side, if I am aware of what has caused me to fall, I do not
think I will let it happen again, especially if the consequences have
been rather severe. This is the way God works with us through
testing. He allows negative consequences that result from our
worldly behavior in order to lead us to Him

Now we turn to the powerful positive consequences of
testing. Perhaps I tend to dwell on the positive because I have
been immersed in God's Word for so many years. The positive
rewards are abundant blessings. When we turn to God for help
and He answers, we are more apt to turn to Him again...and again.

The more we emerge from testing experiences in a positive
way, the more we change to become like our Lord Yeshua, who is
holy and righteous and pure. After all, we are called to change.
One of my favorite verses about change is in Romans where Paul
cries,

I urge you, brethren, by the mercies of God, to
present your bodies a living and holy sacrifice [not a dead
animal like those placed on the altar], acceptable to God,
*which is* your spiritual service of worship.

And do not be conformed to this world [shaped to
the ways of the world like a potter with clay], but be
transformed [that is, changed] by the renewing of your
mind, so that you may prove what the will of God is, that
which is good and acceptable and perfect. (Rom 12:2)

Can you see yourself being formed to the ways of the world like a potter shaping wet, sticky clay? However, we can change and become more like our Lord Yeshua when we put the Word of God in our minds and learn to walk in godly ways.

Again, let me share another personal image about this process of testing. I see an onion. As I peel away an outer layer, which is a worldly part of me, it causes me to cry because shedding something long-standing and comfortable can be difficult. Just when I adjust to the "new me," which results from peeling away this layer, lo and behold! There is another layer...and then another layer. The more worldly layers I shed, the more Christ-like I become. Of course the layers are endless, but I am confident that God will complete the process sometime in the future. And, as I peel away layers in my life, I grow closer and closer to God.

We are ready now to return to the Joseph story to examine the process of testing there. Before continuing, you should stop and read Genesis 41:50-42:24.

## Joseph Tests His Brothers

After Joseph had been made second in command to Pharaoh, who had set him over all the land of Egypt, a seven-year famine began that affected not only Egypt but also the land of Canaan where Jacob lived with his eleven sons. Because Joseph had stored an abundance of food during the preceding seven years of plenty, both Egyptians and foreign people from outside Egypt were coming to Joseph to purchase food.

> Now Jacob saw that there was grain in Egypt...and he said, "Behold, I have heard that there is grain in Egypt; go down there and buy *some* for us from that place, so that we may live and not die." (Gen 42:1-2)

Immediately we are drawn to Jacob's words, "so that we may live and not die." Of course bestowing life to God's children is a role of the Messiah. It is natural for us to think of this life as a static condition in contrast to the state of death. However, there is another aspect of life that is "living now" in contrast to the "process of dying." In the first case, the state of death is a complete action, but in the second, dying is an ongoing process that is not yet complete. Thus, "living" and "dying" are related to our daily walk.

Sometimes we are walking in life, which is "living," and at other times we are walking in the ways of the world, which is "dying." The verse we have just seen in Genesis refers to the first life, which is in contrast to a final death by starvation. Yet, an underlying meaning in the Joseph story will also address the process of living and dying in our daily lives as we will see shortly.

Jacob sent ten of his sons to Egypt, leaving behind Benjamin because, Jacob explained, "I am afraid that harm may befall him" (Gen 42:4). We remember that Rachel, the wife that Jacob dearly loved, had born only two sons, Joseph and Benjamin. Jacob thought his son Joseph was dead, leaving only Benjamin.

When the ten brothers came before Joseph, the ruler of Egypt under the authority of Pharaoh, they did not recognize their brother although Joseph recognized them. So, Joseph initiated the first of three actions that would test his brothers as a method of instruction and judgment. How they heard Joseph's words would be the instruction. How they responded would lead to judgment.

First Joseph accused his brothers of spying, which would have resulted in a penalty of death.

"You are spies; by this you will be tested: by the life of Pharaoh, you shall not go from this place unless your youngest brother comes here!"

"Send one of you that he may get your brother, while you remain confined, that your words may be tested, whether there is truth in you. But if not, by the life of Pharaoh, surely you are spies."

So he put them all together in prison for three days.

Now Joseph said to them on the third day, "Do this and live, for I fear God."

'If you are honest men, let one of your brothers be confined in your prison; but *as for the rest of* you, go, carry grain for the famine of your households." (Gen 42:14-19)

This narrative is more than a plain story. There is, of course, a simple story of what happened to Joseph and his brothers in Egypt. However, we are interested in the deeper meaning that is conveyed through the artistic nature of the language. Eventually you will learn to ask your own questions in order to penetrate a depth of understanding. But for now, try answering the following questions that I will pose based on Genesis 42:3-24.

1.  Is there any evidence in the text that the brothers are spies?

2.  Why does Joseph accuse them of spying?

3.  What is the symbolic imagery of being put in prison?

4.  What is the symbolic imagery of being released from prison after three days?

5.  What is the significance of Joseph's words when he warns his brothers to return to Egypt with Benjamin. "Do this and live, for I fear God." And then we hear an expanded repetition: "Bring your youngest brother to me, so your words may be verified, and you will not die" (Genesis 42:18, 20).

6.  How do the brothers respond in Genesis 42:21?

7.  What is the specific response of Reuben, the firstborn son of Jacob, which you will find in Genesis 42:22?

After pondering answers to these questions, which will undoubtedly generate an emotional response, you will perceive Joseph's first act of testing. However, let us return our attention to questions 3-5.

The symbolic imagery is exquisite. Prison represents bondage to the world. If that is not enough, the brothers were also subjected to bondage in Egypt, which is a pagan nation. Of course release from bondage after three days brings to mind the resurrection of Yeshua. It also points to the promise of *our* resurrection from death to life when we believe in the blood of the lamb. This is the first aspect of life, which is a completed act, in contrast to the state of death. That is, God's promise of eternal life with Him at some time in the future cannot be annulled. Therefore, the promise is a completed act.

Then, after releasing his brothers from prison and thus giving them life, Joseph exhorts his brothers to return to Egypt with Benjamin. "Do this and live," he adds. This is the second aspect of life, which is a "process of living." What does Joseph require of his brothers in order that they may walk in newness of life? They must perform some kind of action, in this case returning with Benjamin. But what about believers in Yeshua? Our action is to walk in obedience through the love and faith of our Lord Yeshua.

Let us turn now to one other aspect of this story. All the brothers responded by acknowledging their guilt of selling Joseph into slavery. However, Scripture draws our attention to only one of the brothers, Reuben, Jacob's firstborn son who was born to the birthright. Instead of responding in a worthy manner by saying, "I have sinned," Reuben said, in essence, "I told you so," for he said to his brothers, "Did I not tell you, 'Do not sin against the boy'; and you would not listen? Now comes the reckoning for his blood" (Gen 42:22). We can conclude that Reuben, the firstborn son of Jacob, was not worthy to inherit the birthright because he did not confess his sins.

Although 1 Chronicles 5:1 tells us that God ultimately bestowed Reuben's birthright on Joseph, Jacob's blessings of his sons in Genesis 49 include clear characteristics of the birthright not only on Joseph but on both Joseph and Judah. So, we will soon see that Judah emerges in this story as a righteous leader in addition to his brother, Joseph. We will see that Judah is going to act in a way that is worthy of this inheritance of leadership.

## Joseph Tests His Brothers a Second Time

We are ready now for Joseph's second act of testing his brothers. Before continuing, read Genesis 42:25-43:34. This time practice looking for a depth of meaning by asking yourself questions.

Again, we must read beyond the simple story by looking at the artistic nature of the language. I will now pose questions for you to consider as you explore for deeper meaning.

1.  How did Joseph bless his brothers in Genesis 42:25?

2.  How did the brothers respond to this blessing, and how was it a form of testing?

3. How did Jacob respond to the report about their journey to Egypt?

4. Now look at the two brothers, Reuben who was born to the birthright but does not appear to be worthy to inherit that role of leadership, and Judah. First consider what Reuben offered to his father in Genesis 42:37, but what happened to that offer?

5. Next consider Judah's offer and compare the two offers. Why was Judah's offer superior to that of his brother Reuben?

6. When the brothers returned to Egypt with Benjamin, how did they learn that Joseph had returned their money as a method of testing them?

7. How did the brothers act differently with Joseph when they came before him this second time? What do you think is the spiritual and prophetic significance of their bringing gifts? What do you think the gifts represent?

As the story progresses, the principles we are learning seem to be elevating and expanding. As the brothers left Egypt, only one brother discovered money in his sack, which caused the hearts of all the brothers to sink. They turned trembling to one another, saying, "What is this that God has done to us?" (Gen 42:28). Then, after they arrived in the land of Canaan, the brothers realized there was money in all their sacks, "and when they and their father saw their bundles of money, they were dismayed" (Gen 42:35). Jacob has now been added to the plot initiated by Joseph.

We see a strong contrast between Reuben and Judah as they fight for the life and safety of their brother, Benjamin. Reuben does not offer himself, but offers his two sons, certainly a heavy commitment. However, Jacob rejects Reuben's offer, and Judah then pledges his own life. "I myself will be surety [a pledge] for Benjamin" (Gen 43:9).

Perhaps the most relevant event for our Parable of the Lost Treasure occurs with Joseph's house servant. As the brothers approached Joseph's house on their return to Egypt, they were afraid "because of the money that was returned in our sacks" (Gen 43:18). Yet, the house steward responded, "Be at ease, do not be afraid. Your God and the God of your father has given you treasure in your sacks" (Gen 43:23). What, then, is really in their sacks? Money represents a treasure. Although Joseph placed the treasure there, we know that Joseph is the one who is interceding to bring two treasures to his brothers. The first is life in contrast to death. Second is a life of abundance and blessings.

Thus, in the first test the brothers acknowledged their guilt of selling Joseph into slavery. In this second test they returned to Joseph with a treasure in their sacks. As our study progresses, we will see what the treasure represents. In the next and final test, Judah will emerge as a righteous leader worthy to inherit the birthright.

## Joseph Tests His Brothers a Third Time

The last of three tests appears in Genesis 44:1-13. Again Joseph hid something, but this time it was his own silver cup that was placed in the sack of Benjamin. In the culture of that time, the theft of personal property from Pharaoh's viceroy would have warranted the immediate penalty of death. However, when the seeming theft was discovered, what penalty did Joseph impose? Not death, but servitude. "He with whom it is found will be my slave, and the rest of you shall be innocent" (Gen 44:10).

On the surface Joseph simply wanted to have his brother Benjamin with him. However, were you startled by the penalty of bondage to only one brother and the release of the others? Whenever we are startled it is likely a clue to deeper meaning.

Consider the contrast between Genesis 44:9 and Genesis 41:10.

BROTHERS OF JOSEPH: With whomever of your servants it is found, let him die, and we also will be my lord's slaves (Gen 44:9).

JOSEPH'S HOUSE STEWARD: So he said, "Now let it also be according to your words; he with whom it is found shall be my slave, and *the rest of* you shall be innocent (Gen 44:10).

In the first verse the brothers state a penalty that was not only just but was also in alignment with ancient custom. The penalty for theft was death, and the penalty for those associated with the thief would have been slavery, a cruel and bitter punishment in the ancient world. However, look at the contrast delivered by Joseph's house steward. The penalty for theft was going to be servitude; and the penalty for those associated with him would be a declaration of innocence.

Now look again at the potential servitude of Benjamin, which was not a cruel and bitter punishment but an opportunity to serve a brother, his lord, who would bestow love and grace upon him. What a wonderful mirror of the way the Messiah treats those who submit to him in obedience as loyal servants. If this had been the penalty that Benjamin ultimately received, the other brothers would undoubtedly have been jealous.

## Judah Emerges as a Righteous Leader

We turn now to my favorite part of the story, perhaps the most relevant to our Parable of Hidden Treasure. Judah will emerge as a righteous leader, which is the calling of God to all His children as we read in Deuteronomy. "The LORD will establish you as a holy people to Himself, as He swore to you, if you keep the commandments of the LORD your God and walk in His ways (Deut 28:9).

Carefully read Judah's plea to Joseph in Genesis 44:14-34 where you will find examples of the kind of behavior that God seeks from His children. Make a list of Judah's godly behavior before continuing.

We are now ready to relate Judah's godly behavior to the judgment that follows. Joseph is speaking.

> 5 "Do not be grieved or angry with yourselves, because you sold me here, for God sent me before you to preserve life."
>
> 6 "For the famine has been in the land these two years, and there are still five years in which there will be neither plowing nor harvesting."

> 7 "God sent me before you to preserve for you a
> remnant in the earth, and to keep you alive by a
> great deliverance." (Gen 45:5-7)

In the first verse 5, God sent Joseph, a type of Messiah, to preserve life. This is the first aspect of life, which is in contrast to the state of death that the brothers were facing from famine in the land of Canaan. Joseph has preserved the life of all the brothers, whose descendants will become the children of Israel.

Verse 7 is a parallel to verse 5 by the repetition of "God sent me before you to preserve life." However, there is a significant change in verse 7 that the ancient ear would have heard. "God sent me before you to preserve for you a remnant." I suggest that the parallel verse 7 selects a remnant out from the brothers, that is, Judah, who represents a righteous remnant out of Israel. To be worthy of the remnant, Judah must exhibit the second aspect of life which is a walk of righteousness. This concept of a remnant is a dominant theme in the Hebrew Scriptures.[102]

## Conclusion

I was led to the echo in the Hebrew Scriptures by the repetition of the word "hidden." However, this word was merely the clue. The question became this. *What* is hidden? And the answer is, of course, a treasure. This concept of a hidden treasure led me to the money (a treasure) that Joseph had hidden in his brother's sacks. However, when I went to the Hebrew Scriptures to carefully consider this passage, I found Joseph, who is a type of Messiah, and who is testing his brothers as a form of instruction and a method of judgment. This process of testing in the Joseph story went through three stages. In the first, all the brothers repented of their sin of jealousy that committed their brother Joseph to a life

---

[102] Many consider all the brothers a remnant because they were rescued from death by famine. However, of what would they have been a remnant, because all of Jacob's family went to live in Egypt. So, the remnant in this passage seems to be referring to a remnant out from the brothers.

of cruel bondage in Egypt, from which only God could rescue him. In the second, the brothers must return to Egypt despite the appearance that they were thieves. This second test highlights the failure of Reuben to be worthy of his birthright, and the emergence of Judah as the likely substitute. God's choice of who will inherit the birthright is a process of selecting the righteous remnant. In the third test, the choice of Judah becomes more evident, and we are awed by Judah's performance on behalf of his brothers.

What, then, is the significance of the chiastic center in Genesis 45:5-7? Chiasm is an ancient literary device that uses parallel lines to point toward a chiastic center, which contains the main idea of the chiasm. Carefully read Genesis 45:6, which is the chiastic center.

In the following construction we see two parallel lines labeled A. The chiastic center is B.

A.  Do not be grieved or angry with yourselves, because you sold me here; for God sent me before you to *preserve life*.

B.  For the famine has been in the land these two years, and there are still five years in which there will be neither plowing nor harvesting.

A.  And God sent me before you to *preserve for you a remnant in the earth*, and to keep you alive by a great deliverance (Gen 45:5-7).

I have added italics to identify the concept of preserving life in the two parallel lines (verses 5 and 7), which are related by the English translation "preserve." The first is preservation of life in contrast to death. The second A line draws us in because not only will a remnant be saved (preserved), but sometime after God selects His remnant He will apparently rescue them by a great deliverance. We are glimpsing the future with these prophetic words about a great deliverance.

Let us now look at the chiastic center in line B (verse 6). We find there are still five years of famine remaining. During this time of intense trouble, God's people will need leaders who will speak and act for God. Certainly they have a leader in their Messiah, who is Joseph. But the Messiah must also rely on his servants, a righteous remnant who have submitted to their Lord as faithful servants.

So, we ask, who was the one who found the hidden treasure? In the Joseph story it was all the brothers who represent all of God's children. Then what is the treasure? God is the treasure, whose gift replaces the penalty of death with life. In our parable in the Gospel of Matthew we are only told that a "man" found a treasure. However, the parable goes on to say that the man hid the treasure again until he could buy the field. This, I suggest, is someone like Judah, who stands in faithful obedience before Joseph, his Messiah. Judah represents those children of God who make the Messiah their lord. They desire and receive more than the treasure of life that overcomes death, although that gift alone is extraordinary. They have also been granted the opportunity for a second aspect of life, which is joy and spiritual abundance. These faithful ones are walking in a way that is worthy of the righteous remnant.

The parable began with the opening words "the Kingdom of Heaven is like." Then, in a way that is characteristic of all the parables, it exhorts God's children to walk in righteous ways that will allow them to draw near to God in a close and harmonious relationship as faithful servants.

## Mystery #10 in the Kingdom of God

The treasure is the gift of life that God gives to all those who belong to Him. In the parable, a man found this treasure as those who believe in God's son also find the treasure, which is God. However, the key to the parable is what follows. The man then hid the treasure until he could purchase the field in which it was located.

Hiding the treasure initiated a process of testing and judgment in the Joseph story. We can imagine the person hiding God's gift in his or her heart where it can grow and mature. Those who respond successfully to this process of "living" and "walking" with God are a smaller number of God's children, who are growing closer to God by submitting in humble obedience to their Lord Yeshua. These are a remnant who are worthy to be leaders of God's people. They are servants who are in preparation for a future role in God's plan to redeem all those who belong to Him.

Therefore, the treasure of God is life, which is given to all God's children. However, the treasure only shines brightly through those who hide it in their hearts, and undergo a process of "living" by walking with God as a faithful servant.

# Chapter Eleven

# Parable of the Unforgiving Servant

As always, begin by reading the parable that you will find in Matthew 18:21-35. Then work through the seven steps on your own before reading the commentary below.

## Facing the Challenge

The Parable of the Unforgiving Servant is one of the most troubling of all the New Testament parables. The context is Peter's question about forgiveness, and Yeshua's answer states the extreme importance for his disciples to forgive. "I do not say to you, up to seven times, but up to seventy times seven" (Mat 18:1-2). Carter has captured some of the disturbing aspects of the parable that follows. "In the actions of both the king and the official, the parable exemplifies the very opposite! The king forgives initially (v. 27), but then refuses to forgive again (vv. 32-34). And worse, by imprisoning the slave, the king withdraws the forgiveness that he had previously extended (v. 34). Of course, the official does not forgive at all."[103]

Perhaps even more unsettling is the common symbol of a king or some authority figure who represents God, and a slave/servant who stands for a faithful follower of the king/God. How could God throw His servant in prison for a debt that would have been impossible to repay? And how could God hand him over to the torturers? Schottroff sets the parable in the cultural and historical context of a ruthless, high-debt culture where slavery and near-slavery were brutal facts, and frightening power lay in the hands of a small elite.[104]

---

[103] Warren Carter, "Resisting and Imitating the Empire: Imperial Paradigms in Two Matthean Parables," *Interpretation* (July 2002): 260-72.

[104] Luise Schottroff, *The Parables of Jesus*, tr. Linda M. Moloney (Minneapolis: Fortres, 2006), 198f.

## Getting Started

We will be using our first century methods to hear and respond to the parable as the people of ancient Israel would have reacted. This will necessitate both a linguistic study and an appreciation for the ancient culture of that time.

There are three elements that may be relatively new to you. First, besides the connection to the Hebrew Scriptures ("forgiveness up to seventy times seven" which refers to Gen 4:24), there is another allusion that is not part of the halachic midrash. However, the first century listeners would have taken notice of this concept of judgment, and so must we. Our challenge is to understand judgment, not from the perspective of traditional Christian theology. Instead, we must undertake a serious study of judgment in the Hebrew Scriptures, which we will do shortly.

Second, there is the ancient custom of debt and its consequences. We read in the parable about an inability to repay and the resulting prison internment until what is owed can be returned. Yet, how can one repay a debt from prison, especially when the amount owed is so high that it would have been impossible to raise this money (10,000 talents)? We are also deeply troubled by the king (the servant's lord) who hands his servant over to the torturers until he can restore all that he owes. The king is a common symbol for God, and the servant is one who submits in service to his king.

Finally, we will have to understand how the language of prophecy operates in this passage. Prophetic language uses extreme exaggeration and intense emotional tactics to admonish grievous sinful behavior. Without this knowledge of prophetic language we will likely interpret the meaning literally, which will probably result in a serious misunderstanding. Alternatively, and perhaps even more undesirable, we can "jump to a conclusion" that will be, essentially, a guess.

## Setting

Although we will begin with the setting, which is usually a simple exercise, the task in this parable will become quite challenging. The setting begins in Matthew 18:1. What follows are four troubling scenarios that are not only introductory but also related by content to our parable in Matthew 18:21-35.

1. Mat 18:3-6. Humble yourself as a child or your punishment will be a heavy millstone hung around your neck and you will be thrown into the sea to drown.
2. Mat 18:7-11. Cut off what causes you to stumble or you will be cast into the eternal fire.
3. Mat 18:12-14. Ninety-nine go astray but only one is found that prevents him from perishing.
4. Mat 18:15-20. Those who refuse to repent will be bound on earth and in heaven.

These disconcerting and even frightening words will give us an opportunity to learn more about the language of prophecy. But first, look carefully at Mat 18:1-2. To whom is Yeshua addressing all this condemning language? It is not to all those who came to hear him, but specifically to those who claimed to be his disciples. This startling observation of strong language directed to Yeshua's disciples requires our careful attention.

## The Language of Prophecy

We will turn now to the nature of prophecy. For more in-depth instruction you can find an eight-part teaching series called "The Language of Prophecy" on the BibleInteract website. But for now, I will offer only a brief overview.

The Hebrew Scriptures are teeming with words of prophecy. The New Testament not so much, but nevertheless the New Testament also contains prophetic passages.

The first thing you must understand is what biblical prophecy actually is, and you may be surprised by my explanation. Yes, some prophecy foretells future events, which is the most common (and often exclusive) understanding. However, this form of prophecy is fairly rare in the Hebrew Scriptures. True, there is a higher percentage of future prophecy in the New Testament, but even there, the predominant form of prophetic words takes another form. This second, more common aspect of the language of prophecy corrects sinful behavior in our lives today, and has nothing to do with foretelling the future.

Who is a prophet? A prophet has been selected by God to speak for Him in whatever form and manner God chooses. For example, God said to Moses, "I make you *as* God to Pharaoh, and

your brother Aaron shall be your prophet" (Ex 7:1). So we see that
a prophet speaks for God.

We know from Deuteronomy 34:10 that Moses was a
prophet whom the Lord knew face to face (Deut 34:10). However,
in tour verse in Exodus 7:1 Aaron is identified as the prophet. For
whom does Aaron speak? He speaks for Moses, who is as God to
pharaoh. If you read all the words that Aaron speaks as a prophet,
you will find that they are not about anything future.

All words of prophecy, most commonly referring to the
present time but occasionally to the future, are meant as loving
guidance and instruction. Future prophecy encourages us to stand
for God now, because we know what is coming. On the other
hand, in our daily lives, if a child is walking in ways that are
contrary to righteous living, then the instruction must be
immediate, strict and demanding. Therefore, most words of
prophecy pass judgment on God's people when they are walking
in sinful ways in their daily lives. The purpose of prophecy, then, is
exhortation, correction and restoration of a loving relationship,
whether speaking of something future or correcting sinful
behavior in our lives today.

Now that you know that prophecy is God speaking to His
people for the purpose of restoring and building a right
relationship, it will be easier for you to understand the nature of
prophetic language. God catches the attention of His people by
employing extreme exaggeration, vivid (sometimes frightening)
imagery, powerful symbolism, and mysterious expressions that
require thoughtful consideration. When a prophet speaks about
something future, the purpose is not to frighten or to lead us to
smug confidence. Instead, knowledge of the future causes us to
stand for God now in this present world. When we stand for God
we are standing in righteousness.

We see a classic example of this prophetic language in the
introductory passage that precedes our parable (Mat 18:3-6).
Yeshua is speaking for God. If a disciple fails to humble himself
like a child, the consequence is expressed in prophetic language.
"It would be better for him to have a heavy millstone hung around
his neck and to be drowned in the depth of the sea" (Mat 18:6). A
heavy millstone around one's neck is certainly vivid imagery, and
the thought of drowning by a kind of terrifying suffocation is too

horrifying to contemplate. This language is extreme exaggeration with vivid imagery. The symbolism of water is intentionally provocative because water not only drowns and destroys (an echo of the flood at the time of Noah), but also purifies (only righteous Noah and his family were left after the flood).

When we turn to our Parable of the Unforgiving Servant, we will see similar prophetic language. But first, we must consider the ancient custom of debt and its consequences.

## Ancient Custom of Debt

Ten thousand talents is an extraordinarily high number that stands in sharp contrast to the fellow-servant's one hundred talents. According to some estimates, one talent was the equivalent of fifteen years of a laborer's wage.[105] Then we read that the lord of this unworthy servant "threw him in prison until he should pay back what was owed."

In the ancient world, the goal of creditors was not to punish but to recover the debt. Since a subsistence economy was common for most people, one person could never expect to raise enough money to satisfy a debt. However, the ancient world knew nothing of the individualism that characterizes our modern western world. Everything was done "in community." Since most people lived in small villages (even Jerusalem at the time of Yeshua had only about 40,000 residents), the community was responsible collectively for agricultural activities, enforcing religious and social customs, and major civic decisions. The community would also have been responsible for raising the money to restore its citizen to a free status. However, raising ten thousand talents would have been impossible for any village or town in ancient Israel.

We remember that something strange or puzzling can be a clue to deeper meaning. Therefore, the immense sum appears to be intentional. This suggestion is reinforced by the action of the lord who "handed him [the servant] over to the torturers until he should repay all that was owed him." We remember that

---

[105] Cleophus J. LaRue, "What Are You Afraid Of?" *Princeton Seminary Bulletin* (27/3, 2006): 196-200.

punishment was not necessarily the goal of the creditor. Torture could only be effective if it encouraged the community to repay the debt. However, no amount of torture could have raised ten thousand talents.

What we have here is the extreme exaggeration of prophetic language. Therefore, what we must do is understand the "meaning of the message."

## Returning to the Parable

Our parable is unique because Yeshua is addressing only one person. Peter, one of his disciples, comes to him and asks, "Lord, how often shall my brother sin against me and I forgive him? Up to seven times?" Yeshua answers, "I do not say to you, up to seven times, but up to seventy-times seven." This is the setting for the parable that follows. So, we know that the topic of the parable will be about forgiveness. Furthermore, our forgiving others is so important that Yeshua's response is expressed through hyperbole (extreme exaggeration). Seven is the number of perfection, but our forgiveness must be seventy times seven.

## Tension in the Narrative

The parable tells the story of a slave whose king forgives him a debt. But then the servant behaves in such a way that his actions cannot be forgiven. This scenario creates a tension in the narrative. On one hand, God forgives completely – up to seventy times seven, because that is what He asks of us. On the other hand, forgiveness is apparently not automatic, and perhaps there are some things that God will not forgive.

The tension extends to the concept of judgment. We learn that the king "wished to settle accounts with his slaves," which suggests a final judgment. We remember that Yeshua was talking to his disciple, Peter, and that slaves (or servants) represent those who have dedicated themselves to serving their lord. These are the dedicated followers of Yeshua. So, the judgment seems to be directed toward Peter and the other disciples.

We must stop and consider that judgment is operating now, in our daily lives, for each and every thought and action. We tend to think of judgment as something that will occur only in the future to determine who will have "eternal life with God."

However, the parables are concerned with daily living, and are encouraging God's people to "walk now in the kingdom of God." So, the tension is caused by God's desire to forgive, while at the same time He is constantly judging our daily actions.

## Judgment and the Hebraic Sense of Time

Let us stop for a moment and review the comparison between the Greek sense of time in our modern western world and the Hebraic sense of time, which was first introduced at the beginning of this book.

The Greek sense of time is linear, so it can be viewed as points on a line. Therefore, past events are behind us; they may have consequences in the present but what occurred in the past is essentially over. Future, then, is ahead of us, and has not yet happened. How are we experiencing time today according to the Greco-Roman concept? The past can only be experienced second-hand; we have history textbooks and oral history and artifacts from the past. We experience the future through our imagination. Thus, our only real and immediate experience is in the present.

However, since time is part of God's creation, God can be viewed as inextricably part of time itself. Because God is infinite and ever-present, so time cannot be finite points on a line. As we read in Scripture, "With the Lord one day is like a thousand years, and a thousand years like one day" (2 Pe 3:8 citing Ps 90:4).

We can extend this concept of God's nature in time to the way He is working with His people. In the beginning God created mankind in His own image, which is perfect and holy and righteous (Gen 1:27). At the end of time God's people will be perfect and holy and righteous in His presence. But now, we have righteousness in us (a gift from God when He made us His) so that we may *walk* in righteousness. When do we walk in righteousness? We walk in righteousness when our hearts are focused on God. Unfortunately, that does not happen all the time. Perhaps we can say that a righteous walk is possible in part now, because we have God's righteousness in us. The completion of our walk of righteousness is still future.[106]

How, then, does the Hebraic concept of time apply to God's judgment? First, we must reflect on the judgment of God that discerns between good and evil, sin and perfection, righteousness and unrighteousness, truth and falsehood. Additionally, as the infinite nature of God is in time, so also His judgment is complete from the beginning. "God has chosen you from the beginning for salvation (2 Th 2:13). That is, in the beginning of time God judged His people to be righteous because He created them in His own image. However, not until the end of time will He bring all of His children to Him in righteousness. We remember that the Kingdom of Heaven (or the Kingdom of God) is a future time (in the linear Greek aspect) when mankind will be in a righteous condition in peace and harmony with God. Thus, God's children were righteous in the beginning and will be righteous in the end of times.

But what about now? We will turn once more to what is important to this study of the parables as haggadic midrash, which is righteous living in our lives today. We remember that many of the parables begin, "The Kingdom of Heaven is like..." and we understand that we can only enter the Kingdom of Heaven when God judges us as holy and righteous. So, when is the Kingdom of Heaven according to the Hebraic sense of time? That is, when are we righteous? God judged mankind righteous in past linear time when He created them in His own image. He will judge them righteous at some future time when His work is complete. But now God is judging His children on a daily basis. So, the parables encourage us to walk in righteousness in our lives today, that is, to enter the presence God in His Kingdom in our daily walk.

## Judgment in the Parable

To fully appreciate this parable it is essential that we comprehend the concept of judgment in the Hebrew Scriptures. After all, there

---

[106] The New Testament attributes the Holy Spirit as the guide to a righteous walk.

are two aspects of judgment. One is positive (rewards) and the other is negative (punishment). The tension is caused by the unresolved conflict between these two aspects of judgment.

Our parable is about forgiveness. When does God forgive and when does He not forgive? We must begin to answer this question by looking for linguistic clues.

There are two repetitions in the parable, "forgive" and "repay." Other key words seem to be "compassion" and "mercy." Therefore, we must identify the equivalent Hebrew words, and then we can search in a concordance for a verse or passage that seems to be related to our parable.

Forgive (סלח *salach*) – to pardon for a crime

Repay (שלם *shalem*) – to make whole or complete (by restoring the money borrowed)

Compassion (רחם *racham*) – to feel deeply with love and caring

Mercy (חן *chen*) – favor, approval, affection for someone

Your work in a concordance will be more meaningful if you can search for the Hebrew words rather than the English translations. The reason is simple. One Hebrew word has been translated various ways into English depending on the context of the passage. Furthermore, translation is a form of interpretation, and this process of interpretation is compounded by the numerous ways that one Hebrew word can be translated into English. Appendix I will help you learn how to use a concordance.

Here is a practical example for working with a Hebrew word, not the English translation. If you search for the word "forgive," you will miss the other English translation for this one Hebrew word, which is "pardon." So, if you use a concordance exclusively in English, you will miss some relevant verses.

## Possible Connecting Verse

When I was searching the Scriptures to understand the biblical concept of judgment, I was drawn to one passage that seemed especially relevant to our parable. Despite the fact that there seems to be no linguistic clue that leads us to this verse, the concept in

Exodus 34:6-7 appears to be a perfect fit. The light it sheds on the Parable of the Unforgiving Servant I found quite meaningful, so I offer it here.

I have constructed in a visual way what the ancient ear would likely have heard and memorized. Besides rhythm that evokes emotion, there are two lists, each with three items followed by a powerful conclusion. The two lists compare the loving nature of God and the sinful nature of mankind. The clashing conclusion contrasts God's forgiveness with the judgment He imposes as penalties. So, I suggest you read this verse aloud and listen to its parts.

> Then the LORD passed by in front of him [Moses] and proclaimed,
>> "The LORD, the LORD God,
>>> 1. compassionate and gracious,
>>> 2. slow to anger, and
>>> 3. abounding in lovingkindness and truth;
>> who keeps lovingkindness for thousands,
>> who forgives
>>> 1. iniquity [עון *avon* – guilt that demands punishment],
>>> 2. transgression (פשע [ *pesha* – rebellious act], and
>>> 3. sin [חטא *chattaah* – a sin is anything contrary to God];
>> Yet He will by no means leave *the guilty* unpunished, visiting the iniquity of fathers on the children and on the grandchildren to the third and fourth generations." (Ex 34:6-7).

This verse demands explanation, which is characteristic of the provocative nature of the biblical text. We remember that there are mysteries in Scripture that people of the first century believed God had placed there to be uncovered by those with a heart to know Him. So, we ask questions that might lead us to a deeper understanding. How can God forgive on one hand and punish on the other? What is required for God's forgiveness? Do all sins lead to judgment? Do all sins have an effect on following generations? What can we learn about God in this verse? How is God instructing us about forgiveness and sin?

The parable we are studying, which Yeshua spoke to Peter, is undoubtedly intended for all those with a desire to serve their Lord and who seek answers to these questions. This is the nature of haggadic midrash, which takes a passage or concept from the Hebrew Scriptures and brings it to life through a fictional narrative that applies a verse or passage to our daily lives. The fact that many of the parables begin, "The Kingdom of Heaven is like," is an indication that only those with ears to hear will understand its meaning. Furthermore, the parables are steeped with linguistic devices and subtle clues that require work to dig for the depth.

## Another Connection to the Hebrew Scriptures

As we ponder the meaning of God's judgment, which forgives in love at the same time it condemns with punishment, we turn to the clear allusion to Gen 4:24. Peter asked Yeshua, "How often shall my brother sin against me and I forgive him? Up to seven times seven?" Early in the Genesis narrative, God protected Cain, who had murdered his brother Abel by declaring, "Whoever kills Cain, vengeance will be taken on him sevenfold" (Gen 4:15). Thus, God withheld the penalty of death for Cain's murder of Abel.

Cain's descendant, Lamech, scorned God's loving act of withholding the penalty of death from Cain. Lamech killed not one, but two people, and then declared:

> I have killed a man for wounding me,
> And a boy for striking me.
> If Cain is avenged sevenfold,
> Then Lamech seventy-sevenfold (Gen 5:23).

Numbers have significance in Scripture, and seven is the number of completion. Seven expanded and multiplied with extreme exaggeration to seventy-sevenfold evokes overwhelming emphasis of completion. Since our parable's connection to the Hebrew Scriptures echoes this story of Cain and his descendant Lamech, we must look more closely at this passage in Genesis as it relates to judgment.

Cain's crime was murder, and there certainly is no more heinous sin in God's eyes. Nevertheless, God's judgment was not a penalty of death. Cain received a severe penalty as the consequence for his murder of Abel when God cursed Cain from the ground, so it would no longer yield its strength for him. This caused Cain to become a vagrant and a wanderer on the earth. Although death would have been a just penalty for killing another person, God withheld this judgment while, at the same time, inflicting a severe penalty. In this next verse we read about the withheld judgment.

> "Whoever kills Cain, vengeance will be taken on him sevenfold." And the LORD appointed a sign for Cain, so that no one finding him would slay him. (Gen 4:15)

Withheld judgment is an important concept in Scripture. God gives the gift of life to all His children despite the penalty of death for sin. Allowing Cain to live seems to signify this gift of life. Nevertheless, even though God appointed a sign for Cain to prevent his death, God imposed a severe penalty. Therefore, God withheld judgment from Cain that gave him life while, at the same time, He imposed a harsh penalty as a consequence for the sin. For us He has also withheld judgment for life, but he imposes penalties for sinful actions.

Rather than responding to God's gift of life with gratitude, and accepting the correcting punishment that God might impose, Lamech flaunted the loving nature of God. He assumed that God would withhold judgment for his murders as God had done for Cain. Since Lamech had committed two murders, he assumed God would doubly protect him, that is, seventy-sevenfold. The text leaves God's response to Lamech's sin of flaunting the Heavenly Father tantalizingly silent.

Thus, we see God withholding the penalty of death with a gift of life. However, sinful actions require God's judgment that leads to penalties. We learned this earlier with the process of testing as a form of instruction.

## Still More Connections to the Hebrew Scriptures

So far, all the connections to the Hebrew Scriptures have been related to judgment. There are still more. Our parable ends, "My heavenly Father will also do the same to you, if each of you does not forgive his brother from your heart." (Mat 18:35). There are two concepts that we must consider in this verse. First is the idea that we bring the same consequences upon ourselves that we inflict on others. Mark explains, "By your standard of measure it shall be measured to you" (Mark 4:24). Matthew phrases the same idea in the context of judgment. "In the way you judge, you will be judged (Mat 7:2). The Lord's Prayer captures the same notion in a positive context. "Do unto others as you would have them do unto you." Thus, we bring the same kind of consequences on ourselves that we inflict on others, both positive and negative.

There is a second concept in the conclusion of the parable's incisive instruction to the Lord's disciples. How are we to judge others in our daily lives? When we repent and turn to God, He withholds judgment as an act of love, so we must do the same. Furthermore, the disciples who are walking as their Master instructs are witnessing godly behavior by their daily lives. However, how does a disciple respond to the sinning actions of others?

If sinful behavior goes unpunished, then God's children will not learn to walk in godly ways. Therefore, we must remember that God allows consequences to fall on others. There may be times when the disciple withholds some aspects of judgment, like Cain who was not punished by death but given life. However, we must remember that God instructs by testing. Thus, the judgment of God, and the judgment of disciples who act on His behalf, must exhibit love when it fosters life. However, they must also allow consequences as a form of loving instruction.

## Conclusion

The Parable of the Unforgiving Servant is giving instruction to disciples, who are servants of their Lord Yeshua, about God's judging them and their judging others. This instruction is so important that it is expressed in prophetic hyperbole.

The unworthy servant owed his Lord a debt of ten thousand talents, which he and his family were unable to repay. So, we must ask an important question. How did the servant (the Lord's disciple) accrue this debt in the first place? A disciple's role is to serve his Lord and bear fruit for God's Kingdom. In return, his Lord bestows grace on his servant and grants rewards of love, joy, peace, patience, kindness, goodness, faithfulness, gentleness and self-control (Eph 5:22). If the servant fails to bear fruit, then the Lord's grace will be withheld. The servant has brought consequences upon himself. As the servant withheld his love from the Master by failing to serve, so his Master withholds the grace of abundance as a penalty that should return the disciple to serving his (or her) lord. The servant has brought these consequences upon himself, and God uses these consequences as loving instruction.

## *Mystery #11 in the Kingdom of God*

It is a privilege and an honor to become a disciple, that is, a committed follower of the Lord Jesus Christ. This privilege is available to all whose hearts hunger to grow close to God. Yet, this elevated position of leadership requires humble obedience that leads to service. If one serves well and bears fruit for God, the wonderful rewards will be abundant – love, joy, peace, patience, kindness, goodness, faithfulness, gentleness and self-control. These spiritual benefits exhibit a close relationship with God in His Kingdom.

However, if the disciple returns to worldly ways, God's punishment will be as severe as the nature of the transgression. The goal of this form of correcting instruction, called testing, is to encourage the disciple to repent and return to God.

This principle of judgment is so important that it is delivered by the parable in the prophetic language of extreme exaggeration, vivid imagery, and powerful symbolism. God desires that all His children become disciples. The closer we grow to God through our Lord Yeshua, the more He demands of us in a walk of righteousness.

Chapter Twelve

# Who are the Remnant?

Some assert that God has rejected all of Israel as a corporate entity. If so, the children of Israel no longer belong to God. Others modify this claim by suggesting that God has selected only those children of Israel who believe in His son, or perhaps those who believed in the coming of the Messiah before the birth of His son.

I would like to offer another suggestion that has been emerging from our work on the parables. It seems that the inheritance of the birthright is at risk of loss instead of God's outright rejection of His people. Going one step farther, I suggest that individuals of Jewish descent are at risk of losing this special inheritance, not Israel as a corporate entity. As God's firstborn son, individuals will be judged by God to be worthy of the birthright or unworthy of this inheritance. However, as I have repeatedly tried to demonstrate, just because a child of God fails to inherit the birthright does not mean that he or she no longer belongs to God. It is the inheritance of the birthright that the person is at risk of losing.

This study further suggests that those who inherit the birthright are associated with the "remnant," those whom God will select a select for some special role in His plan of redemption. The concept of the righteous remnant is pervasive in the biblical text. However, the question becomes this. "What are the qualities required for this selection?" Associating the inheritance of the birthright with the remnant helps us answer this question.

## Inheritance of the Birthright is a Process of Selection

We will begin with my proposal that some individuals out of Israel will inherit the birthright, but many others will lose it. I will offer two features from the Hebrew Scriptures to support this suggestion. First, this study has identified numerous accounts in the patriarchal narrative that not only depict some individuals (firstborn sons) losing the birthright but also show other individuals receiving it. We have seen Esau's birthright transferred to Jacob, Reuben's to Joseph, and Manasseh's to Ephraim. Thus, it appears from the narrative that individuals, not Israel as a corporate entity, will inherit or lose the birthright to which all the children of Israel have been born as God's firstborn son.

Second, we see other examples of individuals losing or receiving the birthright in the genealogical lists in 1 Chronicles 1-9. These lists record several accounts of the birthright passing to a son who was not the firstborn. One example is Perez, the fourth son of Judah who received the birthright. The text tells us that his three older brothers were Er, Onan and Shelah.

> The sons of Judah *were* Er, Onan and Shelah; *these* three were born to him by Bath-shua the Canaanitess. And Er, Judah's firstborn, was wicked in the sight of the LORD, so He put him to death. (1 Chron 2:3)

The biblical narrative then records that the birthright passed from Er, not to Onan or Shelah, but to Perez, the fourth son of Judah.

The sons of Perez were Hezron and Hamuel. Hezron, the firstborn, received the birthright. The sons of Hezron were Jerahmeel, Ram and Chelubain. Although the second son Ram received the birthright, the sons of Jerahmeel, the firstborn, are listed in the genealogical record, so Jerahmeel and his descendants are still in the line of descent, and apparently have not been rejected from some kind of inheritance. What Jerahmeel lost was the special inheritance of the birthright. No reason is given for the birthright passing to Ram (see 1 Chron 2).

## The Narrative Portrays a Process of Selection

We have seen the concept of the birthright conveyed largely through the narrative. Numerous sons were born to the birthright but lost it. Others were selected for this special inheritance because they demonstrated characteristics of leadership. Through the narrative we have already identified five benefits and responsibilities that these leaders will receive: a double portion of land and possessions, a special blessing, the office of high priest with direct communication to God, a position of authority that includes leadership in battle, and procreative vigor both to strengthen the nation and to produce abundant righteous seed.

The Hebrew text employs the narrative in other ways to convey God's process of selection. We will examine two examples. First is the account of the forty years of wandering in the wilderness after the Exodus from Egypt. We have already seen God's process of instruction through "testing." First the bitter water became drinkable when Moses obeyed God, and then manna appeared like morning dew. God was demonstrating consequences for obedience and disobedience.

What is important to this study is God's selection of those who were prepared and qualified to enter the Promised Land and to possess their inheritance. The wilderness experience offered testing and training to obey and follow God. Two groups entered the Promised Land. One was the two spies, Joshua and Caleb, who returned with confidence despite giants and walled cities. The other was all those who left Egypt as youngsters. They had been raised in godly ways in the wilderness without the controlling influence of Egypt, which represents the pagan idolatry of the world.

After conquest of the land, the narrative then presents certain individuals as servants of God,[107] and identifies some of these servants as receiving an inheritance that is characteristic of the birthright. This suggests that the role as a servant of God may be related to, and is perhaps required for, God's selection of a worthy few. Two individuals stand out as servants of God with an inheritance that has attributes of the birthright. These lengthy accounts give us a greater understanding of the circumstances surrounding their inheritance. One is David, and the other is Job.

In the account of David, God told Samuel, "You shall anoint for Me [from the sons of Jesse] the one whom I designate to you. (1 Sa 16:3). The sons whom Jesse assembled passed before Samuel in the order of their birth, from the firstborn to the youngest. God selected the youngest, David, for "God *sees* not as man sees, for man looks at the outward appearance, but the LORD looks at the heart" (1 Sa 16). Thus, David was anointed as

---

[107] Abraham (Gen 26:24), Moses (Num 12:7), Jacob (Is 41:8), David (2 Sam 3:18), Job (Job 1:8), Isaiah (Is 20:3), Paul (Rom 1:1), James (James 1:1).

God's chosen king, the position of leadership that the son with the birthright will inherit, because God has seen David's heart and has found him worthy. The narrative about David expands and illustrates his role as a leader of God's people.

Job is another individual who is identified as a servant of God (Job 1:8; 2:3; 42:7, 8). Job is also shown to receive an inheritance that is characteristic of the birthright. Only after he had "seen" God, repented in dust and ashes, and prayed for his friends did God "give him twice as much as he had before" (Job 42:10). The personal possessions of Job – the sheep, camels, oxen and donkeys – are recorded as twice the number of his original possessions, thus reflecting the double portion of inheritance that belongs to the son who will inherit the birthright.

**Those who Inherit the Birthright are a Remnant**

Through the artistic nature of the language, the biblical narrative reveals information about a righteous remnant, which is often expressed with prophetic poetry. For the remainder of this chapter we will examine these artistic passages, and will see a relationship between the remnant and characteristics of the birthright. This will further explain the requirements for God's selection of a righteous remnant.

We will begin with a passage in Isaiah that is rich with expressions of the remnant. You will probably recognize the context of the passage, because Yeshua cited these verses at the beginning of his ministry by applying them to himself.

> The Spirit of the Lord GOD is upon me,
> Because the LORD has anointed me
> > to bring good news to the afflicted;
> He has sent me
> > to bind up the brokenhearted,
> > to proclaim liberty to captives
> > and freedom to prisoners;
> > to proclaim the favorable year of the
> > LORD. (Is 61:1-2)

Suddenly Isaiah shifts from the singular, Messiah, to "they." Referring to God's victorious army returning to the land after defeating the enemy, we read:

They will rebuild the ancient ruins,
They will raise up the former devastations,
And they will repair the ruined cities. (Is 61:4)

Isaiah continues by describing this victorious army with attributes of the birthright. "You will be called the priests of the Lord" (Is 61:6). We remember that one of the responsibilities of the son with the birthright is to serve as high priest with a direct connection to God.

Finally, in a kind of conclusion, Isaiah describes the double portion of inheritance, which belongs to the sons with the birthright.

> Instead of your shame
>     *you will have a* double *portion,*
> And *instead of* humiliation
>     they will shout for joy over their portion.
> Therefore they will possess a double *portion* in their
>     land,
> Everlasting joy will be theirs. (Isa 61:7)[108]

This will happen "in the favorable year of the Lord and the day of vengeance of our God" (Is 61:2).

## Requirements for a Righteous Remnant

Faithful service to God is an important requirement for the remnant. Proverbs 1-7, for example, contains instructions to the son of the king, most likely the firstborn son, the one destined to succeed to the throne upon the death of his father.

Proverbs 2:21 describes the "upright" and "blameless" who will "live in the land" and "remain in it." "Remain" is from the verbal root יתר (*yatar*), which conveys the sense of being left, thus remaining or spared. *Yatar* is often used for the remnant. Thus, the king's firstborn son, who is upright and blameless, will be a remnant in the land.

---

[108] Italics have been added by the editors of NASB to indicate words that have been added for clarification.

Amos echoes this concept of a righteous remnant by exclaiming:

> Hate evil,
> love good,
> and establish justice in the gate!
> Perhaps the LORD God of hosts May be gracious
> to the remnant of Joseph. (Amos 5:15)

Here we see a second Hebrew word used to identify the remnant, which is שארית (*she'erith*), which is from the verbal root שאר (*sha'ar*) meaning what remains or is left over. Thus, Amos explains that individuals out of Israel, who display righteousness in their deeds and actions, will be a remnant in the land. They shun evil but love what is good, and they maintain justice in the courts.

Giving specific instructions to the remnant of Judah and Israel, Zechariah also exhorts a remnant to manifest similar characteristics. The context of these words is the "remnant of this people" to whom God will give "all these things as an inheritance" (Zech 8:12b).

> These are the things which you should do:
>     Speak the truth to one another;
>     Judge with truth and judgment for peace in
>         your gates.
>     Also let none of you devise evil in your heart
>         against another,
>     And do not love perjury;
> For all these are what I hate, declares the LORD.
> (Zec 8:17)

The prophet Zephaniah also describes the remnant in similar terms that convey righteous behavior. The purpose is to exhort God's children to walk in righteousness so they may be selected as part of God's remnant.

> I will leave among you
>     a humble and lowly people,
>     and they will take refuge in the name of the
>         LORD.

The remnant of Israel [שארית ישראל]
> will do no wrong
> and tell no lies,
> nor will a deceitful tongue be found in their
>     mouths. (Zeph 3:12-13)

Thus, the individuals whom God will select as a remnant must be upright and blameless, meek and humble, hating evil and loving good, maintaining justice in the courts, truthful in speech, and rendering sound judgment. These are the characteristics of the righteous ones who not only know the distinction between good and evil but also walk in the ways of righteousness. They are exalted ones, exalted by God, and they display the characteristics of those worthy to inherit the birthright.

## God's Righteous Judgment

A description of the remnant is often given in tandem with God's righteous judgment. Thus, all of Israel, God's firstborn son, will not inherit the birthright because of God's judgment of His children. This judgment will distinguish between the righteous and the unrighteous.

For example, pride becomes a stumbling block to righteousness because God chooses the humble. The prophets warned Israel of the consequences of their prideful behavior.

> Woe to the proud crown of the drunkards of
>     Ephraim,
> And to the fading flower of its glorious beauty,
>     Which is at the head of the fertile valley
> Of those who are overcome with wine!
>
> In that day the LORD of hosts
>     will become a beautiful crown
>     and a glorious diadem
> To the remnant of His people;
>     a spirit of justice for him who sits in
>         judgment,
>     a strength to those who repel the onslaught at
>         the gate. (Is 28:1, 5-6)

This passage offers a contrast between worldly behavior (drunkards overcome with wine and a fading flower in God's fertile valley) and God's selection of a remnant. The children know they wear the crown of honor bestowed on Israel, God's firstborn son. Yet, haughty pride in their chosen status has made them drunk, and they cannot see that God will be a glorious king to those He selects. The purpose of God's selection is not the rejection of His people, but an act that "strengthens" a righteous remnant so they can "repel the onslaught at the gate." This stimulates a vivid picture of the weak point in a walled city where the enemy most often attempts an attack. The remnant will be prepared to repel that enemy just as those after forty years of wilderness wandering were prepared to defeat the Canaanites.

The concept of rewards that God will bestow on His remnant can be seen in an interesting passage in Jeremiah, again in connection with Ephraim. However, this time Ephraim does not represent all the children of Israel, but stands for the second son of Joseph who was chosen to inherit the birthright.

Before continuing with the passage in Jeremiah, we must first stop and examine the various ways in which Ephraim is used in Scripture. Carefully read each verse below in its context.

1. Second son of Joseph who received the birthright (Gen 46:20; 48:20)
2. The tribe that descended from Ephraim (Num 2:24)
3. The land inherited by the tribe of Ephraim (Josh 17:15)
4. After the death of Solomon the northern kingdom called Israel, as distinct from Judah the southern kingdom (Is 11:13)
5. All of Israel (Is 28:1; Hos 4:17)
6. The son with the birthright (Jer 31:9,18,20)
7. The descendants of Ephraim who will also, like their forefather Ephraim, inherit the birthright (Jer 31:9; Zec 10:7)

Now that you have examined the different ways Ephraim is used in the Hebrew Scriptures, we can turn to a passage in Jeremiah that refers to the descendants of Ephraim who will inherit the birthright (#6 and #7). In the context of Jeremiah 31:7-

20, the prophet is talking about the future. "Proclaim, give praise and say, 'O Lord, save Thy people, the remnant of Israel'" (שארית *she'erith*, Jer 31:7b). Jeremiah continues with a description of this remnant.

> With weeping they will come,
>> and by supplication I will lead them;
> I will make them walk by streams of waters,
>> on a straight path in which they will not stumble;
> For I am a father to Israel,
> And Ephraim is My firstborn. (Jer 31:9)

The passage ends with a parallel construction that identifies God as Israel's "Father," and then presents the relationship of Ephraim as God's "firstborn son." Ephraim in this passage conveys the irony of all Israel having been birthed as God's firstborn son, but Ephraim rather than Manasseh having been declared worthy to receive the birthright. God is a Father to all the children of Israel, but Ephraim is now God's firstborn son, not Manasseh, who was born first.

Continuing to speak of the remnant Jeremiah prophesies.

> They will come and shout for joy on the height of Zion,
> And they will be radiant over the bounty of the LORD—
>> over the grain and the new wine and the oil,
>> and over the young of the flock and the herd;
> And their life will be like a watered garden,
>> and they will never languish again.
> Then the virgin will rejoice in the dance,
>> and the young men and the old, together,
> For I will turn their mourning into joy
>> and will comfort them and give them joy for their sorrow.
> I will fill the soul of the priests with abundance,
> And My people will be satisfied with My goodness,
>> declares the LORD. (Jer 31:12-14)

Again, in the context of the remnant in this verse, the abundance seems to represent the double portion of inheritance to which the sons, who are worthy of the birthright, are entitled.

Thus, one sees in the Prophets and the Writings an expansion of the concept of inheritance by the firstborn sons called the birthright. At some future time God will gather a remnant out of all Israel. These individuals will be blameless, truthful and humble in their hearts and God will exalt them. They will have been deemed worthy as the ones who will inherit the birthright.

As God's firstborn son, all the children of Israel have been born to this calling. However, all of Israel as a corporate entity will not be denied the birthright. Those who will lose their double portion of inheritance are individual children of Israel, who lack the characteristics of obedience and service to God. The leaders of God's people will need these characteristics to rule in God's name and to defeat God's enemy.

## The Remnant Responds to God's Testing

As we continue working on this same passage in Jeremiah, we remember that God instructed His children during the forty years of wilderness wandering in two ways, through the Law and by allowing consequences called "testing." This concept of testing, which is instruction that can lead to repentance and righteousness, is captured by Jeremiah.

> I have surely heard Ephraim grieving,
>> You have chastised me,
> I have surely heard Ephraim's moaning:
>> You disciplined me like an unruly calf,
> And I have been disciplined.
> Restore me, and I will return [shuv v'shuv]
>> because you are the Lord my God. (Jer 31:18)

In this verse, Jeremiah does not mean all of Israel because it is in the context of the remnant in Jer 31:7. It is Ephraim, the son who is worthy to inherit the birthright, who has been successfully disciplined. Note the poetic parallel lines. God has disciplined and chastised Ephraim, who was an unruly calf. This has been accomplished only with Ephraim's grieving and moaning.

Yet, aren't we all unruly calves who need discipline? And "what is the purpose of this testing," we ask. Jeremiah explains. God only desires that His son turn to Him in love, humility and obedience. The intensity of God's desire is expressed with a verb expressed twice [שוב] meaning to "turn" away from the world or "return" to God.

This passage in Jeremiah continues. The remnant that will return to the land are identified as the children of Rachel.

> Thus says the LORD,
> A voice is heard in Ramah,
>     lamentation *and* bitter weeping.
> Rachel is weeping for her children;
>     she refuses to be comforted for her children,
>         because they are no more. (Jer 31:15)

All of Israel is not meant here because Rachel had only two children, Joseph and Benjamin. The children of Leah, Bilhah and Zilpah are strangely silent. The context is still the remnant of Israel, and the "children of Rachel" represent those, like Joseph, who have shown themselves worthy to inherit the birthright. All the other children of Israel are like Reuben, the firstborn son of Jacob who was unworthy to inherit the birthright.

Jeremiah continues.

> Thus says the LORD,
> Restrain your voice from weeping
>     and your eyes from tears;
> For your work will be rewarded," declares the
>     LORD,
> And they will return from the land of the enemy.
> (Jer 31:16)

Why were the children of Rachel missing? They had left to fight the enemy. "They will return from the land of the enemy," Jeremiah explains, and they will be rewarded for faithful service.

Thus, God will judge between those children of Israel who will inherit the birthright and those who will lose it. Those children of Israel who serve God in willing and loving obedience will be strong in the might of God to defeat the enemy, and they will be rewarded for their work (Jer 3:16).

## Rewards and Punishment

God's judgment is both positive and negative. In the context of positive judgment, which is rewards, Isaiah describes the abundance of the birthright to those on whom God bestows "a crown of beauty...the oil of gladness...and a garment of praise," which is descriptive of the birthright (Is 61:3). These loyal servants are identified with characteristics of the remnant.

> For I, the LORD, love justice,
>> I hate robbery in the burnt offering;
>> And I will faithfully give them their recompense [reward]
>> And make an everlasting covenant with them.
>> Then their offspring will be known among the nations,
>> And their descendants in the midst of the peoples.
>> All who see them will recognize them
> Because they are the offspring *whom* the LORD has blessed. (Is 61:8-9)

There are two major points we need to identify in this passage that are relevant to our study. First is the concept of descendants. We remember that the sons with the birthright will bear abundant seed after their own kind, which is righteous. Here Isaiah claims that all the peoples of the world will recognize these descendants, that is, acknowledge them with distinction. Second, there will be a reward.

Let us stop for a moment and consider the English word "reward." We have seen that Jeremiah declares of Rachel's lost children, who have left for war, "Restrain your voice from weeping, and your eyes from tears; for your work shall be rewarded" (Jer 31:16). Isaiah also speaks of rewards. "I will faithfully give them their recompense [reward]" (Is 61:8). These verses use two different words translated "work" and "recompense," but they both refer to wages earned for work. The work of the remnant is to serve God, and the work of the remnant will be rewarded for this work of service.

Thus, God's words convey the concept of receiving back in judgment the very thing that one has given in daily actions. In a positive sense, the recompense at the time of judgment is a reward for loving work performed. In a negative sense, the judgment can be mercy withheld when God allows us to bear the consequences of our sinful behavior. Together (positive rewards and negative punishment) they constitute God's judgment. Thus, individuals of Israel, who comprise the remnant that Jeremiah identifies symbolically as Ephraim, have permitted themselves to be disciplined by God, and so are deserving of a reward (Jer 31:16,18). As Ephraim has been disciplined and deserves a reward, so the remnant is also truly repentant by turning to God. Thus, God rewards those who are disciplined through testing and repent, and turn to him in faithful service. They will be a people the Lord will bless.

Yet, the recompense for deeds and actions has a negative connotation as well because of God's righteous judgment. Talking about his persecutors Jeremiah cries, "Bring on the day of disaster; destroy them with double destruction" (Jer 17:18b). Again, as a result of God's judgment, "I will repay them double for their wickedness and their sin, because they have defiled my land with the lifeless forms of their vile images and have filled my inheritance with their detestable idols" (Jer 16:18). As the double portion of inheritance is a blessing for work performed, so double destruction is the just penalty for wickedness and sin.

However, the purpose of such negative recompense is never to annihilate God's children, but to bring them back to God. Immediately after these harsh words of judgment for sin, Jeremiah concludes that God's faithfulness to His children will nevertheless follow His judgment of punishment.

> Therefore behold, I am going to make them know.
> This time I will make them know
>> My power and My might;
> And they shall know that My name is the LORD.
> (Jer 16:21)

The ones who refuse to obey God will have their own actions returned upon them. They will earn double for their sins by failing to receive the double portion of inheritance. In this way, God's judgment will return to them the consequences of their sinful actions. Nevertheless, God continues to hold out the option of repentance.

In conclusion, we see in the Prophets and the Writings an expansion of the concept of the birthright, which was first introduced in the patriarchal narrative. At some future time God will gather a remnant out of all Israel. These individuals will be blameless, truthful and humble in their hearts, and God will exalt them. They will have been deemed worthy to inherit the birthright to which all the children of Israel have been born as God's firstborn son. However, individuals must demonstrate by godly behavior that they are worthy to receive this special inheritance. It is not all of Israel as a corporate entity that will be denied the birthright. Instead, individuals who lack the characteristics of obedience and service to God will lose their double portion of inheritance. These are characteristics required of the leaders of God's people, who will be prepared to rule in God's name and to defeat God's enemy.

## Rewards for Service in This Life

We have seen that the Hebrew text gives a rich description of the future inheritance for those individuals whom God will select as a remnant. However, their rewards are portrayed not only as a future promise, but also as present blessings.

In their lives today, God gives the remnant prosperity of life and lengthening of days.[109] The purpose seems to be to enable them to serve God. The Book of Leviticus sets forth the daily rewards for obedience and the consequences of disobedience, which is stylistically comprised as a litany of "if" clauses followed by specific results. These are the blessings in this life, which God

---

[109] "You shall walk in all the way which the LORD your God has commanded you, that you may live and that it may be well with you, and that you may prolong *your* days in the land which you will possess" (Deut 5:33).

bestows on those who freely choose to serve and obey Him, and the consequences of losing those blessings if one disobeys God.

> If you walk in My statutes and keep My
> commandments so as to carry them out,
> Then I shall give you rains in their season,
> so that the land will yield its produce
> and the trees of the field will bear their
> fruit....
> But if you do not obey Me and do not carry out all
> these commandments,
> If instead you reject My statutes,
> And if your soul abhors My ordinances
> so as not to carry out all My commandments,
> *and* so break My covenant,
> I, in turn, will do this to you:
> I will appoint over you a sudden terror,
> consumption and fever that will waste away
> the eyes and cause the soul to pine away;
> Also, you will sow your seed uselessly, for your
> enemies will eat it up. (Lev 26:3-4; 14-16)

This same sense of abundance and well-being as a daily reward for obedient service is found elsewhere, especially in the Psalms (Ps 35:26; 119:17; 106:4). Repeatedly those who are rewarded are the servants of God. Joy is a result of obedient service (Ps 86:2, 4, 16), and the promised abundance includes eating, drinking, rejoicing and singing (Is 65:8, 9, 13, 15).

However, much of the heritage of God's servants appears to be a promise of something that is still future. Certainly their reward will be great (Ps 19:11, 13; Is 49:11). God will save His servants because they trust Him (Ps 34:22). Daniel describes the rising of God's servants at the end of days to receive their allotted inheritance (Dan 12:13). God's servants will come into His presence and His face will shine upon them (Lev 26:12; Ps 31:16; 119:135).

God's blessings and prophecies are rewards to His servants who will live in the land that God has given to Jacob (Ex 37:25), the land that God will give to His servant Israel (Ps 136:22). His servants will possess the land after a great victory, and

God will give them rest (Lev 26:6-8; Dan 12:13). The servants of God will have great strength, and none will be able to prevail against them (Ps 86:2, 4, 16; Is 54:16, 17).

There will be abundance from the land as well as an abundance of well-being and great joy (Lev 26:4-5; Ps 35:26; 86:2, 24, 26; 106:4; 119:17; Is 65: 8, 9, 13, 15). This abundance will flow upon the servants of God. Zechariah describes this inheritance.

> *There will be* peace for the seed:
> > the vine will yield its fruit,
> > the land will yield its produce
> > and the heavens will give their dew;
> And I will cause the remnant of this people to inherit all these *things.* (Zec 8:12)

Isaiah describes the way of the Lord to those who will trust in the Lord God and obey Him rather than acting according to their own will and walking in the ways of the world (Is 58:12, 13). Their promised inheritance is proclaimed.

> Then you will take delight in the LORD,
> > And I will make you ride on the heights of the earth;
> > And I will feed you *with* the heritage of Jacob your father,
> For the mouth of the LORD has spoken.    (Is 58:14).

Thus, we see that the remnant of Israel, individuals who have committed themselves to serve God, will not only receive a double portion of inheritance but will also be honored by special blessings from God that are characteristic of the birthright. Under the testing instruction of God they are being prepared to lead God's people and to fight God's battles. From them will come an abundance of godly progeny. The remnant are the sons who are worthy to inherit the birthright.

# *Mystery #12 in the Kingdom of God*

Once we understand the requirements of the sons who will inherit the birthright, it is easy to see that these same requirements apply to the remnant. Those who are the remnant permit themselves to be disciplined. They become servants of God. The remnant are "priests of the Lord" who will possess a double portion in the land. They sit in judgment and repel the onslaught at the gate. They are humble and lowly, doing no wrong and telling no lies. Their reward will be great.

In their lives today God gives the remnant prosperity of life and lengthening of days. At some time in the future the remnant will inherit "peace for the seed, the vine will yield its fruit, the land will yield its produce, and the heavens will give their due." God will make His remnant "ride on the heights of the earth."

Part Four

# Parables of Judgment

Chapter Thirteen

# Parable of the Tares

Again we have a parable about judgment that the harvest represents. The appearance of "tares" (eight repetitions in this one passage) conveys the heart of the parable, which views these plants as undesirable, ungodly and unworthy to be gathered into God's barn.

The Parable of the Tares occupies seven verses in Matthew 13:24-30. However, what follows are two more parables, the mustard seed and the leaven, before we come to what appears to be an explanation of the Parable of the Tares. The explanation begins,. Yeshua "left the multitudes and went into the house" where "his disciples came to him, saying, 'Explain to us the parable of the tares of the field'" (Mat 13:36). Do you remember the earlier words of Yeshua? "To you [disciples and followers of the Lord Yeshua] it has been granted to know the mysteries of the kingdom of heaven, but to them [pointing to the multitudes] it has not been granted" (Mat 13:11). The disciples were asking Yeshua to tell them the mystery. However, do you think the explanation that follows is the deeper meaning?

By failing to see the connection to the Hebrew Scriptures, which is a basic principle of midrash, many have concluded that the parable and its explanation is an allegory.[110] Allegories use fictional characters, figures or events to represent an abstract idea. I do not agree with this suggestion. Disciples have a heart to grow in their knowledge and wisdom of God, which occurs not by rote memory or simple explanation or even explanation by others. Instead, the disciple must search the Scriptures to uncover its depth and disclose its mysteries. So, what many Bible versions call "the tares explained" simply offers additional clues.

We must learn to always start with questions. Others have taken this path. Kiehl, for example, asks, "Why did Jesus begin to

---

[110] See, for example, Richard E. Strelan, "A Ripping Yarn: Matthew 13:24-30," *Lutheran Theological Journal* 30/1 (1996): 22-29.

speak in parables? What is a parable? How is a parable properly interpreted? What did Jesus mean by Kingdom of God?"[111] You should have your own set of questions for this parable. One should certainly be, "What is the connection to the Hebrew Scriptures?" The answer in this case is easy because there is a direct citation from Scripture (Daniel 12:3). We will need to carefully examine this verse in its context in the Hebrew Scriptures. But first, let us consider the imagery of the tares.

## Imagery of the Tares

We will begin with the words that Yeshua was speaking to a great multitude that had gathered to hear him (Mat 13:24-30). As I began to read this parable I thought the tares might be alluding to the "thorns and thistles" in Genesis 3:18. However, assumptions are dangerous and can often be misleading. So, I examined the repetitive word "tares," which in the original Greek is ζιζάνιον (*zizanion*). I was surprised to find that the Septuagint translation does not use this Greek word for either thorns or thistles in Genesis 3:18. Furthermore, the only place this word appears throughout all of Scripture, including the Septuagint translation of the Hebrew text, is this parable in Matthew.[112] Therefore, the use of the word in the Parable of the Tares is enough to tweak our curiosity, but the meaning of *zizanion* is also quite distinct and applies in a penetrating way to this particular parable.

*Zizanion* is a troublesome weed that resembles wheat. It is not surprising that our parable employs this plant with graphic imagery and incisive symbolism. In fact, this worthless and despicable plant was called by the rabbis זנה (*zonah*), meaning a harlot or prostitute.[113]

---

[111] Erich Kiehl, "Jesus Taught in Parables," *Concordia Journal* 7/6 (1981):221=28.

[112] Matthew 13:25, 26, 27, 29, 30, 36, 38.

[113] Simcha Fishbane, *Deviancy in Early Rabbinic Judaism* (Leiden: Brill, 2007), 85.

Harlotry was symbolic of mixing with the pagan, impure world. Because of the prevalence of this ungodly behavior, God had told Moses to instruct the Israelites:

Make for themselves tassels on the corners of their garments throughout their generations, and that they shall put on the tassel of each corner a cord of blue.

It shall be a tassel for you to look at and remember all the commandments of the LORD, so as to do them and not follow after your own heart and your own eyes, after which you played the harlot,

So that you may remember to do all My commandments and be holy to your God. (Num 15:38-40)

Playing the harlot is a metaphor for failing to "remember all the commandments of the Lord, so as to do them" (Num 15:39). Since the Jewish literature uses the imagery of the *zizanion* plant for playing the harlot, these unwanted plants that resemble wheat convey a striking picture of joining oneself to pagan idolatry in the world that harlotry represents. This image is compatible with the Parable of the Tares.

## The Figurative Language of a Metaphor

We must stop here and consider the figurative language of a metaphor. I have just said that "playing the harlot" is a metaphor for failing to walk in the ways of God by "doing all the commandments."

A metaphor is an extended symbol that uses one concept to represent another in a totally non-literal way. If the relationship is literal, it is a symbol. For example, we all recognize the symbolism of the words that Yeshua spoke at the last supper. "This is My blood of the covenant, which is poured out for many" (Mar 14:23-24). Thus, wine is a commonly recognized symbol for blood. However, a metaphor extends the concept of a symbol by making the representation obscure and even puzzling.

Scripture is teeming with metaphors that the people of ancient Israel would have "heard." They would have been startled by the vague words, which would have required them to consider the deeper meaning. We too must learn to recognize a metaphor, to visualize the vivid picture it portrays, and to stop and ponder the deeper meaning to which it is pointing.

The subtle association of harlotry with tares stimulates the graphic image of a woman beckoning us to "turn aside, my master, turn aside to me" (Jdg 4:18). This language is common in the biblical text as words spoken by harlots. Thus, the parable would have stimulated deep emotion among the original listeners. In present times we are also taken aback when we learn the ancient association of tares with harlots. The deeper meaning of the metaphor is guiding us to know the Law and to walk in its ways so we can avoid playing the harlot. The men in the ancient crowd, who were listening to Yeshua tell this parable, might well have nervously fingered the four tassels on their shawls. These tassels were knotted with 613 knots, one for each of the 613 commandments.

## Imagery of Tares among the Wheat

We are still in the portion of the parable that Yeshua was speaking to multitudes on the shore (Mat 13:24-30). As we continue to let the imagery blossom, we have not left the plain and simple meaning. Nevertheless, the imagery is exquisite and contributes greatly to the flavor of the parable. So, let us look further at the figurative nature of these tares.

We learn that the tares are an enemy, and there seems to be a struggle or battle between two forces. On one hand we have a man who sowed good seed in his field that is now producing wheat. On the other hand the enemy is working to thwart his good work. The two are certainly symbolic. The man who sowed seed represents those children of God who have learned the Law and are exhibiting the elements of godly behavior. The enemy is the god of this world and all the worldly enticements that lure God's children to play the harlot. However, we must admit that this would have been no great revelation to people at the time of Yeshua, nor is it particularly remarkable to us today. Therefore, we are still in the plain and simple meaning that the figurative language conveys.

The enemy is using a method of warfare that necessitates further scrutiny. The *zizonion* plant looks just like a stalk of wheat, thus making it hard to distinguish between the good and the bad.

This method of attack is deceit, and an echo from the Hebrew Scriptures is undoubtedly the serpent in the Garden of Eden. Another interesting and related element in the parable is the sower, who was sleeping when the enemy sowed the threatening tares. Therefore, not only must we know the ways of God that He reveals in Scripture (the Law) but we must also be alert to any deceitful worldly tactics.

## Judgment and the Language of Prophecy

Let us now turn to additional symbolism in the parable that we must consider before continuing to the depth of meaning. There are two symbols that point to judgment. One is reaping, which occurs at the time of the harvest, and the other is burning the unwanted weeds.

God uses prophetic language of extreme exaggeration and vivid imagery when He is speaking to His people about judgment. Thus, the language of judgment is like an emotional carrot and stick. On one hand God dangles a carrot and says, in essence, you will be with Me in peace and harmony and righteousness in a wonderful future kingdom. But beware of the stick! There will be consequences for your sinful actions.

We have seen earlier, in the Parable of the Unforgiving Servant, a graphic vision of the language of prophecy that uses a reprimanding stick. In that parable the king and the landlord represented God, who cast His servant into prison without a way of being released, and turned him over to the torturers. Here, in the Parable of the Tares, we are going to see the same kind of vivid and startling prophetic language with the imagery of reaping and burning.

## Symbolic Imagery of Reaping

Reaping is an agricultural task that harvests the grain crop. Israel has two grain harvests, barley in the spring and wheat in early summer. After cutting the grain stalks, the grain kernels must be separated from the outer husks, called chaff. The husks, or chaff, are unwanted and need to be destroyed. In ancient Israel separation of the grain from the chaff was accomplished by tossing wheat stalks into the wind with a pitchfork, thus allowing the lighter chaff to blow away and the heavier kernels to fall to the ground. The chaff was then burned.

This imagery of separating the kernel from the chaff and then burning the unwanted husks is common in Scripture. Read each of the following verses in their context to gain a better understanding of this powerful imagery and symbolism of judgment. Then answer the provocative questions that follow.

> Ex 15:7
> Job 21:18
> Ps 35:5
> Is 33:11
> Dan 2:35
> Mat 3:12; cf.. Lk 3:17

1.  Matthew 3:12 (cf. Luke 3:17) is probably a familiar verse. Use the internet to find a picture of winnowing with a winnowing fork. Then consider the verse as a metaphor because the fork is in God's hand. How is this imagery a metaphor and how does a metaphor convey a powerful meaning?

2.  Make a list of the characteristics of those who experience God's wrath in judgment. Start with "rising up against God" in Exodus 15:7. What does it mean to "rise up against God?" Continue making your list and consider the various characteristics of those who experience God's wrath (you will need to read each verse in its context).

NOTE: I use the term "wrath," as it applies to God's judgment, as any kind of penalty that fails to produce a response of repentance for a sinful action.

3.  The verse, Isaiah 33:1, can apply to all of us at some time in our lives. How do we conceive chaff and give birth to stubble? What does this figurative language represent? Whose breath will consume us like a fire? What is the Hebrew word for breath?

We can see from these verses that God is separating His people for some purpose, as wheat is separated from chaff. So we ask, "Who is He separating and why?" Turn to the explanation in Matthew 13:36-43 and re-read this passage. Then continue reading the commentary below.

God's judgment, which is conveyed metaphorically by the image of reaping, is separating the "good seed" from what is unwanted and useless. "Good seed" gives us two clues. We have "good" as opposed to "bad," and "seed" bears "fruit." Who bears fruit for God? Those who bear fruit "do good" by walking in righteousness. By contrast, those who do not bear fruit for God are not walking in righteousness. They are the bad seed that is not bearing fruit. They are the unwanted tares.

The context of this explanation is important. Yeshua "left the multitudes...and the disciples came to him, saying, 'Explain to us the Parable of the Tares.'" So, Yeshua is talking to his disciples. They are his followers and he is instructing them to "do good" by walking in the ways of the Law so they will "bear fruit" for God. If they do not bear fruit from good seed, they are like the tares and must bear God's wrath in judgment. However, do not jump to the conclusion that these disciples have lost their eternal life. Read on.

## Symbolic Imagery of Fire

Now we turn to the metaphorical method that God uses to separate the "good" (those who are walking in righteousness) from the "bad" (those walking in the ways of the world). Fire is a powerful symbol that conveys a purification process, which destroys the unholy and leaves only what is righteous and good. Take, for example, gold ore, which can be heated with an intense heat to destroy all impure materials, thus leaving pure gold. The Parable of the Tares uses graphic imagery to convey this purification by fire. "The tares are gathered up and burned with fire" (Matthew 13:41). Thus, the unholy is gone, leaving only what is holy and pure, which is the remnant or what remains.

The following verses portray the imagery of fire as it is used in the biblical text. Read each verse in its context, and then answer the questions below.

Exodus 29:25
Deuteronomy 9:3
Deuteronomy 32:22
Job 1:16
Psalm 18:8
Isaiah 5:24
Isaiah 10:17
Jeremiah 6:29
Ezekiel 22:20

1. How is a burnt offering, which is described in Exodus 29:25, symbolic of the best gift that the children of Israel could give to God? What does the burnt offering symbolize?

2. How does Job 1:16 echo the Noah account?

3. We cannot read Psalm 18:8 literally. Instead the language is teeming with prophetic language. Be sure and read this verse in its context. How is the language both prophetic of the future *and* prophetic of God's work in our lives today?

4. In the two verses in Isaiah, how does fire act both to destroy and to purify?

Scripture tells us that God will purify (and is purifying) His people by judging their actions. If they walk in godly ways, they bear fruit for God and God rewards them with joy and peace in a relationship with Him. If they walk in worldly ways, God will allow them to go through a process of testing, which can be likened to a fiery furnace. Ultimately God will select those who respond to testing by repenting and abandoning their worldly ways. In this way, God will select those who are worthy as a remnant. The remnant are God's chosen leaders now, and will also participate in a future battle to destroy God's enemy as we will see in more detail in Chapter Sixteen.

Purification by fire and the burning of tares are graphic metaphors that convey a powerful emotional message. We cannot take these images literally because the artistic language conveys a vivid metaphorical meaning. In the parable we read that, in the place of the "furnace of fire," there will be "weeping and gnashing of teeth." These are the ones whom God has *not* selected. Their bodies have not been destroyed because they are capable of weeping and gnashing their teeth. However, they are outside God's kingdom and separated from Him because they cannot come into God's righteous presence in their sinful condition. Inside the Kingdom are those whose sins have been purified. They are the righteous ones who can come before the brilliant glory of God. Metaphorically, those in the Kingdom have been refined and purified. Metaphorically, the others are the tares because of their unrighteous behavior.

## The Parable's Conclusion

The parable's concluding verse cites Daniel 12:3. "Then THE RIGHTEOUS WILL SHINE FORTH AS THE SUN in the kingdom of their Father." (Capital letters identify the citation, and the remaining words are an explanatory commentary). Thus, *where* will the righteous shine forth as the sun? They will be in "the kingdom of their Father." But *when* will the righteous shine forth as the sun? All the parables, which I believe are haggadic midrash, are exhorting God's people to walk in righteousness now. When they do, they will be walking in the kingdom of their Father and witnessing, by their light and fruit, the glory of God to others.

We remember that people in ancient Israel memorized the Holy Writings from early childhood, so a brief citation would have stimulated the memorized block in their minds. Therefore, we must turn to Daniel 12:3 to identify the likely memorized block, which I also call "the contex.t"

I suggest you read Daniel 12:1-3. "Now at that time" introduces a new conceptual thought whereas verse 4 begins with a contrast. So, the immediate context seems to be Daniel 12:1-3 (the memorized block would undoubtedly have also included the contrast, but for our purposes we will work only with verses 1-3).

> Now at that time Michael, the great prince who stands *guard* over the sons of your people, will arise. And there will be a time of distress such as never occurred since there was a nation until that

time; and at that time your people, everyone who is
found written in the book, will be rescued.

Many of those who sleep in the dust of the
ground will awake, these to everlasting life, but the
others to disgrace *and* everlasting contempt.

Those who have insight will shine brightly
like the brightness of the expanse of heaven, and
those who lead the many to righteousness, like the
stars forever and ever. (Dan 12:1-3)

"Those who have insight" are the ones who will shine
brightly like the "brightness of the expanse of heaven." What role
has God given them? We see that they will "lead the many to
righteousness." I suggest that the ones who shine brightly are
God's chosen remnant. They are the leaders of God's people both
now and also in the future. They are guiding God's people to
righteousness, which is the requirement for standing in the
presence of God. We cannot see clearly *how* they will perform as
leaders in the future. However, it appears that this prophetic role
of bringing God's people to Him will occur *after* the Millennial
Kingdom. Thus, the Millennial Kingdom seems to be a period of
preparation for what will follow.

These are only my thoughts, so I suggest you use your
online interlinear Bible to learn more about two Hebrew words in
Daniel 12:3. One has been translated "insight," and the other is
"shine brightly." This exercise may help you gain a glimpse of this
prophetic future.

# Mystery #13 in the Kingdom of God

The Parable of the Tares uses graphic language to vividly portray a symbolic process of destroying what is unwanted (chaff represents all our sinful acts), thus leaving only what is pure and righteous. What remains is a kernel or seed, which represents the beginning of new life. We can begin a new life now, in our lives today, by following the instructions of the parables that lead us to walk in righteousness in the kingdom of God.

The parable is also teeming with future prophetic imagery that portrays God's selection of a righteous remnant. This remnant has a leadership role to play, both now in this life and also in some future activity. In our glimpse of the future in the Book of Daniel, we see the chosen leaders of God's people (a remnant) who will guide them to their God.

Chapter Fourteen

# Parable of the Fishing Net

I had a wonderful time with this parable. Of course, as with many of the parables I started in confusion. I have not memorized the Hebrew Scriptures as people in ancient Israel would have done. So, I simply began by reading a story about some fishermen who caught a lot of fish in the Sea of Galilee, and then they came to the shore to separate their catch and prepare it for sale or consumption. At this point I could have drawn some kind of moral message about separation and selecting the best. After all, the Hebrew Scriptures exhort the people of God to separate *from* the world *unto* God. However, the parable ends with a furnace of fire, so the separation has something to do with judgment. Without perceiving the connection to the Hebrew Scriptures, any attempt to draw some moral message about judgment will likely fall short of its depth of meaning, and may even become a personal interpretation.

## Where to Begin

I assume that my initial response of puzzlement to the parable also describes your experience. So, what should we do next?

1. Start by carefully reading the Parable of the Fishing Net in Matthew 13:47-52.
2. The setting is important. You will find it in Matthew 13:36. Yeshua is *not* talking to all of God's people. To whom is he addressing this parable? Why is the answer to this question important for a proper understanding of the meaning of the parable?
3. Read verses 47-48 again, this time listen carefully to the rhythm and let your voice rise for important words. What visual image emerges from this reading? What are the important words and phrases?
4. Did you hear the list in the rhythm of your reading? "Drew it up on the beach...sat down...gathered the good into containers." Do you think there is a progression in these three phrases? What might they symbolize?

5. Following the list is the word "but," which signifies a contrast. However, what follows the list is emphasized not only by "but" but also by standing alone at the end of the list. Listen again to the rhythm. Pause after "but" and then let your voice rise for "bad" and again for "away." "But...the *bad* they threw *away*." What is the relationship between this last phrase about throwing away something bad and the list that precedes it?

Now it is time to go back and carefully consider the repetition, "to gather." This is going to be our clue for finding the connection to the Hebrew Scriptures.

## "Gather" in the Hebrew Scriptures

Using the Septuagint translation, we can see there are two possible Hebrew words that mean "gather." One is לקט (*laqat*), which means to pick up or glean as in picking up wheat sheaves after they have been cut. For example, Ruth was a widow with a mother-in-law to support, so she asked permission to pick up wheat from the fields of Boaz. "Please let me glean and gather after the reapers among the sheaves," she politely asked the servant of Boaz (Ruth 2:7). "Glean" is לקט (*lakat*) meaning to gather, but we also have a second word that means to gather, which is אסף (*asaph*).

| Hebrew | English translation | Examples |
|---|---|---|
| לקט (*laqat*) | Gather together, amass | 1. Jacob said to his kinsmen, "Gather stones." (Gen 32:46) 2. Joseph gathered all the money that was found in the land of Egypt. (Gen 47:14) |
| אסף (*asaph*) | Assemble together | 1. The flocks were gathered there. (Gen 29:3) 2. They will gather together against me and attack me and I will be destroyed. (Gen 34:30) |

As I pored over verses in the Hebrew Scriptures that use these two words meaning "to gather," I was drawn to one in particular where Jacob bestows prophetic blessings on his twelve sons. "Jacob summoned [called] all of his sons and said, 'Assemble yourselves that I may tell you what will befall you in the days to come'" (Gen 49:1). The word for "assemble" is אסף (*asaph*), and two things caught my attention. First, in the Parable of the Fishing Net, all were gathered; that is, Jacob gathered all his sons. The parable then follows with prophetic consequences.

The second thing that drew me in was this. In the same Genesis passage we will see that Jacob's prophetic blessings identify two sons who are worthy to inherit the birthright, hence righteous in the eyes of God and prepared for a leadership role. The other ten sons are unworthy of the birthright, and are therefore perceived as unrighteous. This is prophetic information about the time that Matthew calls "the end of the age."

## Judah and Joseph Inherit the Birthright

Turn to Genesis 49:1-28 and read Jacob's prophetic blessings to his twelve sons. Then review the five characteristics of the birthright from Chapter Four (summarized on page 81).

You are now ready to examine the blessings of Judah and Joseph in Genesis 49:8-12; 22-26. We will start with Judah. How are the following descriptions characteristic of the birthright?

1. Your brothers shall praise you.
2. Your hand will be on the neck of your enemies.
3. Your father's sons shall bow down to you.
4. The scepter shall not depart from you.
5. The ruler's staff [shall remain] between your feet.
6. To you shall be the obedience of the peoples.
7. Imagery of a lion.

It is time now to turn to the prophetic blessing of Joseph in Genesis 49:22-26. How are the following descriptions characteristic of the birthright?

1.  A fruitful bough whose branches run over a wall...
2.  Archers attacked but his bow remained firm.
3.  The God of your father helps you and blesses you.
4.  You will be blessed with the breasts and the womb.
5.  You will wear the crown of leadership that will distinguish you among your brothers.

## Reuben's Loss of the Birthright

We will turn next to Reuben, who was born to the birthright as Jacob's firstborn son, but lost this inheritance because of unworthy behavior. You will find a description of his unworthy behavior in 1 Chronicles 5:1, which you should review now. So we ask, "How did Reuben defile his father's bed?" We learn that, "while Israel was dwelling in the land [Israel refers to Jacob whose name was changed to Israel], Reuben went and lay with Bilhah his father's concubine and Israel heard *of it*" (Gen 35:22). So what, then, is Reuben's prophetic blessing in Genesis 49:3-4??

As you read the blessing of Reuben, the artistry of the language conveys a contrast between the inheritance to which Reuben was born and a description of his character that led to the loss of the birthright. Let us review Gevirtz' conclusion from his extensive linguistic study of Reuben's blessing and his translation of these verses:[114]

> Reuben, my first-born,
>> you are my strength
>> and the beginning of my vigor:
>> pre-eminent in authority
>> and pre-eminent in power.
> But, checked like water,
>> you may not lead!
>> When you ascended your father's bed,
>> then you fouled the suckler's couch (Gen 49:3-4).

---

[114] Translation by Stanley S. Gevirtz, "The Reprimand of Reuben (Gen 49:3)," JNES 30 (April, 1971): 98.

Gevirtz' rendering of שאת as "authority" helps clarify Reuben's loss of leadership that the birthright conveys. So does his understanding of "checked like water, you may not lead!"

How, then, would you explain from Genesis 49:3-4 how and why Reuben was unworthy of the birthright?

## Remaining Sons of Jacob

Carefully re-read the prophetic blessings of Jacob's remaining sons who, like Reuben, did not receive the birthright. You will find this information in Genesis 49:5-7, 13-21, 27. Start by making your own list as you read and note the ungodly action or actions of each son and the consequences of these actions. Then consider how these words of prophecy can be applied to your lives today.

Now you are ready to use my list below for your further (and hopefully deeper) examination of this passage.

1. Simeon and Levi (Gen 49:8-7) - Review Gen 34:1-31.

2. Zebulun (Gen 49:13) – Consider the location and inhabitants of Sidon.

3. Issachar (Gen 49:14-15) – This is prophetic and therefore fuzzy as to its meaning. Concentrate on imagery and symbolism that has general application.

4. Dan (Gen 49:16-18) – Much discussion has revolved around Revelation 7 where the list of the twelve tribes does not include Dan (the tribes of Manasseh and Ephraim inherited Joseph's double portion).

5. Gad (Gen 49:19) – There are two parts to this verse. Could the second be an echo of Gen 3:15?

6. Asher (Gen 49:20) – Is rich food and royal dainties a biblical blessing or curse?

7. Naphtali (Gen 49:21) – The Book of Proverbs deals extensively with the power of the tongue, both for good and for evil.

8. Benjamin (Gen 49:27) – Apply the powerful imagery to actions of some people today.

## Returning to the Parable

This account of Jacob gathering his sons together to tell them what will befall them in the days to come seems relevant to our parable. "What will happen at the end of the age?" the parable asks, and words of prophecy follow. The fishermen have gathered all the fish into the net, as Jacob gathered all his sons to hear the future consequences of their actions. However, only two of Jacob's sons have been selected to inherit the birthright, Joseph and Judah.

During a judgment of God (notice I say "a" judgment because there will be more than one)[115] the parable declares there will be a separation between the righteous and the πονηρός (poneros). English versions of the Bible interpret the Greek word πονηρός as "wicked." However, I think this translation is too strong because it implies a final judgment, which may or may not be the case. With a first century mind, I suggest it is better to perceive and consider the contrast this parable portrays. One group is "good" (Mat 13:48) and "righteous" (Mat 13:49). With typical Hebraic parallelism, the other group is "bad" and "unrighteous."

My conclusion, that Jacob's prophetic blessings in Genesis 49 are an echo that the parable evokes, describes Judah and Joseph as "good and righteous" and the remaining ten sons as "bad and unrighteous." The consequences of their actions will affect the *nature* of their inheritance. There will be a judgment that leads to an inheritance for a remnant whom God considers worthy of leadership, as Judah and Joseph were a remnant chosen from Jacob's twelve sons. This remnant will defeat the army of Satan which, I suggest, will then allow God to deal with all His children who have been "bad and unrighteous."

---

[115] There are numerous possible interpretations about the Great White Throne Judgment that this study will not address (Rev 20:11).

## Conclusion

We must remember the setting of the parable. Jesus was talking to his disciples, those whose hearts desired to live in a way that is good and righteous. He asked these disciples, "Have you understood all these things?" Although they answered "yes," he gave them additional words of instruction, which leads us to believe that there was still more for them to understand. "Therefore," he began, which suggests the practical application of this parable. "Every scribe who has become a disciple of the kingdom of heaven is like a head of a household who brings forth out of his treasure things new and old" (Mat 13:52). "Things new and old" seems to relate to uncovering "the mysteries of the kingdom of heaven" (Mat 13:11).

Thus, the deeper meaning of the parables is not for all of God's children. All may hear them, perhaps when they go to church on Sunday morning or read their Bible at home. However, not all God's children will understand what they hear. The deeper meaning in the parables is for those who hunger to know God, who want to grow closer to Him, and who desire to serve their Lord in humble obedience. These are the disciples. However, the disciples are not only being prepared for a future prophetic role but also have an important part to play now. They are to be like the "head of a household" who guides and instructs its members. As they serve in this way, they will bear fruit for God and will produce from His treasure.

If you respond to this parable of judgment with fear and concern, perhaps you are not yet a disciple. However, if you hunger to know God and desire to walk in His ways, then you *are* a disciple, and you should respond to this parable with excitement and anticipation. God will be selecting a remnant out of all His children just as He chose Judah and Joseph. The requirement is to be "good and righteous." Fortunately, as we learned in God's selection of David, God only sees the heart (1 Sam 16:7). So, righteousness in God's eyes is not complete perfection, but one whose heart truly desires to serve in humble obedience. The psalms capture this concept with poetic rhythm.

Be glad in the LORD and rejoice, you righteous ones,
And shout for joy, all you who are upright in hear.
(Ps 32:11)

The righteous man will be glad in the LORD, and will
take refuge in Him;
And all the upright in heart will glory. (Ps 64:10)

Did you catch the emotional excitement? "Upright" is parallel to "righteous," which expands our understanding of what God is asking of us. Upright (יָשָׁר *yashar*) is to be conscientious, straight, and to do what is right. Where is this righteousness? It is in the heart. When will these upright ones shout for joy? They glory in part now. However, at some time in the future, which the parable calls the end of times, they will shout for joy when God selects those who are good and righteous. What is the purpose of this selection? The remnant will play an important role that will ultimately defeat God's enemy.

---

## Mystery #14 in the Kingdom of God

God is in the process of gathering all His children to Him. However, from all His family He is selecting a few to play a special role of leadership both now and in the future.

God is seeking those who are upright and righteous. His selection is based on their hearts, the innermost part of their beings. Like Judah, those who belong to the remnant display righteousness in their thoughts and actions so others will praise them. Like Joseph, those in the remnant are leaders of God's people and can withstand attacks by the enemy.

You too can walk in righteousness if your heart overflows with love for God and you desire to serve Him in humble obedience.

Chapter Fifteen

# Parable of the Wedding Feast

"Many are called but few are chosen." These are enigmatic words in the New Testament that have led to confusion and several possible interpretations. Who are the called? Perhaps more important, who are those whom God has chosen, and what is the significance of their selection?

I always assumed that the called were Jews whom God invites to believe in Yeshua, the promised Messiah. With a sense of deep concern I thought that only a few believed, so these few are the only ones whom God has chosen to be "saved." When I asked others what they thought this verse meant, some suggested that the calling was for God's children to submit, obey and serve, and only a few answer this calling to become servants of their Lord Yeshua. However, most agreed with what I had been led to believe, that the verse refers to the requirement to believe in Yeshua in order to be saved.

When I was browsing online to look at the "chat" on this verse, I found an article by Allen Ross, a scholar and professor who supports the traditional thinking that only Jews who believe in Yeshua will be saved. However, he then extends this interpretation to a conclusion that I found quite disturbing. "The meaning of this parable is pretty clear – it condemns the contempt that Israel as a whole (and everyone in general) had (and has) for God's gracious invitation through Jesus the Messiah."[116] All Israel according to Ross have rejected Yeshua and are condemned for their contempt. Apparently, Ross believes that believing Jews are no longer Jews but Christians. This is strong language. The unsettling conclusion by a respected scholar stimulated, perhaps more than anything else, my intense curiosity and desire to dig into

---

[116] Allen Ross, *Parable of the Wedding Banquet,* http://bible.org (accessed 6/3/11).

the parable that concludes, "Many are called, but few are chosen."[117]

As always, before you continue with my commentary, please stop and carefully read the Parable of the Wedding Feast in Matthew 22:1-14. In fact, you may wish to read it more than once while asking, "How and why does this parable lead to the conclusion, many are called but few are chosen"?

## The Setting

The setting of the parable is significant. Yeshua was teaching in the temple grounds in Jerusalem shortly before his death and resurrection. The chief priests and elders of the people were questioning his authority, so he began to speak to all of them in parables (Mat 21:23). One of these is our parable about the wedding banquet. So, the focus and purpose of this particular parable is directed to these religious leaders, but the multitudes are listening. As for what is startling, let me ask you some questions.

1. Who had originally been invited to the wedding feast? In the context of Israel's ancient culture and tradition, why was it startling that they refused the invitation?
2. Do you see the three categories of those who refused the invitation to attend the wedding banquet for the king's son? What are these three categories?
3. Whom did the king invite next? In the context of Israel's ancient culture and tradition, why is this so startling?
4. One of the wedding guests came without wedding clothes and was cast into outer darkness. Are you startled by the consequences of attending a wedding without proper clothing? What do you think this means?

---

[117] This chapter is a brief summary of a more in-depth study that is available on bibleinteract.tv. It is entitled, "Many are Called but Few are Chosen."

## Who are the Called?

The repetition in this parable is so strong that we cannot ignore it. One Greek word is used repeatedly (καλέω pronounced *kaleo*). However, this one Greek word has been translated to English with two different words, "called" and "invited." Yet, the parable uses the same Greek word a total of six times.

> Verse 3: *call* those who have been *invited*
> Verse 4: those who have been *invited*
> Verse 8: those who were *invited*
> Verse 9: *invite* to the wedding feast
> Verse 14: many are *called*, but few are chosen

We are learning to think with a first century mind, so we ask, "What would the original listeners of this parable have "heard"? Those who listened to Yeshua speak this parable in the temple grounds were, of course, Jews. Their Holy Writings were the Hebrew Scriptures because the New Testament had not yet been written. So, what did they "hear" when Yeshua said, "Many are called?" They heard echoes from the Hebrew Scriptures. However, for us to hear the same echoes we must first identify the equivalent Hebrew word that means "called," and examine how it is used in the Hebrew Scriptures.[118]

The Hebrew word is קרא (*qara*), which first appears in the creation account in Genesis.

> God *called* the light day.
> God *called* the expanse heaven.
> Whatever the man *called* a living creature, that was
> its name.
> The man *called* his wife's name Eve.

---

[118] The *Septuagint* is a translation of the Hebrew Scriptures from Hebrew to Greek that was completed in the late 2nd century B.C. To find a Hebrew word, which is the equivalent of a NT Greek word, we can use the *Septuagint* to locate where the Greek word is used and then identify the original Hebrew.

## 1. Most Common Usage: Called by the Name of God

Thus, קרא is first used in Scripture to mean "called by name." God named the light "day," and to the expanse He gave the name "heaven." This concept of naming is even more evident when Adam called his wife's name Eve. That is, קרא does not mean to "invite" in these verses and, in fact, in almost all the usages of קרא in the Hebrew Scriptures. קרא means "to be called by name."

As I was poring over the many appearances of קרא, which means to be called by name, I suddenly remembered where Paul had cited Genesis 21:12 in his letter to the Romans. "Through Isaac your descendants will be named [καλέω]" (Rom 9:7). which means to be called by name. The cited verse in Genesis reads, "Through Isaac your offspring will be called [קרא]." That is, the descendants of Isaac would carry the name of Abraham.

Then I discovered what would become a pivotal verse in my search to understand the concept of being "called." "I have called you by name; you are Mine!" declared God to His children, Israel. So, to be called by the name of God means to belong to Him by bearing His name. Since God calls Israel His firstborn son in Exodus 4:22, all the children of Israel are called by the name of the Lord and belong to Him. He is their Father and they are His firstborn. This would have been the understanding of the first century listeners who heard Yeshua conclude his parable with these words, "Many are called." The children of Israel are called by the name of God and belong to Him.

However, Hebrew is a language that often has several words to convey the same or similar meaning. Furthermore, what is important to this study on the NT parable, one Hebrew word often expresses more than one concept. All languages do this, but Hebrew does it to an extreme. This allowed the biblical authors to use the language in artistic ways to convey a depth of meaning. We see this artistic handling of the language with our word קרא. In most cases it means "called by name." However, we will now see two additional meanings that this one Hebrew word can convey.

## 2.  Second Usage: Call on the Name of the Lord

Those who belong to God, who bear His name, can call on the name of the Lord in times of need. For example, Elijah declared to the prophets of Baal, "You call on the name of your god, and I will call on the name of the Lord" (1 Kings 18:24). In his letter to the Romans, Paul cites the prophet Joel who proclaimed, "Whoever calls on the name of the Lord will be delivered" (Joel 2:32). So, those who belong to God, who bear His name, can call on the name of the Lord in times of need and God will respond.

## 3.  Third Usage: Called as an Invitation

There is a third way that קרא is used in the Hebrew Scriptures. This third way only occurs twice, which draws our attention to it. Its appearance is important for the understanding of our parable and its concluding words, "Many are called but few are chosen." The third usage is to be "invited to a banquet." We see this understanding of קרא in two important passages.

> Jacob offered a sacrifice on the mountain, and called [קרא] his kinsmen to the meal; and they ate the meal and spent the night on the mountain." (Gen 31:54)

> He [Jethro] said to his daughters, ""Where is he then [referring to Moses]? Why is it that you have left the man behind? Invite [קרא] him to have something to eat. (Ex 2:20)

In the first verse, Jacob had just left Padan Aram to return to the land of Israel, taking with him his four wives, eleven sons (Benjamin had not yet been born), a daughter, all their children, and an abundance of livestock and other property. Jacob's father-in-law chased after him to try to capture and take back (both people and property) what he believed rightfully belonged to him. However, Jacob and Laban came to an understanding, which is why Jacob celebrated this covenantal pact by "calling [inviting] his kinsmen" to a special banquet meal.

In the second verse, after killing an Egyptian overseer, Moses fled to the wilderness. There he came to a well where he met the daughters of the priest of Midian. Hostile shepherds were preventing their access to the well, so Moses rescued the women and drew water for their sheep. Their father, Jethro, then sent his daughters to "call" [invite] Moses to a special meal.

There is one more significant feature in the Hebrew Scriptures and subsequent sacrificial practices that relate to this invitation to a banquet meal. One of the prescribed sacrifices, which was first conducted in the tabernacle and then in the temple, was called a peace or fellowship offering. For this particular sacrifice, an unblemished animal was given to the Lord simply because the participant wanted to express his love for his wonderful God. The priests would burn the fat portion of the animal as a sweet aroma to God. Then, after roasting, half of the animal would be distributed to the priests and the other half returned to the giver. The giver would then share a "banquet of thanksgiving" by calling [inviting] his family and close friends. This fellowship offering to God is expressed as a special banquet meal.

We can now conclude, from our understanding of the Hebrew word "call" (קרא), that Yeshua was referring to all the Jews who, as  God's firstborn son, were called by the name of God. They belonged to God, who called Himself their Father (Deut 32:6). Thus, many are the children of Israel. However, what follows in the NT parable is "few are chosen." So, now we must turn to the Hebrew Scriptures once more to understand what it means to be chosen.

**Few are Chosen**

We are beginning to penetrate our parable's conclusion, "Many are called but few are chosen." When Yeshua was teaching in the temple compound, where the chief priests and elders were questioning his authority, he was addressing both those who came to hear him, and also those who came to criticize him. They were probably all Jews who had come to Jerusalem for the Passover. Thus, they were all called by the name of God and belonged to God as His children. They all had the privilege of calling on the name of God.

However, according to the parable, only a few would be invited to the banquet given by the king for the wedding of his son. This is prophetic imagery of the celebration after the defeat of God's enemy. So, now we must search the Hebrew Scriptures to understand the word "chosen." Who are the few who will be chosen? Why will God choose them and not others? For what purpose will they be chosen?

Let us start by looking at the two Greek words, one for "called" and the other for "chosen." We remember that "called" is the Greek καλέω (*kaleo*), which has the Hebrew equivalent of קרא (*kara*). "Chosen" is the Greek word ἐκλεκτός (*ekklektos*), which is the same verb καλέω with the preposition ἐκ attached in front of it. Thus, ἐκλεκτός means "called out," or chosen for a special role.

Now, we need to identify the Hebrew equivalent so we can work to understand the concept of "chosen" in the Hebrew Scriptures. We remember that the New Testament had not yet been written, and the Jews listening to Yeshua would have heard echoes from the Hebrew Holy Writings.

The Hebrew word for "chosen" is בחר (*bachar*), which conveys a very important concept in Scripture. With typical Hebrew artistry this three-letter verbal root can be modified to create other similar words that are nevertheless related to the meaning of the verbal root.

| | HEBREW | ENGLISH |
|---|---|---|
| 1 | בחר (*bachar*) | Chosen (verbal root) |
| 2 | בכור (*b'chor*) | Firstborn |
| 3 | בכורה (*b'chorah*) | Birthright |
| 4 | בכורים (*bekurim*) | First fruits |

1. Who, then, is chosen? The firstborn son is chosen for a special role. He is entitled to an inheritance known as the birthright. However, he must prove himself worthy of this special inheritance, which bestows a role of leadership, by becoming a kind of first fruits to God that is unblemished and holy. This firstborn son, who is worthy to inherit the birthright, is the one who will be chosen. I have underlined each word that is derived from the verbal root *bachar*.

2. We will turn now to the concept of the firstborn son. Our attention is drawn to God declaring Israel, meaning all the

children of Israel, to be His firstborn. "Israel is My son, My firstborn [b'chor]. Let My son go so he may serve Me; but you [pharaoh] have refused to let him go. Behold, I will kill you son, your firstborn [b'chor]" (Ex 4:22-23).

3.    Thus, all the children of Israel, as God's firstborn son, are born to this special inheritance known as the birthright. However, they must show that they are worthy. Listen again to God. "You are a holy people to the Lord your God; the Lord your God has chosen you [bachar] to be a people for His own possession out of all the peoples on the face of the earth" (Deut 7:6). Thus, God first sees His children as holy, and then encourages them to walk in this holiness. However, they must be guided to walk in righteousness, which is why God has given them His law.

4.    We turn now to those few out of Israel who will be worthy to inherit the birthright. They give themselves to God as "first fruits," that is, a gift that is holy, pure and unblemished. God describes these worthy ones as "righteous," and identifies them as a "remnant."

For example, we have seen that Noah is identified as the first remnant after the flood destroyed unrighteousness on the face of the earth. "Only Noah was left [שאר sha'ar, a word for the remnant], together with those that were with him in the ark" (Gen 7:23). God chose Noah because "Noah was a righteous man, blameless in his time; Noah walked with God" (Gen 6:9). The word translated "blameless" is the Hebrew תמים (tamim) meaning unblemished, as the sacrificial animal was unblemished, perfect, and given to God as a first fruit (bekurim).

Another example of a righteous remnant is Abraham to whom God declared, "I have chosen him [bachar] so that he may command his children and his household after him to keep the way of the Lord by doing righteousness and justice" (Gen 18:19). Abraham was righteous by doing righteousness. As one whom God has chosen, he served the Lord God by instructing his children and his household by his righteous example.

## Gentile Believers are Called by the Name of God and Chosen

God treats Gentile believers in Christ no differently than He is treating Israel. Peter cites from the Hebrew Scriptures to convey this message. "You are A CHOSEN RACE, A royal PRIESTHOOD, A HOLY NATION, A PEOPLE FOR *God's* OWN POSSESSION, so that you may proclaim the excellencies of Him who has called you out of darkness into His marvelous light" (1 Pe 2:9). The actual citation is identified by small capital letters. I have highlighted "chosen" and "called" by underlining. We recognize God's children Israel as chosen and holy. "Chosen," in chosen people, is the Greek *ekklektos* (Hebrew equivalent *bachar*). That is, the children of Israel are called out or chosen as God's firstborn son who is born to the birthright, and whom God encourages to be holy.

In this same citation (1 Pe 2:9) we also recognize "called," which is *kaleo* (Hebrew equivalent *qara*). God has called Gentile believers in Christ, not as an invitation, but calling them by His name as He had earlier called the Jews by His name, thus making them His. He has taken believers in Christ out of darkness into His marvelous light to be His children.

But now, God's children must learn to walk in righteousness. To guide them in this endeavor we remember that the Jews had the Law; Gentile believers in Christ have the Law carved on their hearts by the Holy Spirit (Rom 2:15; 2 Co 3:3). James further explains about believers in Christ, God "brought us forth by the word of truth, so that we would be a kind of first fruits among His creatures" (Jam 1:18). We become holy, righteous and worthy of giving ourselves in service as a kind of first fruits when we walk in righteousness.

Thus, all believers in Christ are "called" by the name of God. However, God will only select the few who are unblemished and who walk with God like Noah, those who do righteousness and justice like Abraham, and those who become a kind of first fruits that are unblemished and holy as a gift to God. These righteous ones are disciples and followers of their Lord Yeshua. They are the chosen ones.

## Imagery and Symbolism

After spending considerable time on the conclusion that declares, "Many are called but few are chosen," we are finally ready to return to the parable. Stop now and re-read the parable in Matthew 22:1-14. Look for the following linguistic devices:

1. Repetition
2. Vivid imagery
3. Intriguing symbolism
4. Anything strange or startling

We have already seen the repetition of "called" (*kaleo*) and "called out" (*eklektos*) but did you also notice the repetition of slaves? These servants are in the service of the king, which suggests the role of a disciple who humbles himself to obey his lord and serve his master. How many times do you see the repetition of "slaves" (or servants in some translations) in this passage? Do you agree with me that they represent faithful and obedient followers who are serving the king?

We turn next to the wedding feast, which is symbolic of a future celebration after God's people defeat the enemy and proclaim the Kingdom of God. Those who expect to be invited are the Jews, who know they are God's firstborn son, and they are called by His name. Do you see the three categories of their responses? Do you recognize the escalating nature as the first response progresses to the second, and then to the third and final response?

We turn now to the symbolism of the battle that is being waged by God's army, which is represented in the parable by the army of the king (undoubtedly comprised of those who are worthy and prepared to obey their commander). The victorious army sets the enemy's city on fire, which likely symbolizes the baptism by fire that will purify by destroying all that is impure, thus leaving only what is pure.

Next we see a sudden intrusion to the story. The expectation would have been that only those close to the king would have been invited to the wedding banquet of his son, but the servants called both the good and the evil.

> When the king came in to look over the dinner guests, he saw a man there who was not dressed in wedding clothes,
>
> And he said to him, "Friend, how did you come in here without wedding clothes?" And the man was speechless.
>
> Then the king said to the servants, "Bind him hand and foot, and throw him into the outer darkness; in that place there will be weeping and gnashing of teeth." (Mat 22:11-13)

Why would failure to wear the proper clothing lead to such devastating consequences? What does the clothing represent? To answer these questions we must return to the Garden of Eden at the time of the fall of mankind. Before continuing, read Genesis 2:25-3:21. Then answer the following questions:

1.  When and why were Adam and Eve *not* ashamed?

2.  Their subsequent shame was caused by sin, which destroys righteousness and causes an unholy condition. Mankind must be righteous to come into the presence of the Righteous God. So, how does sin cause shame?

3.  What does shame represent?

4.  How, when and why did Adam and Eve try to clothe themselves?

5.  How did God clothe Adam and Eve? What does the clothing represent?

6.  How does the blood of Yeshua clothe a believer in Christ?

7.  What does the failure to wear proper clothing at the wedding banquet represent?

The abundance of imagery and symbolism in this parable is especially rich with meaning. I will leave you with a list to ponder. As you consider the imagery and symbolism in the list below, ask yourself the following questions that will help lead you to a depth of understanding.

1. How does each symbol portray vivid imagery (imagery activates the five sense – see, hear, taste, touch, smell)?

2. What does each symbol stand for or represent? Why do you see this particular association?

3. Can you find one or more passages in the Hebrew Scriptures that clarify the symbolic meaning?

4. How does each symbol relate to the entire story of the parable?

5. How does each symbol relate to the conclusion, "Many are called but few are chosen"?

Now I will guide you with my own list of symbols, but I will not insert a commentary. You should have the skills to conduct the last exercise. What is the rich meaning of each of the following symbols, how are they used in the Parable of the Wedding Feast, and how does each apply to "many are called but few are chosen?"

1. Wedding feast
2. Slaves or servants
3. Two armies
4. Judgment by fire
5. Binding
6. Outer darkness
7. Wailing and gnashing of teeth

# *Mystery #15 in the Kingdom of God*

Many are called by the name of God - Jews who are born to the inheritance of the birthright as God's firstborn son and Gentiles who believe in God's son, the Messiah. However, only a few of God's children will be chosen by God as worthy to inherit the birthright, a special role that requires submission and obedience in order to defeat God's enemy in a final battle. These are the remnant.

There will be a celebration and a wedding banquet after the battle. However, only those who are properly clothed in righteousness will be allowed to participate. Many who expect to be invited, because of their prideful sense of self-righteousness, will be wailing and gnashing their teeth. They will be able to see those who have entered God's presence in His kingdom, but they will remain separated from God in darkness. They have not been chosen as worthy and prepared to inherit the birthright to defeat God's enemy under the command of their leader, Yeshua.

Chapter Sixteen

# The Role of the Remnant

We have seen that the remnant is comprised of those whom God deems worthy to inherit the birthright. We have also spent considerable time in the artistic sections of Hebrew poetry to learn how God is instructing His servants to walk in His ways. We discovered that there will be rewards, both now and also in the future. Of course our curiosity draws us to the mysterious future, so we ask, "What is the future role for which God is preparing His remnant?"

The most important aspect of our study, and the purpose of the parables, is what God expects of us today. However, we must also appreciate the future role of those whom God is selecting. This glimpse of the future is the "carrot" of prophetic language. The idyllic anticipation of the Kingdom helps us stand firm in our lives today.

We find that the future is conveyed in two ways, through the metaphorical nature of the narrative and through the artistic language of prophecy.

## The Army of Satan

Let us begin with the narrative, which portrays two mighty armies that are struggling for ultimate control and power. One represents the world, ruled by Satan, and the other is the army of God. Both are identified as a powerful remnant.

We first meet the remnant of Satan before the flood when "the Nephilim were on the earth...those were the mighty men who were of old, men of renown" (Gen 6:4). The Nephilim were giants of huge proportion who are identified as גברים (*gibborim*), that is, exceptionally strong and powerful (translated "mighty men"). We see that these Nephilim were mighty men with a name (translated "of renown"). Whose name? The name is implied; the name is Satan. That is, they belong to Satan.

The purpose of the flood was to destroy this giant enemy, as well as to preserve a godly remnant in Noah and his family. Here, at the beginning of the biblical narrative, we see the initial formation of the two armies, because all the giants were not destroyed; some remained as a remnant for Satan. The contrast between the two armies is stark and startling. The army of Satan is comprised of physical giants. The army of God will be like Noah - righteous, blameless, and walking with God.

We will first explore this army of Satan by searching for the Hebrew word for "mighty men," which is גברים (*gibborim*). We see, for example, that Goliath, who was one of these giants, is described as *gibbor*. "David ran and stood over the Philistine and took his sword and drew it out of its sheath and killed him, and cut off his head with it. When the Philistines saw that their champion was dead, they fled" (1 Sa 17:51). "Champion" is the Hebrew word *gibor*, meaning very strong and powerful, hence a hero or champion. Goliath was part of this remnant of giants.

We often wonder how large Goliath actually was. Ancient Jewish commentaries, such as Josephus and the Dead Sea Scrolls, give his height as somewhere between seven and ten feet tall. However, the message is what is important. David's victory was due, not to worldly weapons or tactics, but to his confidence that God was directing the battle.

We see another encounter with these giants at the time of the wilderness wandering when God began to instruct His people with the Law. This account helps us understand God's method of warfare, and instructs us how to stand against this giant enemy.

Moses sent twelve spies into the Promised Land to gather information about the enemy. When the spies returned their report bred fear among the Israelites.

> The people who live in the land are strong, and the cities are fortified [walled] *and* very large; and moreover, we saw the descendants of Anak there…The Nephilim (the sons of Anak are part of the Nephilim); and we became like grasshoppers in our own sight, and so we were in their sight (Num 13:28, 33).

After hearing this terrifying news about giants in the land, God's children refused to enter the Promised Land in battle. This account occurred shortly after the Exodus from Egypt, and it would take forty years of training in the wilderness before Moses sent Joshua and Caleb to spy out the land once again. This time the people were ready to fight the enemy.

Then we see Og of Bashan, the king who was defeated by Moses and the children of Israel as they were approaching the Promised Land in what is today Jordan. We learn that "only Og of Bashan was left of the remnant of the Rephaim" (another name for the Nephilim; Deut 3:11). That "only Og was left" does not mean he was the only remaining giant. "Left" in Hebrew is a word for the remnant (שאר, *shaar*). Thus, Og was one of the giants in the remnant army of Satan. He was so large that he required an iron bedstead whose dimensions were six feet wide and thirteen feet long (Deut 3:11).

Later in the narrative we meet "Ishbi-benob, who was among the descendants of the giant" (2 Sam 21:16). There were also "descendants from the giants of Gath [the city of Goliath], who fell by the hand of David"(1 Ch 20:8). Could there be giants among us now, we ask? Probably so. The army of Satan is alive and active in our lives today.

## The Army of God

As we continue to explore the metaphorical nature of the biblical narrative, God's army begins to emerge. We are continuing to search for the Hebrew word גברים (*gibborim*), which describes God's remnant as well Satan's, although the two have distinctly different characteristics. Satan is cultivating a remnant of giants who are mighty men. God is also at work to build up an army of mighty men, although the might and power of God's army is not in physical size but in righteous faith in God.

We see, for example, that all the men who left Egypt under the leadership of Moses were *gibborim* (Ex 12:37). They were not yet an army. That would take forty years of wilderness training before they could enter the Promised Land. However, they were "mighty" as they left Egypt because they were a serious threat to Pharaoh, whose army was drowned in the Sea of Reeds. Furthermore, obeying God by picking up and simply walking away from their servitude had to have taken immense courage and faith in the Lord. This helps us see them as "mighty men."

David is another example of one who was *gibbor*. When God selected a king from the sons of Jesse, David was that son. Scripture describes David as "a skillful musician, a mighty man of valor, a warrior, one prudent in speech, and a handsome man" (1

Sa 16:18). A "mighty man of valor" is גבור חיל (*gibbor chayil*), two words that both mean very strong, thus forming double emphasis for very, very strong. David was also "a warrior" whose defeat of the Philistines led to the formation of the kingdom of Israel. We remember that the remnant must overcome the enemy in battle in order to initiate the future Kingdom of God. We also see in this passage that David was "prudent in speech" (Hebrew בון דבר , *bin davar*). *Davar* refers to speaking, and *bin* conveys an ability to discern between good and evil, truth and falsehood, what is of God and what is not. David was prepared to speak for God. He was a "mighty man" (*gibbor*) who led his people in battle to defeat the enemy and to possess the land of his inheritance.

Many others in the biblical narrative are described as *gibor*, and these mighty men all exhibit characteristics of the remnant. David gathered around him mighty men (1 Chr 28:1), and he staffed his army with these *gibborim*. King Hezekiah stands as tall as David in the biblical narrative, and his accomplishments are described as *gibor* (2 Ki 20:20). The priests who served in the house of the Lord were *giborim,* and the four Levite gatekeepers at the temple were also *giborim* (1 Chr 9:13, 28).

By examining the appearance of *gibor* in the Hebrew Scriptures we see physical giants that belong to Satan. We also see God's "mighty men" who are like Noah, "a righteous man, blameless in his time; Noah walked with God (Gen 6:9).

## The Battle of the Remnants

The biblical narrative portrays the victorious battle against God's enemy in the account of the battle of Jericho, which is a prophetic event pointing to a future battle that has not yet occurred. At Jericho, the army of God included all those who had successfully passed through forty years of instruction in the wilderness. The army was led by priests who were carrying the Ark of the Covenant that contained the Law of God. The battle was won, not by worldly might and measures, but by faith in the Lord God.

The Prophets offer further information on the coming battle between the two remnants with artistic prophetic language. For example, although Isaiah prophesies of a battle that would overcome the Babylonians, his poetic language is intentionally mysterious. In these enticing words we discover that the language of prophecy often points to more than one future event.[119]

Returning to Isaiah, we can hear the clash of two armies.

> I have commanded My consecrated ones, I have even called My mighty warriors, My proudly exulting ones, to execute My anger.
> A sound of tumult on the mountains, like that of many people! A sound of the uproar of kingdoms, of nations gathered together! The LORD of hosts is mustering the army for battle.
> (Is 13:3, 4)

The "consecrated ones" are set apart and holy, dedicated to serving the Lord. The "mighty warriors" are *gibborim*. It is not just the Babylonians that are gathered against the army of God (one of the pagan nations) but "the nations" (all of the pagan peoples). These prophetic words evoke images of the future battle between the two mighty armies.

The prophet Zechariah also uses poetic language that describes a future mighty battle.

> The LORD of hosts has visited His flock, the house of Judah, and will make them like His majestic horse in battle.
>> From them will come the cornerstone,
>> from them the tent peg,
>> from them the bow of battle,
>> from them every ruler, all of them together.
> They will be as mighty men, treading down the enemy in the mire of the streets in battle; and they will fight, for the LORD will be with them; and the riders on horses will be put to shame. (Zec 10:3-5)

---

[119]The Red Sea parted when the Israelites left Egypt, and the Jordan River parted when they entered the Promised Land. We also see the children of Israel as slaves in Egypt and again in Babylon.

Again we see the "mighty men" (*gibborim*) who are fighting for God. They come from the house of Judah, but it is not necessarily all the tribe of Judah because not all will be *giborim*. The "cornerstone" is the Messiah (see Mat 21:42 citing Ps 118:22). The army wields the "bow of battle" and serves under the command of this Messiah. The "tent peg" is an image of anchoring the tabernacle in a firm and steady way. This house of God is comprised of God's servants who have become the firm foundation for the entire family in God's house.

## The Role of the Remnant

The symbolism of the tent peg, which holds God's house as a firm foundation, leads us to a significant verse in Ezra where the prophet speaks of the remnant that returned to the land from exile in Babylon.

> Now for a brief moment grace has been shown from the LORD our God, to leave us an escaped remnant and to give us a peg in His holy place. (Ezra 9:8)

Here the tent peg is not holding the tabernacle; it is holding the land that belongs to the holy God. What is holding the land? There is a remnant out of all the exiles in Babylon, those who returned to the land of Israel, leaving most of God's people still in exile and bondage in Babylon. It is a remnant that plants this tent peg in the land. Thus, a responsibility of God's mighty remnant is to secure a firm foundation for the remainder of God's people who are still in bondage.

Since the remnant is comprised of the righteous, like Noah, they are the ones who will bear fruit for God. Isaiah expands on this theme.

> The surviving remnant of the house of Judah will again take root downward and bear fruit upward.
>
> For out of Jerusalem will go forth a remnant and out of Mount Zion survivors. The zeal of the LORD of hosts will perform this. (Is 37:31-32)

This powerful imagery portrays a vivid agricultural scene. God has planted the seeds, which are a remnant of His people who have grown into mighty plants. First our attention is drawn down to the roots that are growing thick and firm. These roots hold the plant steady so it cannot be moved. After we see the strong roots, our attention then turns upward where the plant is growing strong and bearing fruit for God. Who are the ones bearing fruit? They are a remnant.

Because the remnant is righteous in God's eyes, they will bear abundant righteous seed (the Hebrew word for seed means descendants). Godly seed produces more godly descendants, seed after its own kind. In this way, God is preparing a righteous army for a future battle that will defeat the army of Satan.

## A Picture of the Future Battle

We will return once more to the narrative for a commanding glimpse of the final battle. We have seen that *gibborim*, meaning very strong and mighty ones, refers to giants in the army of Satan. However, the very same word *gibborim* also applies to God's opposing army, which is comprised of a powerful righteous remnant.

We can glimpse a picture of the future battle in the account of Daniel's three friends, who were thrown by the Babylonian king Nebuchadnezzar into a blazing furnace. English translations are misleading. The word *gibor* appears eight times in Dan 3:20-27, but the English translations (KJV, NIV, NASB) have merely given us "men" for the three friends who are *gibborim* in the Hebrew text, and "soldiers" when referring to Nebuchadnezzar's prison guards, who are also *gibborim*. Only once, where the Hebrew text employs two words with similar meanings (גברי־חיל, *gibborae-chayil*) does the translation appear as "mighty men" (KJV), "valiant warriors" (NASB), and "strongest soldiers" (NIV).

The story begins in Dan 3:19. The visual image of Nebuchadnezzar, who represents Satan, is intense and dramatic. He has worked himself into a rage, and the "image of his face has changed." We can see this evil monster. His hatred of the true God is so strong that he gives orders to "heat the furnace seven times more than it was usually heated" (Dan 3:19). Seven is the number of finality. This will be a future battle to the death.

> He [Nebuchadnezzar] commanded certain valiant warriors who were in his army to tie up Shadrach, Meshach and Abed-nego in order to cast them into the furnace of blazing fire.
>
> Then these men were tied up in their trousers, their coats, their caps and their other clothes, and were cast into the midst of the furnace of blazing fire. (Dan 3:20-21)

Nebuchadnezzar's army is comprised of "certain valiant warriors." The Hebrew is גברין גברי־חיל (*gibborim gibor-chayil*), a construction that is emphatic by its repetition and also by the doublet of two words that mean the same thing. These soldiers in Nebuchadnezzar's army represent the army of Satan. We are then presented with "these men," Daniel's three friends. "These men" in Hebrew is אדין גבריא אלך (*adon gibborei elech*). *Adon* is the word for men, but an adjective follows, which is *gibbor*. These mighty men, who are opposing Satan's army, are the mighty army of God.

I will let you read the rest of the story in Daniel 3:19-28, which is teeming with exquisite imagery and a powerful message. However, I want to draw your attention to one more important and tantalizing aspect of this account. The blazing furnace is a dramatic symbol of the baptism by fire. God's army is being purified and prepared for the battle that will follow. We will spend more time on baptism by fire in Chapter Twenty.

# Mystery #16 in the Kingdom of God

For those who are disciples and servants of the Lord, God portrays the future as a "carrot" that generates eager anticipation and a commitment to stand for God now. Those who are not walking in godly ways experience the "stick" of discipline. They will likely perceive the future with trepidation, concern, and sometimes even fear (like the spies who returned from the Promised Land).

God wants his loyal followers to uncover His mysteries. Certainly one of the most important mysteries is an accurate understanding of the prophetic future, which portrays a fierce struggle between two mighty armies. Those who are fully prepared to participate in this battle are a remnant, those who have complete confidence in God and are ready to obey without hesitation.

Part Five

# Parables for The Remnant Today

## Chapter Seventeen
# Parable of the Good Samaritan

We all know the story of the Good Samaritan, which often leads to these wise words of wisdom: "Do unto others as you would have them do unto you." As we work to uncover the connection of this parable to the Hebrew Scriptures, this simple message of compassion is not going to change. However, your understanding of the message will be so much deeper that the simple meaning will remain only for children, and your life will undoubtedly never be the same.

## Context

The context of the story is extremely important, especially at this point in your study of the parables. The goal of haggadic midrash, which employs an account from the Hebrew Scriptures, exhorts us to walk with Yeshua in the Kingdom of Heaven. To accomplish this godly walk we must be a disciple, a devoted follower of the Lord Yeshua. We must be committed to submit and obey in service to God's people.

Although the Parable of the Good Samaritan appears in Luke 10:30-37, I suggest that the context actually begins in Luke 9:28. Take time now to read Luke 9:28-10:29 that precedes our parable.

1. How does Luke 9:28-36 instruct us about discipleship? What role do Moses and Elijah play? What is the connection between the transfiguration of Yeshua and the Parable of the Good Samaritan?
2. I suggest that the key words in Luke 9:38-45 are these: "I begged your disciples to cast it out, but they did not" (Lk 9:40). Why do you think I drew this conclusion, that these are key words?
3. What is the relationship of these words, "I begged your disciples to cast it [an evil spirit] out, but they did not," to the transfiguration of Yeshua? What is their relationship to the Parable of the Good Samaritan?

In Luke 9:51-56 we see an encounter of Yeshua and his disciples with Samaritans, who lived in the hill country north of Jerusalem. Use the internet to learn more about these Samaritans at the time of Yeshua - where they lived and what were their religious beliefs. Then answer the following questions.

1.  Why would these Samaritans have refused to receive the disciples of Yeshua whom he had sent to make lodging arrangements on his journey to Jerusalem?
2.  List and discuss the instructions that Yeshua gave to his disciples in Luke 9:46-50, 57-62; 10:1-29.

The immediate context of our parable is Luke 10:25-30a. However, we must remember the general context of discipleship that began in Luke 9:28. Yeshua is headed toward Jerusalem, and he knew that "the Son of Man was going to be delivered into the hands of man" (Lk 9:44). Nevertheless, his death would not end the Kingdom of God that he had initiated because he was leaving behind his disciples. The Parable of the Good Samaritan continues to instruct his disciples, this time for understanding the commandment to "love your neighbor as yourself."

## Inherit Eternal Life

I would like to stop at this point and comment on the lawyer's question, "What shall I do to inherit eternal life?" Christian theology tends to equate the term "eternal life" with "those who belong to God." That is, only those who belong to God will inherit eternal life. Furthermore, Christianity sees eternal life as existing exclusively in the future. Therefore, Christians are often anxious about whether or not they belong to God so they can inherit "eternal life."

The parables have been leading us to a somewhat different conclusion. The Hebraic sense of time views God in time, so the Kingdom of God exists at all times. Certainly the Kingdom was present when Yeshua was here on this earth. However, Yeshua has been instructing his disciples that, when he leaves, his disciples will be able to heal others, rebuke evil spirits, and tread upon the power of the enemy *as long as* they follow their Master's instructions to walk in godly ways. Therefore, the Kingdom of God is present now when disciples of the Lord Yeshua come in his name. So, we ask, when is "eternal life" according to the Hebraic sense of time? It existed in past time in the Garden of Eden. It was present when Yeshua was here on this earth. It will exist at some time in the future when God brings all of His children to Him in righteousness. Nevertheless, eternal life is also present now when we walk in the Kingdom of God.

Let us look next at the English translation "eternal life." We must approach this exercise by first purging from our minds any preconceived theological ideas. The original Greek term is ζωὴν αἰώνιον (*zoaen aionion*). If we use the ancient Septuagint translation from Hebrew to Greek, we will see that the Hebrew equivalent is נפש חיה (*nephesh chaya*), and you will remember that those who first heard Yeshua speak the Parable of the Good Samaritan were Jews who knew the Hebrew Scriptures well. The New Testament had not yet been written, nor had Christian theology emerged as a belief system. So, we are interested in what the original listeners would have heard. I suggest that *zoaen aionion* would have stimulated in their minds the term *nephesh chaya* from the Hebrew Scriptures, which means a "living soul" or "living being." Where does this Hebrew expression first appear?

> The LORD God formed man of dust from the ground, and breathed into his nostrils the breath of life; and man became a living being [*nephesh chayai*].
> . (Gen 2:7)

With the Hebraic sense of time we see that God is the only source of life. From searching the Scriptures we understand that He brings about this life in three ways. First, He breathed life into mankind at the time of creation. Second, the parables have been teaching us that He breathes life into the disciples of His son when they walk in His ways. Finally, the term *zoaen aionion* conveys the wonderful prophetic truth that God will breathe life into all those who belong to Him at some time in the future, that is, He will bring all of His children to Him in righteousness.

The Greek NT term, *zoaen aionion,* can be translated literally as "life of the age," hence eternal life, which implies a future time. However, as with all of Scripture, there can be a simple, plain meaning and a deeper, richer meaning. We remember the words of Yeshua. "To you it has been granted to know the mysteries of the kingdom of heaven" (Mat 13:11). Thus, we perceive that God gives "life" to His children in their daily lives when they walk in righteousness, and this understanding is one of those mysteries. The Parable of the Good Samaritan helps us understand this mystery.

## Who are the Samaritans?

Samaria was the capital city of the northern kingdom of Israel that was captured by the Assyrians in 723 B.C. The ten northern tribes, who occupied the northern kingdom, were then taken into captivity and dispersed throughout the Assyrian empire.

In the ancient world, people believed that their gods ruled the land in which they lived and were, in essence, tied to that land. So, the strategy of the Assyrians was to sever the connection of the conquered people from their gods by moving them to other parts of the empire. The Assyrians not only removed the Israelites from their homeland and transferred them to other parts of the Assyrian empire, but they also brought other conquered peoples to Samaria (the capital of Israel's conquered northern kingdom) and its surrounding areas in the northern hill country.

> The king of Assyria brought *men* from Babylon and from Cuthah and from Avva and from Hamath and Sephar-vaim, and settled *them* in the cities of Samaria in place of the sons of Israel. So they possessed Samaria and lived in its cities.
> (2 Ki 17:24)

These were the Samaritans, a foreign people who were brought to northern Israel by the Assyrians. However, there is more to the story.

When they were first transported to the land of Israel, these foreign people who became known as Samaritans believed that their gods were still in the original land from which they had been deported. So, they were without the help and power of the gods they had left behind. The story of these Samaritans continues.

At the beginning of their living there, they did not fear the LORD; therefore the LORD sent lions among them which killed some of them.

So they spoke to the king of Assyria, saying, "The nations whom you have carried away into exile in the cities of Samaria do not know the custom of the god of the land; so he has sent lions among them, and behold, they kill them because they do not know the custom of the god of the land."

Then the king of Assyria commanded, saying, "Take there one of the priests whom you carried away into exile and let him go and live there; and let him teach them the custom of the god of the land."

So one of the priests whom they had carried away into exile from Samaria came and lived at Bethel, and taught them how they should fear the LORD. (2 Ki 17:25-28).

Thus, the Samaritans learned about the God of Israel and became, in essence, Jews by their religious beliefs. However, they retained some of their previous idolatrous practices, so their Judaism was mixed with pagan ideas and customs.

At the time of Yeshua there were a significant number of these Samaritans who lived in the northern hill country. Their holy writings were the Torah, although their religious practices were a mixture of Judaism and paganism. Their holy city was not Jerusalem on Mount Zion, but a holy place on Mount Gerizim. This explains the words of Yeshua to the Samaritan woman recorded in the Gospel of John.

"Woman, believe Me, an hour is coming when neither in this mountain [Mount Gerizim] nor in Jerusalem [Mount Zion] will you worship the Father.

You worship what you do not know [Samaritans do not know the pure religion of Judaism]; we worship what we know, for salvation is from the Jews.

> But an hour is coming, and now is, when the
> true worshipers will worship the Father in spirit
> and truth; for such people the Father seeks to be
> His worshipers.
> God is spirit, and those who worship Him
> must worship in spirit and truth." (John 4:21-24)

When Yeshua spoke to the Samaritan woman he was deviating in a dramatic way from Jewish tradition. In the first century the Jews perceived Samaritans as unholy, and did everything in their power to avoid contact with these idolatrous people. By contrast, the Samaritans viewed themselves as people of the God of Israel, and perceived their worship as the proper service to Israel's God.

## Connection to the Hebrew Scriptures

Several scholars have suggested an allusion to a story in Chronicles. Isaac Kalimi, for example, explains that in 2 Chron 28:8-15, following the civil war between King Ahaz of Judah and King Pekah of Israel, Judean captives were taken to Samaria. In Samaria they were released after the involvement of the Prophet Obed, who also encouraged the Israelites, Judah's enemies, to care for the captives. This certainly sounds like a possible candidate for the parable's connection to the Hebrew Scriptures.[120]

Kalimi further suggests that the midrashic lesson is moral kindness, and points to the law in Leviticus 19:18b. "You shall love your neighbor as yourself; I am the Lord." Kalimi concludes that "even a Samaritan's behavior is according to the Torah [in contrast to] the behaviors of the people of high hierarchy from Jerusalem."[121]

Kalimi's observations may be valid. However, I have come to a different conclusion as to the relationship of the Parable of the Prodigal Son to the Hebrew Scriptures. Kalimi's suggestion is more in alignment with Isaiah's condemnation of the people of

---

[120] Isaac Kalimi, "Robbers on the road to Jericho," *Ephemerides Theologicae Lovanienses* 85/1 (2009): 47-53.

[121] Ibid.

Judah at the time of the civil war between Israel and Judah. Furthermore, Kalimi fails to convincingly show the relationship of the account in Chronicles to the NT parable in Luke.

Instead, I considered the geographic and cultural setting of the parable, which would have been quite startling and puzzling to the first century listeners. The setting of the parable was a radical departure from what would have been expected. I also discovered some interesting linguistic anomalies that drew me in to what I perceived as the deeper meaning of the parable. I will share these thoughts with you now.

## Going Down from Jerusalem to Jericho

To fully appreciate the parable we must have a sense both of geography and of the customs of ancient Israel. As you visualize this physical setting, you will perceive what is strange and puzzling.

God commanded the children of Israel to travel to Jerusalem three times a year for the annual festivals of Pesach (Passover), Shavuot (Pentecost), and Sukkot (Tabernacles). Coming from Galilee in the north there were two roads to Jerusalem. The most direct was through the hill country. However, this route passed by the unholy Samaritan settlements, which the Jews wanted to avoid. The other road traveled on the east side of the Jordan River, crossing at the ford at Jericho and then continuing west through the Wadi Kelt, also called by the psalmist, the Valley of the Shadow of Death. During the time of Yeshua a Roman road had been built in the Wadi Kelt to help travelers pass through this deep and hostile ravine that connected Jerusalem and Jericho. Nevertheless, cracks and caves in the steep cliffs harbored threatening thieves and robbers.

Now we turn to what is strange and puzzling. Since the Wadi Kelt was such a dangerous road, why was "a certain man" traveling alone? After "he fell among robbers, and they stripped him and beat him, and went off leaving him half dead," a Samaritan was there to help him. However, which of the two roads would the Samaritan have taken on any journey between Samaria and Jerusalem? It would not have been the Wadi Qelt to Jericho where one could cross a ford in the Jordan River to reach the Roman road on the east side of the river. In fact, since Mount Gerizim was the holy mountain for the Samaritans, why was the good Samaritan even traveling on a road that led to Jerusalem? Could these strange and puzzling situations be intentional for the purpose of encouraging us to ask questions?

1. Use a biblical atlas to locate the Wadi Kelt. Then use the internet to see pictures of this deep and hostile canyon.
2. Do you ever feel alone and find yourself in frightening places like the Wadi Qelt (or what the Wadi Qelt represents)? If so, do you turn to God? How does God respond by sending disciples of the Lord Jesus Christ? Give a specific example in your life of how God has helped you by sending one of His disciples.
3. The Samaritan represents a disciple of God. How is this irony?

We now must ask, "Why would the Samaritan have been traveling on the road to Jericho instead of the road through the hill country that connected Samaria and Jerusalem"? This aspect of the parable seems strange and puzzling. The Samaritan seems to have chosen "the road less traveled by" to use the poetic words of Robert Frost. That decision placed the Samaritan in a position to help one of God's people. Should disciples today take "the road less traveled by?" What does this mean?

## Symbolism of "The Other Side

We are now ready to consider repetitions that attract our attention. The priest saw the man who had been beaten and robbed but "passed by on the other side." The Levite also came to the place and saw him, but "passed on the other side."

The term "other side" was used by Jews in the Galilee to refer to the east side of the Sea of Galilee where large Roman cities were located that were populated by Gentiles, that is, by those who were pagans of the Gentile world. Jews of the Galilee lived on the west side of the Sea of Galilee and avoided contact with these unholy people on "the other side."

We have a wonderful story in the gospels about "traveling to the other side." When Yeshua "came to the other side into the country of the Gadarenes [east of the Jordan River in the land of the pagan Gentiles], two men who were demon-possessed met Him as they were coming out of the tombs." (Mat 8:28). Gadara was one of the Roman Decapolis cities,[122] and the two possessed men were pagans from that unholy city. Yeshua healed them by driving out the demons. Another time Yeshua commanded that his disciples get in a boat to go to "the other side" (the land of the pagan Gentiles) while he remained with the Jewish multitude on the Jewish side. When he was finished teaching he came to his disciples by walking on the water, and the words he spoke to his disciples were these: "Take courage, it is I; do not be afraid." Thus, disciples are not to fear going into strange and unholy places like "the other side."

As we return to the Parable of the Good Samaritan, there is irony in the priest and the Levite passing "on the other side." Instead of serving God as holy leaders, they were acting like the unholy Gentiles who lived on "the other side," which was the pagan side. The Samaritan, on the other hand, whom the Jews considered to be an unholy pagan, was actually behaving as a holy disciple of God who did not pass by "on the other side."

**Who is Your Neighbor?**

Dr. Randall Buth has suggested a play on words, which I think is an interesting possibility.[123] We can only understand this linguistic artistry in Hebrew since the context of the parable is God's commandment in Leviticus 19:18. "Love your neighbor as yourself." "Neighbor" in the verse in Leviticus is רע, pronounced *re-ah*. However, the very same letters can be pronounced differently as *rah*, meaning "bad" or "evil." In its first usage in the

---

[122] Decapolis in Latin means ten cities. The Romans built these large and powerful cities on the eastern frontier of their empire to anchor their military and political authority against threatening tribes to the east. When we visit the archaeological ruins of these Decapolis cities today, even the remains are impressive and convey the magnitude and power of the Romans. The ten cities are Jerash, Gedara, Pella, Philadelphia, Beit Ras and Raphana in Jordan, Qanawat and Damascus in Syria, and Beit Shean and Hippos in Israel.

[123] Dr. Buth made this suggestion to me in a recent conversation. He is a linguist who resides in Israel where he develops resources and refines methodology for the study of biblical languages.

Torah, where it means "bad or evil," we read, "The LORD saw that the wickedness of man was great on the earth, and that every intent of the thoughts of his heart was only evil [רע pronounced *rah*] continually" (Gen 6:5). This evil nature of mankind led God to initiate the flood. However, after the flood, when God smelled the soothing aroma of Noah's sacrifice He declared, "I will never again curse the ground on account of man, for the intent of man's heart is evil [רע] from his youth; and I will never again destroy every living thing, as I have done" (Gen 8:21).

Therefore, God acknowledges bad and evil behavior in mankind, even in those who belong to Him. However, Yeshua is teaching in parables to those who desire to act in godly ways as disciples of their Lord Yeshua. Thus, in the Parable of the Good Samaritan we have a play on words. *Rah* means "bad" or "evil," and *re-ah* (same Hebrew letters) means a neighbor or someone close to you. So we ask, "Who then is the *re-ah* (the neighbor)? We expect the neighbors in the parable to be the priest and the Levite, but they are *rah* by passing by "on the other side."

At the end of the parable Yeshua asks, "Which of these three do you think proved to be a neighbor?" Of course, the answer is the Samaritan, and this answer is contrary to what would have been expected. Not only was the Samaritan perceived by the Jews as an evil pagan (*rah*) who was on the other side, but Jews also considered their neighbors (*re-ah*) to be exclusively other Jews. Yet the two who should have been neighbors (*re-ah*), the priest and the Levite, were actually acting like bad or evil ones (*rah*). With this ironic twist, the one who was perceived as bad or evil turned out to be the true neighbor, that is, the Samaritan.

Who, then, is *your* neighbor? Stop and seriously consider this question by considering these thoughts.

- Who do I treat with judgmental condemnation?
- Who do I perceive as "outside" my circle of acquaintances because I am condemning them in some way?
- Are these people in need of help? As a disciple of Yeshua, is there some way I can bring blessings to them without condemning them?

## *Mystery #17 in the Kingdom of God*

The parables encourage all believers in Christ to become disciples who feel compassion for all people as the Good Samaritan "felt compassion and came to him and bandaged up his wounds, pouring oil and wine on *them*; and he put him on his own beast, and brought him to an inn and took care of him" (Lk 10:34).

The world rarely recognizes the true "neighbor," but tends to honor those with titles and positions of power. Disciples should not be concerned with worldly perceptions, but should live quietly in harmony with God, and care for all who are in need of compassion and comfort.

Turning to the other side of the coin, during those times in our lives when we feel alone and in need of help, we must trust God that He will send one or more disciples who will act on behalf of the Master. Keep your eyes open for that person. Sometimes it is hard to ask for help, but we are learning from the parables that God will always be there with His disciples, who will come in the name of the Lord.

Chapter Eighteen

# Parable of the Rich Man and Lazarus

The Parable of the Rich Man and Lazarus is found in only one of the gospels, Luke 16:19-31. Before moving forward in this chapter, stop and carefully read these verses. Continue to practice "listening to the text."

About a year ago one of my students asked me what the parable meant. I was a little unsettled by his question because I had not yet spent time working on this particular parable. So, I gave him a truthful answer. "I don't know," I replied. But of course I went right to work, rolled up my sleeves, and tried to unravel its mysteries. It took me a while to identify the connection to the Hebrew Scriptures, so I want to share with you the process I went through to uncover the deeper meaning. But first, let us begin with the setting.

## The Setting

Carefully consider the following questions. Go deeper by asking your own questions. Enter into discussion with your study partner, and encourage your partner to go deeper by asking questions.

1.  What is the setting in which Yeshua spoke this parable?

2.  As you look for the setting, what verses must be considered in addition to the actual parable in Luke 16: 19-31? We will not address the meaning of these preliminary verses until the end of this chapter, but you should identify them now.

3.  What two groups of people were listening to the parable? How do you think each of the two groups would have responded?

4.  What do you think is strange and puzzling about this parable?

## Use the Internet to Learn More about the Setting

We hear in the setting to this parable that the Pharisees were lovers of money. Does this peak your curiosity? Do we need to know more about the culture of the first century that would have prompted this accusation? Since haggadic midrash takes a biblical principle and applies it to current life conditions, might we also apply this accusation of loving money to our own life and world today? Let us spend a little time pursuing this question. In the process we will gain a better understanding of the setting of our parable.

Turn now to the online interlinear Bible to find the Greek word used in Luke 16:14 for "lover of money."

- Where else in the NT does this word appear?
- What is the sense of the word that you learn from reading these usages in their context?
- Were you surprised to discover that φιλάργυροι (*philarguroi*) is used in only one other verse in the New Testament?

Now you can return to the internet to further your understanding about this Greek word. The internet is an easy resource for quick information. You must learn to use the web responsibly, so the information you will be using is reliable and meaningful. Here are some guidelines for obtaining information from the web.

1. Start by asking yourself, "What am I looking for?"

2. Who is the author or owner of the site? What is the purpose of the site? How is the site funded? Is there a real person to contact?

2. What is the reliability of the site? Is the purpose of the site to inform, sell, or persuade? What is the accuracy (spelling, grammar)? Is the site current or stale?

You will now practice analyzing and judging a website, one that relates love of money to a modern situation. Go to http://www.gty.org/Blog/B100119. Before listening to the audio recording, scrutinize the site following the steps above. Then answer these questions:

1. What are you looking for?

2. Who is John MacArthur? Try to learn more about him from other websites. Does he have a particular doctrinal approach?

3. What is the purpose of the site? Is it to inform, sell, persuade, or a combination of these? If a combination, which one is predominant?

Now listen to the audio teaching on the love of money by John MacArthur. First assess the reliability of the teaching. What points does he make? Does he support these points with evidence? Is the teaching in alignment with Scripture? Finally, how might you apply this teaching to your life?

## Artistry of Language: Clues to the Hebrew Scriptures

The clue that unlocked the mystery of this parable for me was the repetition. I will try to lead you through the process I followed by asking you the same questions I asked.

1. How many repetitions do you see in the parable? Since people in the first century were "listening" to the text, the important repetition will likely be near the beginning.

2. What is the repetition that you think might be most significant to the story?

## The Setting

People in first century Israel believed that God had placed sufficient information in His Holy Writings for everything they would ever need to know. If one word or verse or passage seemed puzzling, then other portions of Scripture could clarify what otherwise seemed unclear. Since people at the time of Yeshua had memorized the Scriptures, they would let their minds roam around what they had memorized until an illuminating passage appeared in their minds.

By now you probably know that the repetitive word, which has caught our attention, is "sores." So, I let Scripture interpret itself by looking for other related passages that contain the original Greek word for "sores," which is ἕλκος (*helkos*). I always begin by considering equivalent Hebrew words and phrases in the Torah because these five books of Moses would have been the first thing that people of ancient Israel had memorized. They perceived the Torah as a direct communication from God to Moses.

The people also understood the Prophets and the Writings as commentary on the Torah. So, after considering related words and phrases in the Torah, I turn to the Prophets and the Writings.

Today you have may not know the Scriptures well enough to recall passages that comment on "sores." However, you can use a concordance, which tells you where this Greek word appears both in the New Testament and in the Septuagint translation of the Hebrew Scriptures. In the case of our parable, our repetitive word is "sores," which is the Greek ἕλκος. So, try now to conduct your own search in a concordance to find the equivalent Hebrew word before reading my observations below.

1.  The concept of sores on the skin first appears in the Exodus account. One of the plagues that God brought upon Egypt was "boils breaking out with sores on man and beast through all the land of Egypt." If you truly desire to learn how to uncover mysteries in the parables by thinking with a first century mind, then you must carefully read this account in Exodus 9:8-17 before considering the next question.

2.  Having internalized the Exodus account into their lives, how do you think the children of Israel would have responded when boils broke out on their skin or the skin of their neighbors?

3.  The Hebrew Scriptures instruct the children of Israel how to walk in holy ways because they could only come into the presence of the Holy God in a righteous condition. We read, for example, "I am the LORD your God. Consecrate

yourselves therefore, and be holy, for I am holy. And you shall not make yourselves unclean" (Lev 11:44).  How do the sores on the skin relate to the Parable of the Rich Man and Lazarus?

What is relevant to our parable is that anyone with an outbreak of sores on the skin was considered unclean, that is, unholy, because this condition had been one of God's plagues in Egypt.

Now you can begin to understand the response of those who heard the parable of The Rich Man and Lazarus. They had been taught that any eruption of a skin disorder was unclean in God's eyes. Furthermore, they had to avoid this person because physical contact would make them unclean as well. That is the setting for our parable.

## Looking for the Connection to the Hebrew Scriptures

As I was roaming around the Hebrew Scriptures thinking about other accounts concerning sores on the body, I thought of Job. So, I spent some time in the book of Job wondering if this was the intended connection. However, I finally concluded that it probably was not.

Then I considered the account of Jezebel, the pagan wife of King Ahab. Prophecy declared that at her death dogs would eat her flesh (the prophecy actually came true). Our parable says of Lazarus, "even the dogs were coming and licking his sores." Yet, that didn't work either.

When I found the connection I had to chide myself. It was in the Torah, the heart of the Hebrew Scriptures. In fact, it was in Leviticus, which contains many of the "laws" that give instructions about walking in holy ways.

4. Read Leviticus 13:18-23. You will see here God's instructions regarding the break-out of skin diseases.

In the ancient world, skin diseases were often a sign of leprosy, a hideous disease that ate away parts of the flesh including the face. Furthermore, leprosy was highly contagious. So, when the sores of leprosy appeared on a person, the response was repulsion and fear. In our modern world of medicine, a cure was not discovered until about 100 years ago. Yet Scripture, composed thousands of years ago, reports that healing of leprosy did occur from time to time. People of the ancient world believed that God could bring about healing.

5.  Now re-read Leviticus 13:18-23. What was the physical sign that healing had occurred?

6.  How does Leviticus 13:18-23 appear to be the passage that creates the midrash in the Parable of the Rich Man and Lazarus? What is the resulting meaning in the parable?

## Practical Application

The rich man was only concerned with his comfort in life, and in death he was still only concerned with his wants.

1.  In life, what was the rich man's perception of his relationship to Lazarus? What was his perception in death?

2.  What is your perception of Lazarus?

3.  In life, what was the rich man's belief about mercy? What was his belief in death?

4.  What is your belief about mercy?

5.  What effect did the first century image of tormenting in hell have on the rich man?

6.  How does Yeshua's concluding words relate to this parable? "They won't be convinced even if someone rises from the dead."

## How Much More

Yeshua often took a principle from the Hebrew Scriptures and elevated it to a higher level of understanding. Sometimes we see the phrase "how much more," which illustrates this principle. I think the midrash in the Parable of Lazarus and the Rich Man is doing just that. It is teaching us "how much more."

True, sores could be an indication of leprosy, a highly contagious disease. Also true, Scripture considered such sores as unclean, hence unholy. However, there is a higher principle. God heals. God can restore us to a holy and clean condition when we turn to Him in prayer and repentance. Read the parable one more time with this thought in mind, and with the rich man as a contrast to Lazarus.

---

## Mystery #18 in the Kingdom of God

Followers and disciples are serving their Lord in the Kingdom of God. So, our hearts must approach this parable with a desire to help others. As we look around us, we see so many who are suffering terrible unholy conditions like addiction, sexual deviations, low self-image and the like. Should we condemn them? No. Yeshua did not. Should we put guilt in their hearts? Certainly not. Will God have mercy on them? God had mercy on Lazarus, and so should we have mercy on others who are suffering unclean conditions.

## Chapter Nineteen

# Parable of the Landowner and his Tenants

You can find the Parable of the Landowner and the Tenants in Matthew 21:33-45, but locate and read the context that begins much earlier.

Christian tradition tends to interpret the tenants as people of Israel who kill the landowner's son (identified as Yeshua). Unfortunately this common understanding has reinforced a separation between Christians and Jews. However, there is much more to this parable than a simple story with a moral message. As only one example, there are two citations from the Hebrew Scriptures (Isaiah 5 and Psalms 118) as well as one clear allusion (Isaiah 8). Furthermore, the parable's imagery and symbolism is rich with meaning, and the opportunity for proper practical application is abundant.

## Context and Main Characters

The context alone alerts us that the parable conveys something other than God's rejection of His people Israel. Furthermore, we must be careful not to equate rejection with loss of eternal life, or with God's dismissing those whom He has birthed as His firstborn son, or as God turning away from Israel. We will see in this parable not only the concept of selection for the purpose of inheritance (some will inherit the birthright and others will not), and also powerful exhortation for God's children to walk in righteousness, which brings them into God's presence as servants in the Kingdom of God.

The setting begins in Matthew 21: 23 where we read, "When He had come into the temple, the chief priests and the elders of the people came to Him as He was teaching, and said, 'By what authority are You doing these things, and who gave You this authority?'" Jesus was instructing Jews who had come to Jerusalem for the Passover, and his words of criticism in this parable were directed to these self-righteous leaders. As we proceed through this parable, we will not direct our attention to his words of criticism, but to a powerful message for all of God's people.

**Connection to the Hebrew Scriptures**

The Parable of the Landowner and His Tenant begins with a citation, which is identified by capital letters

> There was a landowner who PLANTED A VINEYARD AND PUT A WALL AROUND IT AND DUG A WINE PRESS IN IT AND BUILT A TOWER, and rented it out to vine-growers and went on a journey. (Mat 21:33)

The first thing we must do is to compare this citation in Matthew with the passage it is citing in Isaiah. We ask, "Are there any changes, additions or deletions? If so, could they be intentional in order to convey meaning? Compare the citation in Matthew with what it has cited from Isaiah.

> Let me sing now for my well-beloved a song of my beloved concerning His vineyard. My well-beloved had a vineyard on a fertile hill.
> He dug it all around, removed its stones, and planted it with the choicest vine. And He built a tower in the middle of it and also hewed out a wine vat in it. Then He expected *it* to produce *good* grapes, but it produced *only* worthless ones. (Is 5:1-2)

Carefully compare the passage in Isaiah 51:1-2 with the verse in Matthew 21:33 before continuing.

I will now make the following observations.

- In Isaiah, God has carefully prepared a vineyard for His people. He has placed the vineyard on a fertile hill (the ancient Israelites lived in the central hill country), dug around it (possibly a system of irrigation), removed its stones (the hills were littered with rocks and stones that were used to construct terraces on the hillside), built a watch tower to protect the vineyard from animals and enemies, and carved out a wine press from the rocky ground. The vineyard represents the children of Israel, and God has cultivated His people so they can bear abundant fruit.

- Instead of abundant fruit, the vineyard (children of Israel) have produced worthless (Hebrew word meaning "wild") grapes rather than cultivated ones.

- In the New Testament parable, we can identify the landowner with God. It is also God who is tending His vineyard in the Isaiah passage.

- The citation in Matthew has added something significant. The landowner puts a wall around the vineyard, which undoubtedly represents the Torah, because the Torah was viewed as a "protective wall around God's people." When Jews observed the commandments of the Law, God would protect them.

We remember that it is important to read a citation in its context because people of the first century had memorized the Holy Writings, not verse-by-verse but in blocks that included many verses. In the context of the two verses in Isaiah that the parable has cited, God announces consequences to Israel because it has produced only wild grapes. "I will remove its hedge and it will be consumed. I will break down its wall and it will become trampled ground. And I will lay it waste" (Is 5:5-6). When we return to the NT parable we see it reinforcing these consequences by announcing, "When the harvest time approached...." The harvest symbolizes God's judgment.

Before we look at the second of two citations in this parable, we will turn to the artistry of language in the parable.

## Artistry of Language

We must identify the symbolism of the characters in the parable. In Isaiah, the vineyard represents the children of Israel whom God was cultivating and tending so they could bear fruit. In Matthew's parable, the landowner represents God, who owns the vineyard and rents it out to tenants. It is the tenants who are expected to cultivate and tend the vineyard, which stands for God's children. The tenants represent the leaders of God's people.

God expects His tenants, as steward of His people, to obey and act in righteous ways. These tenants (leaders of God's people) instruct and guide by their actions, not merely by their knowledge of the Law. However, the tenants want to seize the land and take possession of it by killing the landowner's servants and his son, who is the father's heir entitled to inherit the land. By killing the heir they could illegally take ownership of the land. So, we have the landowner (God) and the tenants (unrighteous leaders of Israel). However, we also have slaves or servants of the landowner, and this third group is especially important to the symbolism of the parable.

We remember that servants are loyal workers for their lord. When the Israelites obeyed the Law in righteous living, they were perceived as honorable servants of God.[124] The same imagery can apply, of course, to Christian believers in Christ. In the parable, the slaves (or servants) are those righteous children of God who are bearing fruit for God and are worthy to be leaders of God's people. By contrast, the tenants, who are self-professed leaders, are bearing unproductive and wild grapes.

## Second Connection to the Hebrew Scriptures

After the tenants have beaten, killed and stoned the landowner's servants, and then killed his son, Yeshua cites a second verse, this time from Psalm 118:22.

> Jesus said to them [the chief priests and elders who metaphorically had just passed judgment on the tenants who had killed the landowner's son], "Did you never read in the Scriptures, 'THE STONE WHICH THE BUILDERS REJECTED, THIS BECAME THE CHIEF CORNER *stone*; THIS CAME ABOUT FROM THE LORD, AND IT IS MARVELOUS IN OUR EYES'? (Mat 21:42)

There is no significant difference in the language between this citation in Matthew and the verse it cites in Psalm 118.

---

124 Some Bible versions have translated "slave," others have translated "servant." The Greek word is δοῦλος, which means slave or servant. "Servant" is the common translation in the New Testament to convey an honorable choice to serve God. However, in the passage about the parable of the landowner, the NASB has chosen "slave," perhaps to convey the negative judgment on those who killed the son of the landowner.

However, the context of the cited verse in Psalm 118:22 is important. David was in distress because all the nations (the pagan people who were not Jews) were "surrounding me like bees." Yet, "the Lord is my strength and my song, and He has become my salvation." There is a reason that David has been able to overcome the enemy in victory. "The Lord has disciplined me severely," he explains, so David has learned repentance and submission through God's discipline. For this reason God has "opened to me the gates of righteousness." This language of "opening the gates" evokes a future time when God will reward the righteous by opening the gates so they may enter the presence of God.

Then we hear, "The stone which the builders rejected has become the chief corner stone." This language in the psalm conveys the concept of judgment, separation and rejection. In the context of the cited verse, the judgment is against the pagan nations. However, with ironic humor (undoubtedly perceived as ridicule by the chief priests and elders who were listening to Yeshua), Yeshua was turning the psalm upside-down to apply the judgment, not against the pagan nations, but against Israel's own unrighteous leaders. These leaders perceived themselves as the cornerstone and foundation of Israel.

However, with continuing irony, the new cornerstone will be "the stone which the builders rejected." The rejected stone applies not only to Yeshua whom the leaders rejected, but also (in the context of the psalm) to the pagan nations that would believe in Yeshua the Messiah. The parable concludes, "Therefore, I say to you, the kingdom of God will be taken away from you [leaders of Israel], and be given to a nation [meaning people] producing the fruit of it."

However, the parable does not end here. It then identifies, using an allusion to the Hebrew Scriptures, not only the new cornerstone but also the people who will produce good fruit instead of wild grapes.

## Third Connection to the Hebrew Scriptures

> MATTHEW: He who falls on this stone will be broken to pieces; but on whomever it falls, it will scatter him like dust (Mat 21:44 referring to Is 8:14-15).

An allusion is not a direct citation, but has enough words that are the same or similar in order to activate the memory of those who had learned the Holy Writings by heart.

> ISAIAH: To both the houses of Israel, a stone to strike and a rock to stumble over, *and* a snare and a trap for the inhabitants of Jerusalem.
> Many will stumble over them. Then they will fall and be broken; they will even be snared and caught. (Is 8:14-15)

It is imperative that we examine these verses in Isaiah in their context. First, we will look at the historical context, and then the context of the memorized block or passage.

At the time Isaiah was prophesying, the powerful and cruel Assyrians were approaching Jerusalem, and the leaders at that time were "devising a plan" instead of trusting in the Lord. That is, they were aligning themselves with Egypt, a pagan nation, in hopes that the Egyptians would defeat their enemy, the Assyrians. However, Isaiah the prophet declared that God "instructed me not to walk in the way of this people, saying, 'You are not to say *it is* a conspiracy!'...It is the Lord of hosts whom you should regard as holy. And He shall be your fear. And He shall be your dread." Then follows the allusion to which the parable is referring: "He [God] shall become a sanctuary; but to both the houses of Israel, a stone to strike and a rock to stumble over." Yet, we cannot stop here, because the greater context of the passage continues to identify the righteous ones who "regard God as holy and fear Him."

> Bind up the testimony, seal the law among my disciples, and I will wait for the Lord who is hiding His face from the house of Jacob; I will even look eagerly for Him.
> Behold, I and the children whom the Lord has given me are for signs and wonders in Israel from the Lord of hosts, who dwells on Mount Zion. (Is 8:16-18)

"Bind up the testimony, seal the law among my disciples." These are powerful words that apply not only to the ancient Israelites as the Assyrians were approaching but also to God's children today. In the Isaiah passage, the disciples are the *talmidim*, the devoted followers of their master. They are the righteous ones. According to Isaiah they are the only ones who can understand the mystery. "Seal the law among my disciples," commands Isaiah.

The author of the NT Book of Hebrews has uncovered this mystery by conducting a midrash on the same passage, Isaiah 8:14-18, which I would like to share with you now. In Hebrews we read, "Both He who sanctifies [Yeshua the Messiah] and those who are sanctified [believers in God's Son] are all from *one* Father; for which reason He [Yeshua] is not ashamed to call them brethren" (Heb 2:11). We have here three separate entities – the Father, the son, and the son's brethren, who are also sons of the Father.

Who, then, are the ones in Isaiah who are "waiting eagerly" for the Lord, which is the tantalizing mystery? The connection between this verse in Isaiah and the passage in Hebrews is the *talmidim*, the disciples, the devoted followers of Isaiah who are now disciples of Yeshua.

With this background we can now appreciate the conclusion of the midrash. Declares the author of Hebrews, "I [Yeshua] and the children whom the Lord has given me are for signs and wonders in Israel from the Lord of hosts." That is, the disciples (*talmidim*) of their Master Yeshua will walk in righteousness, and signs and wonders will follow them. This is the mystery, now revealed, that Isaiah had sealed and bound.

What, then, is the stone that the builders rejected that we see in Isaiah 8:14 and to which Matthew is alluding? The stone that the builders rejected, of course, is Yeshua, who was crucified. He has become the new chief cornerstone. However, the power of the midrash in Hebrews, and the mystery revealed there that Isaiah had sealed among His disciples, is Yeshua coming with his brethren, his *talmidim*, his disciples. Together, Yeshua and his disciples are now performing signs and wonders. This is the mystery that the midrash in Hebrews uncovers and that Matthew is also revealing in his parable.

With this background, we are now ready to return to the parable in Matthew.

## Returning to the Parable

By carefully examining the two citations and the one allusion to the Hebrew Scriptures, and by considering the way in which the people of the first century would have "heard" this parable, we must resist a conclusion that God's judgment is against all the people of Israel who fail to believe in the Messiah. Instead, the judgment in our parable is against those who have made themselves leaders of God's people, but are not following the Law by walking in righteous ways. They are not walking in the Kingdom of God. Instead, they are manifesting ways of the world.

On the other hand, a new group has emerged to serve God. With ironic humor these are people from the very pagan nations, that is, the Gentiles who were not Jews and who were surrounding David in the psalm like bees. They are the now people whom the parable announces, and they will produce good fruit rather than wild grapes.

We can now comprehend the puzzling verse in the parable. "He who falls on this stone [the new cornerstone that is Yeshua] will be broken to pieces." These are the false leaders of Israel who, in Isaiah, are "a stone to strike and a rock to stumble over." By their false leadership they are causing God's people to stumble.

Then the verse in the parable continues with a contrast. "But on whomever it [the new cornerstone] falls, it will scatter him." "Scatter" is the Greek word λικμάω (*likmao*), which can take various nuances of meaning related to "scattering." Various Bible versions translate "grind him to powder" (KJV), "scatter him like dust" (NASB), "on whom it falls will be crushed" (NIV). However, the word can also convey scattering like sowing seed, which I suggest is the most likely meaning in the context of the work that we have just conducted on this parable. The children whom God has given to Yeshua for signs and wonders have been sown as seed. They will bear rich and productive fruit, not wild and sour grapes that have no use.

I would like to offer one last word of caution by citing Paul in his letter to the Romans, "If God did not spare the natural branches [Jews who were born to the birthright but are unworthy to inherit it], neither will He spare you [believers in Christ who now belong to God by their faith in His son]" (Rom 11:21). That is, all the children of God have not become disciples by committing in their hearts to obey and serve their Lord. They will be denied the inheritance of the birthright. However, if your heart desires to grow closer to God, then you are indeed one of the disciples, and the parables are certainly for you. There are mysteries for you to uncover, and you now have the skills to reveal and understand those mysteries.

We conclude this discussion with the recurring theme of the parables that exhorts us to walk in righteousness. When we do, we are walking in the Kingdom of God as witnesses to the world of the Kingdom to come, which will be a new world of peace and righteousness in harmony with God.

## *Mystery #19 in the Kingdom of God*

God wants His children to serve Him with humble obedience. When we do, we bear fruit for God and perform signs and miracles under the lordship of our Master, the Messiah. However, when we produce wild grapes that are sour and of no use to mankind, God allows us to stumble in the snares and traps of the world.

Unfortunately we can also cause snares and traps that bring harm to others. Will we allow the world to rule over us? Or will we submit as faithful servants to our Lord? Will we live our lives in the kingdom of the world, or will we learn to walk in righteousness in the Kingdom of Heaven as witnesses to the glory of God?

Chapter Twenty

# The Remnant and Believers in Christ

All the parables seem to be pointing to God's selection of a remnant, which will be the reward for becoming a disciple today. Furthermore, this remnant is identified as those who are worthy to inherit the birthright. Although all the children of Israel have been born to the inheritance of the birthright as God's firstborn son, God will only select some to fill this leadership role, and they are identified as a remnant.

The question then becomes this. What about Gentile believers in Christ? Will they inherit the birthright, and will they be part of a remnant of God's people?

**Many Believers in Christ: Unworthy to Inherit the Birthright**

We will begin with Paul's letter to the Romans, specifically chapters 9-11. Although Christian theology offers numerous possible interpretations for this portion of Scripture, I think we can agree on one point. These three chapters are talking about God's selection of a remnant.

For example, in Romans 9:6-13 Paul argues with considerable force and emotion that sons born to the birthright have lost it (Ishmael and Esau) and God has given this special inheritance to younger sons (Isaac and Jacob). The passage in Romans 11:2-5 even uses the word "remnant" (λεῖμμα) to refer to Elijah who was the only one "left." Then Paul directs our attention to God's selection of 7,000 "who had not bowed the knee to Baal."

Paul is referring again to God's choice of a select few in Romans 11:7. "What Israel is seeking it has not obtained, but those who were chosen obtained it." Chosen is ἐκλογή referring to a specific selection. The Hebrew equivalent is בָּחַר (bachar), which is used for the inheritance of the birthright.

The concept of selection permeates these three chapters in Romans. Paul expresses "great sorrow and unceasing grief in his heart" wishing he were "accursed and separated from Christ for the sake of his brethren." Apparently those Jews who had not believed that Yeshua was the promised Messiah were "accursed and separated from Christ." Then, citing Isaiah Paul cries, "Though the number of the sons of Israel be like the sand of the sea, it is the remnant that will be saved" (Rom 9:27 citing Is 10:22 and Gen 22:17). Thus, Romans 9-11 is filled with instruction about a remnant.

I agree that there are many enigmatic statements in these three chapters. For example, we read, "not all who are descended from Israel are Israel" (Rom 9:6). Another example is this: "It is not the natural children who are God's children, but it is the children of promise" (Rom 9: 8). We will not address these puzzling passages here, but let me simply suggest that Paul has crafted a legal midrashic argument with exquisite linguistic artistry in Romans 9:6-13.[125] Instead, we will focus on Romans 11:15-21.

Thus, we have seen in the context of Romans 11:15-21 that Paul is talking about God's selecting a remnant from the children of Israel (Rom 9:6-13; 11:2-7). Suddenly Paul delivers a direct declaration to Gentile believers. "I am talking to you Gentiles," he announces in Romans 11:13. What follows is imagery of pruning and grafting an olive tree, which is the task of removing old and exhausted branches in order to generate new life. Much has been written about this agricultural work of pruning to try and make sense of what Paul is attempting to convey. However, I suggest that we must take the imagery at face value and connect it with God's selection of a remnant because that is the topic that precedes and introduces this particular passage.

"Some of the branches were broken off," asserts Paul of those who had been "separated from Christ" by their unbelief. But "you [referring to believing Gentiles], being a wild olive, have been grafted in" (Rom 11:17). Then we hear the most startling statement of all.

> Do not be arrogant toward the branches; but if you are arrogant, *remember that* it is not you who supports the root [referring to the Messiah], but the root *supports* you.

---

[125] See the forthcoming book by Anne Davis, *All Israel will be Saved: Paul's Midrash in romans* (BibleInteract, 2014).

You will say then, "Branches were broken off
[those 'accursed and separated from Christ'} so
that I might be grafted in."

Quite right, they were broken off for their
unbelief, but you stand by your faith. Do not be
conceited, but fear;

For if God did not spare the natural branches,
He will not spare you, either. (Rom 11:18-21)

God's process of selection began with the children of
Israel and is now continuing with Gentile believers. "If God did
not spare the natural branches, He will not spare you either."

Paul offers a subtle explanation of the criteria for God's
selection of a remnant by using imagery that Jews in the first
century would have recognized. Paul has been talking about the
"rejection" of "my fellow countrymen" with a description of olive
branches that have been broken off (Rom 11:14-15). Then, he
suddenly turns to another image of the grain offering given to
God as part of the temple service. "If the first piece *of dough* is holy
the lump is also; and if the root is holy, the branches are too"
(Rom 11:16).

Stop for a moment and consider a revealing aspect of this
terse statement. The grain offering was made with fine flour, olive
oil and incense (Lev 2:1). It was a gift to God that had to be the
very best one had to offer. The "first piece of *dough*" would have
been from the first fruits, and we have seen that "first fruits" is
linguistically related to the concept of selection, that is, being
chosen as worthy of the birthright of inheritance. Thus, we are to
give ourselves in service to God as first fruits that are holy.

Then, with sudden condemning words Paul applies this
same process of selecting what is holy, which has been occurring
with God's people, Israel, to His people who are Gentile believers.
"Do not be arrogant toward the branches… If God did not spare
the natural branches, He will not spare you, either" (Rom 11:21).
God will reject those w ho are unholy and unworthy to inherit the
birthright. They are not prepared to participate in the work of the
remnant.

I suggest that this one passage in Romans 11:13-21 is not
conclusive evidence that many believers in Christ will be unworthy
to inherit the birthright. There are too many other puzzling

passages in the context of the three chapters in Romans. However, what we have just seen is certainly food for thought. So, now we will turn to other concepts in Scripture that contribute to the suggestion that many believers in Christ will be found unworthy to inherit the birthright.

## Yeshua is God's Firstborn Son

Yeshua was a firstborn son, both of Mary and Joseph and of God. Luke observes that Yeshua was the firstborn son of Mary (Lk 2:7); Joseph's name is not mentioned, perhaps because Luke perceived God as his Father. Luke goes on to narrate the subsequent trip to Jerusalem where the parents of Yeshua complied with the law. Luke explains, "Every firstborn male that opens the womb shall be called holy to the Lord" (Lk 2:23). The law required that the firstborn be consecrated as holy because he would serve God as a leader of God's people. Furthermore, the author of Hebrews specifically calls Yeshua the firstborn son of God (Heb 1:6).

We remember that just because a son is born first does not guarantee him the inheritance of the birthright. He has to prove himself worthy, and God will make the final decision. The requirement seems to be spiritual strength and power that comes from obedience leading to righteousness.

We can see this spiritual strength in the Hebrew word for "inherit," which is ירש (*yarash*). Interestingly enough, this word also conveys the sense of "possessing the inheritance. Therefore, the inheritance is a promise, which requires the heir to develop the strength and ability to defeat the enemy in order to conquer the land of his (or her) inheritance. Inheritance required possession, and the firstborn was the leader of God's people in this endeavor.

Now let us consider Abraham, who had no heir (יורש). Yet God told him, "One who will come forth from your own body, he shall be your heir" (יורש). Then God explained that Abraham's descendants would be as numerous as the stars in the sky, and God would give Abraham the land because Abraham would "take possession of it" ( לרשתה from the root *yarash*, meaning to possess the inheritance).

I suggest that the purpose of Abraham's abundant offspring is to inherit by defeating the enemy. To accomplish this,

Abraham's descendants must possess the land, not merely because of their large numbers but because of their righteous obedience to the Lord. As Abraham was a righteous servant whom God had chosen, so his offspring will also be righteous. They will obey the Lord who will act as their leader and commander.

> I have chosen him [explained God, referring to Abraham and using the verbal root for the birthright, *bachar*] so that he may command his children and his household after him to keep the way of the LORD by doing righteousness and justice, so that the LORD may bring upon Abraham what He has spoken about him.
> (Gen 18:19).

How will God accomplish His promise of possessing the land? Abraham's righteous descendants will become a mighty army led by a righteous commander, and together they will possess the land of their inheritance by defeating the enemy.

Let us return now to Yeshua, the firstborn son of God, whom God has declared righteous and worthy of his inheritance. Because he was obedient even unto death he has been seated at the right hand of the Father. However, he must still return to possess his inheritance. When he does, he will gather an army that will be worthy and ready to serve and obey. I suggest that this army will be a remnant from both Israel and from Gentile believers in Christ.

## The Remnant are "in" Christ

The biblical text is filled with metaphorical imagery to help us comprehend spiritual concepts that are otherwise beyond human comprehension. We remember that a metaphor relates two unlike things to each other that nevertheless have something in common. An example of a simple metaphor is food, which we put in our stomachs by eating a meal. This is a literal description of a physical object (food) in a specific place (stomach). Then we metaphorically relate food in the stomach to "eating the bread of life," which is Christ. As bread is the source of life, so the Messiah metaphorically becomes the source of life.

Another metaphor helps us understand a God whom no man has seen or can see" (1 Tim 6:16). We can create this metaphor by placing God "in Christ," which suggests that God and Christ are one. We can now perceive that Christ belongs to God, and whatever Christ says and does is as if God were saying and doing these things. We find this metaphor in 2 Corinthians 5:19. "God was in Christ reconciling the world to Himself."

This metaphor leads to another, which places God, through Christ, in us. We can take this new metaphorical concept and relate Christ to those with faith in him. For example, we learn that God has revealed a mystery, "which is Christ in you, the hope of glory" (Col 1:27). Christ is not physically in those who believe in him, but the metaphorical placement of Christ in Christian believers offers an understanding that Christ and believers are one. We can now perceive that believers in Christ belong to him, and that which the believer says and does is as if Christ were saying and doing these things. We can now extend this metaphorical imagery to declare that, since God is in Christ and Christ is in those with faith in him, then God, who is Spirit, is in those with faith in Christ.

I bring this metaphorical concept to your attention because I suggest that "Christ in you" is a gift from God to those with faith in His son. This gift allows a believer in Christ to enter the family of God and to receive the promise of eternal life because God has placed His Spirit in that person through his (or her) faith in Christ. The author of Colossians expresses this promise as "the hope of glory."

> ...the mystery which has been hidden from the *past* ages and generations, but has now been manifested to His saints, to whom God willed to make known what is the riches of the glory of this mystery among the Gentiles, which is Christ in you, the hope of glory. (Col 1:26-27)

The biblical concept of "hope' is the certainty of something that is still future. The "glory" is God whom we will experience when we come into His presence.

We see this same idea in Romans. "If Christ is in you, though the body is dead because of sin, yet the Spirit is alive because of righteousness" (Rom 8:10). Your body is not literally dead, but you are metaphorically dead with the expectation of death because of sin. Although you are actually physically alive, your physical body is in the process of dying. But now, declares Paul, you have become spiritually alive because Christ is in you.

Finally, we know that God is Spirit (John 4:24). Therefore, as a believer in Christ you have the living Spirit of God in you because Christ is in you by your faith in him. God's gift of the Holy Spirit plays, in a sense, a double role. It is the instrument by which you will obtain future life with God. It also gives spiritual life now when you walk in the love and faith of Christ.

In summary, Christ "in you" is the hope of glory, the promise of eternal life. However, we also understand that you have the privilege, if you choose, of being "in Christ," which means you have the ability to walk in righteousness. When you are "in Christ," you are walking as Yeshua the Messiah walked. We learn about this principle in 1 John. "The one who says he abides in Him [Yeshua] ought himself to walk in the same manner as He walked" (1 Jo 2:6).

I suggest that those who are walking in the same manner as Yeshua, that is, walking in righteousness, are worthy to inherit the birthright. They will be chosen by God because they are prepared to participate in the defeat of God's enemy. The remnant will become an army under the leadership of their lord Yeshua. Together they will possess their inheritance by conquering the land. However, as I often explain, God only sees the heart (remember the story of God's selection of David). That is, there really *are* those who are "walking as Jesus Christ walked" even though sustained complete perfection in mankind is not yet possible at this time.

The parables are instructing us how to walk in righteousness. When we do, we are walking with God in His kingdom, and witnessing to the world the coming glory.

## Requirements to be Worthy of the Remnant

Requirements for inheritance of the birthright are the same for Gentile believers in Christ as they are for the children of Israel; they must submit in humble obedience to their Lord Yeshua. Their work of service is distinct from God's gift of eternal life, and this service will ultimately lead to rewards (in addition to eternal life with God, which is the gift). Thus, the requirement to participate in the remnant is submission to Yeshua as Lord, and willingness to serve in humble obedience.

The verses so frequently cited by evangelical believers as the requirement to receive the gift of eternal life (Rom 10:9-10) is actually an exquisite chiastic structure that captures both aspects, the gift of eternal life with God and a remnant that submits in humble obedience. "If you confess with your mouth Jesus *as* Lord, and believe in your heart that God raised Him from the dead, you will be saved; for with the heart a person believes, resulting in righteousness, and with the mouth he confesses, resulting in salvation (Rom 10:9-10).

To perceive both the gift and the remnant in this passage, we must understand its chiastic structure. Chiasm is a linguistic device that was common in the ancient world, and is quite prevalent in the biblical text. A chiastic structure employs parallel lines that lead to a central focus, which is the main point of the linguistic pattern. The parallel lines also convey a relationship to each other as well as to the central focus.

Before examining Romans 10:9-10 we must consider the English word "saved." Only one Greek word leads to this English translation. The Greek word is σῴζω (*sozo*), which conveys rescue from some undesirable danger. However, there are two aspects of meaning that *sozo* generates in the New Testament. One is to be rescued from death, which is the penalty of sin. This first salvation from death is a gift from God through Christ because all men are sinners, and are therefore condemned to die. This gift of life can be perceived as a promise of something future. The other aspect of salvation is rescue from worldly dangers in our daily lives. When we walk in alignment and harmony with God, we are rescued from the consequences of the world. We identify these consequences as pain, or suffering, or mere temporary happiness. When we are "made whole" by obeying our Lord, we are in the peace and light of God. In fact, the salvation in our daily lives is a foretaste of what is to come in the end of times. So, first we must be "saved" unto eternal life with God by faith in His son Then we can learn to walk as Jesus Christ walked by being "saved" (or rescued) from worldly thoughts and actions.

Let us turn now to examine the chiastic structure of Romans 10:9-10 in a visual way. Start by considering the chiastic center [C]. The salvation here captures both aspects of meaning due to the nature of the chiastic structure, as we will see. Now, ponder the relationship between the two parallel lines labeled [B]. Then consider the relationship between the two parallel lines [A]. Finally, reflect on the relationship between the parallel lines [A] and [B] with the chiastic center [C].

[A] If you confess with your mouth Jesus as Lord
    [B] Believe in you heart that God raised him from the dead
        [C] You will be saved
    [B] For with the heart a person believes, resulting in righteousness
[A] With the mouth he confesses, resulting in salvation.

The [B] lines are parallel because of the repetition of "heart." Their relationship is one of cause and effect. That is, when we believe in our heart that God raised Yeshua from the dead, God sees us as righteous, a requirement for us to belong to Him. This is a gift of righteousness that results in eternal life with God.

The [A] lines are parallel because of the repetition of "mouth." Their relationship is again one of cause and effect. When we make Yeshua Lord in our lives by confessing our submission to him, we have a different kind of salvation. This second use of the word *sozo* in the second [A] line cannot mean salvation unto eternal life because of the parallel structure and its function in the chiastic structure. "Salvation" in the second [A] line is in a parallel relationship with making Jesus Lord. Therefore, this second salvation in the [A] lines is the salvation that is rescue from worldly consequences in our daily lives. We are saved or rescued in our daily lives from pain and suffering and become one with our Lord in peace and harmony.

Now let us focus on the chiastic center. "Saved" in [C] conveys both aspects of salvation because of its relation to the parallel lines [A] and [B]. First we see the closest parallel to the chiastic center, which is the [B] construction. Believing in the son of God comes first (closest to the chiastic center) because it results in the believer belonging to God with the promise of eternal life.

Then we move to the [A] lines, which are farthest from the chiastic center. All believers in Christ have an opportunity to make Yeshua Lord in their lives, but not all will take advantage of this opportunity. Only some believers will make Yeshua their Lord, who will guide us to walk in his ways. Thus, we have a distinction between all the children of God who have Christ "in them," so they belong to God [B]. A smaller remnant has confessed Yeshua as Lord [B], so they are "in Christ." They are serving in the army of God.

The important condition for making your life "whole," which is the second aspect of salvation in the [B] lines, is service, which requires humble submission and obedience. Yeshua is our model whom we desire to imitate. He is a servant of God as Matthew declares from Isaiah. "Behold, My servant whom I have chosen. My beloved in whom My soul is well-pleased (Mat 12:18 citing Is 42:1). We are also reminded of the advice of Yeshua to his disciples. "No one can serve two masters....You cannot serve God and wealth" (Mat 6:24). Wealth represents the ways of the world, so a servant of God must abandon worldly thoughts and actions to serve only God.

Service to God is not a quick and easy path. Paul describes this service as a sacrifice similar to the animal sacrifice at the temple. However, there is one significant difference. Although both the animal and the servant of the Lord must be unblemished as loving gifts to God, the animal is a dead sacrifice whereas the servant is alive with the spiritual life of God. Paul speaks with intense emotion. "I urge you, brethren, by the mercies of God, to present your bodies a living and holy sacrifice, acceptable to God, *which is* your spiritual service of worship" (Rom 12:1).

## Purification by Baptism

Since service to God is not a quick and easy path, we must stop to consider the journey one must travel to become a loyal follower of Christ in service to God. The biblical text employs the concept of baptism, a metaphor that uses literal objects and actions to instruct us in the spiritual principle of purification. For example, water baptism does not literally wash away our sins, but allows us to apply this visual image of washing to understand the importance of replacing worldly ways with godly living.

Many Christian denominations employ water baptism to signify entrance into the Christian faith and a new relationship with Yeshua the Messiah. This practice of initiation for adults and christening for children originates, in large part, from the Great Commission. "Go therefore and make disciples of all the nations, baptizing them in the name of the Father and the Son and the Holy Spirit" (Mat 28:19). However, the biblical concept of baptism is also important for our daily walk. We will look at three points that support this suggestion of baptism as a symbol for walking in righteousness.

First, the Jewish practice at the time of Yeshua (and still today) was not a single event of water immersion, but an on-going repetitive occurrence. Archaeologists have uncovered numerous Jewish ritual baths, called *mikvot*, that were used for ritual purification. Many of them are in the area before the ancient Israelites would enter the temple compound in Jerusalem, and others are in numerous ancient Jewish villages and neighborhoods at the entrance to synagogues. The purpose of ritual immersion was not for entrance into the Jewish faith, but to symbolize the desire of the participant to be pure in God's presence.

Second, this practice of ritual immersion appears in the New Testament. When John the Baptist was baptizing Jews in the Jordan River (including Yeshua), he accompanied this ritual immersion with these words. "Repent for the kingdom of heaven is near" (Mat 3:2). There are two key concepts in these words, "repent" and "kingdom of heaven." Looking first at "kingdom of heaven," we note that Jews were expecting a Messiah who would bring the Kingdom of God to Israel where sin would be destroyed and God's people would be able to live peacefully in His presence. We find this expectation in the book of Daniel. "The God of heaven will set up a kingdom which will never be destroyed" (Dan 2:44).

"Repent" is the required action that accompanies the Jewish rite of ritual immersion. Repent means to change. Water is merely symbolic of eliminating sin in our lives through the act of purification. However, if the person is not committed to change, the symbolism of water is meaningless. Thus, baptism among Jews at the time of Yeshua was not initiation into the Christian faith. It

272 Uncovering Mysteries of the Parables

was a traditional practice of committing to change in order to come into God's presence in a pure and holy condition.

Finally, we should look again at the Great Commission. "Go, therefore, and make disciples of all the nations, baptizing them in the name of the Father and the Son and the Holy Spirit" (Mat 28:19). Note that the ones being baptized are not those who first believe that Yeshua is the son of God, but disciples who have made Yeshua Lord in their lives. These disciples have already believed in the Messiah. Now they are ready to commit to service by representing God and acting on His behalf. As disciples they must purify themselves to act and walk in godly ways. Their witness is their walk, which must be holy and righteous.

We are now ready to examine intriguing prophetic words spoken by John the Baptist about baptism.

> The axe is already laid at the root of the trees; therefore every tree that does not bear good fruit is cut down and thrown into the fire.
>
> As for me, I baptize you with water for repentance, but He who is coming after me is mightier than I, and I am not fit to remove His sandals; He will baptize you with the Holy Spirit and fire. (Mat 3:10-11)

The imagery conveys God's judgment and His selection of those who "bear good fruit," which is consistent with God's choice of a remnant. However, let us focus on the symbolism of fire. John identifies three kinds of baptism – water, Holy Spirit and fire.

All baptisms are a purification process. Water symbolizes purification by washing away what is impure. The Holy Spirit acts as a form of purification by guiding and instructing. "The Helper, the Holy Spirit, whom the Father will send in My name, He will teach you all things, and bring to your remembrance all that I said to you (John 14:26). Finally, fire purifies by refining, that is, burning away what is impure and leaving only what is pure.

The imagery of fire is a metaphor, which is a literal action employed to convey a spiritual truth. The Hebraic sense of time helps us understand that baptism by fire is both prophetic of something future, as well as an activity that is currently in progress. We have already seen the process of testing where God allows His people to receive the consequences of their ungodly behavior in order to encourage them to turn to Him. Using typical Hebrew parallel construction, the Hebrew Scriptures identify testing as a kind of refinement. "You have tried us, O God; You have refined us as silver is refined," cries David (Ps 66:10). "I have refined you, but not as silver; I have tested you in the furnace of affliction," declares God through Isaiah (Is 48:10). Testing is a process that occurs in our lives today. Thus, refinement by fire is both prophetic of something future, as well as a process of purification that occurs in our lives today.

Refinement does not completely destroy. Instead it eliminates what is not pure, leaving only what is completely pure. Applying this literal action of refinement to a spiritual truth, we understand that all unrighteousness will be destroyed at some time in the future leaving only what is righteous and holy. Furthermore, it is not our literal bodies that will be destroyed, but our unrighteous works. "If any man's work is burned up, he will suffer loss; but he himself will be saved, yet so as through fire" (1 Co 3:15). Thus, we can only come into God's presence in a righteous and holy condition, which baptism by fire accomplishes metaphorically through this purification process.

We remember that John the Baptist refers to baptism by fire in the context of judgment where God is selecting those who "bear good fruit," which is compatible with God's choice of a remnant. So, we ask two questions that relate to the Hebraic sense of time. First, who is God refining metaphorically today with the baptism of fire? And second, who will God refine by fire at some time in the future? The answer to our first question is logically simple. All those who desire to change and submit to testing are being refined by fire today. As for future baptism by fire, there is a fascinating passage in Zechariah.

> "It will come about in all the land," declares the LORD, "that two parts in it will be cut off *and* perish; but the third will be left in it."
> "And I will bring the third part through the fire, refine them as silver is refined, and test them as gold is tested. They will call on My name, and I will answer them; I will say, 'They are My people,' And they will say, 'The LORD is my God'." (Zec 13:8-9)

## Joining of the Two Remnants

This passage in Zechariah stimulates some interesting questions. Are there two separate remnants, one for Israel and one for believers in Christ? Or , will there be only one remnant with neither Jew nor Gentile but one people? We probably cannot answer these questions conclusively. However, there is one passage in Ezekiel with a fascinating repetition that requires careful consideration. The repetition forms a chiastic structure.

[A] Take for yourself one stick and write on it,
    For Judah and for the sons of Israel, his companions;
        [B] Then take another stick and write on it,
            For Joseph, the stick of Ephraim and all the house of Israel, his companions.
            [C] Then join them for yourself one to another into one stick that they may become one in your hand.
        [B] I will take the stick of Joseph, which is in the hand of Ephraim,
        and the tribes of Israel, his companions;
[A] And I will put them with it, with the stick of Judah,
    and make them one stick, and they will be one in My hand
(Ez 37:16-19).

The chiastic center joins together Judah and Joseph. We remember that Judah and Joseph were the sons of Jacob who were worthy to inherit the birthright. Furthermore, this understanding, of joining two sticks, which represent two remnants with the birthright, is reinforced by the association of Joseph with his son Ephraim. It was Ephraim who inherited the birthright, not the firstborn son, Manasseh. The stick of Joseph is in the hand of Ephraim. We seem to have, in this terse passage in Ezekiel, the joining of two remnants. However, there is more that suggests this conclusion.

A key word is "companions." It is only the "companions" who will be with Judah and Joseph when the two sticks are joined. Who are the companions?

The verbal root of "companion" is חבר, which means to unite or be joined. For example, the tabernacle was made of "ten curtains of fine twisted linen, and blue and purple and scarlet *material*" that were "joined to one another [חברת אשה, *chaverot echad*]." That is, they became as one. The verb חבר is repeated ten times in this brief passage (Ex 26:3-11). This account of constructing the tabernacle by joining the curtains is recorded again in Exodus 36:10-18 where the verb חבר is again repeated ten times. I suggest that the ancient listener of the Ezekiel passage would have heard this echo of the tabernacle curtains joined as "one," and would have identified it with the joining of the sticks of Judah and Joseph. What is being joined together to become one is something sacred and holy.

The verbal root חבר, in its noun construct, is a word you may recognize if you have spent time in Israel. חברים (*chaverim*) are friends. However, the most common word for friend in Scripture is רֵיע (*re-ah*), meaning a close associate or a neighbor. Our word *chaver*, on the other hand, is seldom used in the Hebrew Scriptues. When it is, it conveys more than a close associate but two friends who are joined together and united as one. In fact, I only found one place in the Hebrew Scriptures that uses the verbal root חבר in its noun construct. That is in reference to Daniel and his three friends Shadrach, Mishach and Abednego. These friends, joined together as one, passed through the baptism of fire and were purified.

There is one other key word that we must recognize because of its repetition. That word is עץ (*etz*), which has been translated "stick." However, *etz* means a tree or any part of a tree. Since we are interested in first century methods of searching the Scriptures, we are drawn to the first usage of this common word where it appears in the creation account. "God said, 'Let the earth sprout vegetation: plants yielding seed, and fruit trees on the earth bearing fruit after their kind with seed in them'; and it was so" (Gen 1:11). The trees are bearing fruit in the creation account just like the righteous remnant is bearing fruit for God. Furthermore, the fruit is "after its kind." Thus, the righteous remnant is bearing righteous fruit.

Thus, it appears that we have in this passage in Ezekiel the joining of two remnants represented by the stick of Judah and the stick of Joseph/Ephraim. The sticks are also representing those who are closely associated with Judah and Joseph/Ephraim in an intimate relationship. They are joining together to become one, and are bearing righteous fruit for God.

We are left with only one remaining question. Who do Joseph and Judah represent? In the parallel lines the companions of Joseph are identified first as "all the house of Israel" and then as "all the tribes of Israel." Thus, the companions of Joseph seem to be a remnant from the children of Israel. However, what about Judah? The parallel lines for Judah are mysterious. In the first parallel line we read "Judah and the sons of Israel, his companions." However, in the second parallel line we are startled by the omission of any reference to the children of Israel. We read simply, "the stick of Judah."

We are aware that the New Testament identifies Yeshua of Nazareth as descended from the line of Judah. Furthermore, we have a tantalizing verse in Isaiah that suggests a remnant from Judah. "The surviving remnant of the house of Judah will again take root downward and bear fruit upward (Is 37:31). Therefore, I think we can ponder the parallel construction in Ezekiel, which startles us by deleting any mention of Israel, as apparently a reference to those Gentile believers joined and united to Yeshua the Messiah. The stick of Judah seems to be the remnant of believers in Christ who will take root downward and bear fruit upward under their Lord Yeshua, the Messiah.

## Conclusion

There is no explicit verse in the New Testament that clearly and literally states there will be a remnant from those who belong to God by their faith in His son. However, as we consider the artistic nature of the biblical language, we have seen there are numerous suggestions of this concept. Furthermore, God tells us that He is "not one to show partiality" (Acts 10:34). Therefore, it is a reasonable conclusion that God is treating His children in Christ in the same manner that He is treating His children, Israel. Furthermore, as we examined the artistic nature of the intriguing passage in Ezekiel about two sticks, it appears that the two remnants will be joined together, at some time in the future, to become one remnant.

# Mystery #20 in the Kingdom of God

The evidence in Scripture for a righteous remnant of Israel, which is comprised of those who are worthy to inherit the birthright, is quite strong and convincing. The question about a remnant from those who belong to God by their faith in Christ is not so obvious. However, there are two convincing arguments.

First is the understanding that God is "not one to show partiality." Thus, He is treating believers in Christ in the same way He is treating His children Israel. Even more convincing is an abundance of artistic passages that suggest there will be a remnant from believers in Christ. If we apply our first century methods and think with a first century mind, the artistic nature of the biblical text comes to life with rich meaning.

# Concluding Thoughts

These conclusions will be most meaningful if you read them *after* you have completed the entire book and worked through the various exercises. However, I know we are all human, so you have likely turned to this chapter before finishing the book. So, I suggest you return to this list periodically as you work through the book. And I trust my concluding thoughts will have a rich impact on your life.

1.  As a disciple of Christ you know with a firm certainty that you belong to God. He is your Father and you are His child. You perceive this gift as a treasure beyond words to describe, so you express your deep gratitude with an intense emotional outpouring of joy that is manifested in a new life with God. This life of joy becomes a witness to the world.

2.  As a disciple of Christ it has been granted to you to know the mysteries of the Kingdom of Heaven (also known as the Kingdom of God). The only requirements are a hunger to grow closer to God and a willingness to roll up your sleeves and work. God has stored these mysteries in the depth of His Word, so how well do you know the Holy Writings? If you have worked through this book, taking time to ponder the questions and join in the process of discovery, then you have acquired the skills necessary to uncover a depth of meaning. You have become a "steward of the mysteries of God" (1 Co 4:1), so use your understanding wisely. "Whoever has, to him shall more be given, and he shall have an abundance; but whoever does not have, even what he has shall be taken away from him. (Mat 13:12).

3.  As a disciple of Christ you bring the Kingdom of God both to your own life and to the lives of God's people. You are a Good Samaritan. When anyone is in need of help you do not pass on the other side by behaving in worldly ways, but you feel compassion which leads you to stop and help. How do you help? You bring healing words and actions by offering your own resources, whether they are money or time or skills, and you give these resources as a gift.

4. As a disciple of Christ you want to be like Abel, who offered to God the first fruits of his flock. In the New Testament, James tells us that we are a kind of first fruits (James 4:7). We offer ourselves to God as loving children who desire to glorify Him. However, there will be times in our lives when we separate ourselves from God by sinning (a sin is anything contrary to God). At these times we must remember Cain. "If you do not do well, sin is crouching at the door; and its desire is for you, but you must master it" (Gen 4:7)

5. As a disciple of Christ you respond to the knowledge of future prophetic events with growing excitement and firm confidence in God. Your excitement comes from a desire to be with God to participate in His future work. Your confidence allows you to respond with calm peace to otherwise unsettling questions. If I am chosen, will my loved ones be there with me? Will God ask me to participate in the Great Tribulation? What role will I be expected to play? The answers are a mystery, but your trust in God allows you to walk forward with confidence.

6. As a disciple of Christ you know that one requirement of the remnant is to be faithful to the end. Therefore, only God knows who will be in the remnant. However, this unknown aspect of your life simply encourages you to grow in your righteous walk with God. With growing desire, you want to participate with God in the future defeat of the enemy.

7. As a disciple of Christ you are growing in your understanding of God's great plan of redemption. God is drawing His children to Him in righteousness, which began at the time of creation. Now we are participating in this great plan by witnessing to the world our wonderful God, the Messiah whom He has sent, and the Kingdom to that is still future. Our vision of the future is beginning to open before us. We want to be there. We want to be part of the remnant that will defeat God's enemy, which has also become our enemy.

# Appendix I:
# How to Use a Concordance

A lexicon is a dictionary that lists biblical words and offers definitions. A lexicon is typically composed in English with English words and English definitions. However, we must remember that "all translations are interpretation." So, I discourage you from using a lexicon because you will be relying on the interpretation of others.

Most lexicons also include a concordance, which will bring you closer to the original meaning of a Hebrew or Greek word. An ancient version of Greek is the language of the New Testament, and Hebrew is the language of the Old Testament, although small portions of the Hebrew Scriptures are composed in Aramaic. A concordance takes key biblical words and lists every verse in the Bible where this word appears. Your task will be to read each verse in its context to gain a comprehensive understanding of how that word is used in Scripture.

However, there is a caveat. If the concordance takes an English word and offers verses where that English word appears, you are still trapped in the interpretation of others. Therefore, you need a concordance that provides the original Hebrew or Greek word, and then offers a list where that Hebrew or Greek word appears in Scripture.

We suggest that you memorize the Hebrew and Greek alphabets. In this way, you will be able to work with Hebrew and Greek words, not English translations. There is an easy tool to help you memorize these alphabets that you will find on the BibleInteract website, http://www.bibleinteract.com.

I recommend to my students an online concordance that is easy to access and use in this way. I suggest http://biblos.com. You will also find an audio file on the BibleInteract website that explains how to use this concordance. Simply go to http://www.biblineteract.com.

We will now offer the steps to follow if you choose to use the online concordance at biblos.com.

1. As you are reading in your Bible, let yourself be curious about certain key words. Select one word for your search in a concordance.
2. Go to http://biblos.com and click on Interlinear Bible in the top navigation. This will bring you to Genesis 1:1.
3. At the top of the page is an empty bar where you will type in the verse that contains your word. Hit "Enter" on your computer.
4. You are now on a page that gives your verse in both the English translation and the original Hebrew or Greek text. Find the English word that captured your curiosity, and then focus on the original Hebrew or Greek word above it. You may wish to practice speaking aloud the original word.
5. At the very top, above the English translation and the original Hebrew or Greek word, you will find a number that refers to Strong's Concordance. Click on this number.
6. You are now on the page that will give you the list of verses where the original Hebrew or Greek word appears in Scripture. You will find this list in the right column of the page.
7. At the top of the right column you will find the number of occurrences where the word appears. Scroll down to see this list of occurrences. Make a list of these verses leaving room for *brief* notes.
8. Your task is now to read each verse *in its context*. Context means the surrounding verses that are needed to convey a complete thought. Take brief notes on your list of verses.
9. When you are finished making this list of verses with brief notes, you must review the list and consider any patterns. For example, the word may be used in more than one way. Or perhaps there is a contrast between two nuances of meaning. Or the order of the list, from the first usage to the last, may offer some kind of pattern.
10. These patterns are only examples. You will undoubtedly find other patterns as you conduct this type of word-study.
11. It is now time to return to the original verse where you were curious about one word. Read this verse again in its context. You will be surprised by the depth and richness of your new understanding.

# Appendix II:
# Recommended Reading

The purpose of *Uncovering Mysteries in the Parables: The Parables as Haggadic Midrash* is to introduce a methodology based on the proposal that the NT parables are a form of haggadic midrash. This methodology focuses on two principles. First, each parable is a commentary on some verse or passage in the Hebrew Scriptures. Second, people in first century Israel would have heard linguistic anomalies that led them to a deeper understanding that resides behind the lain, simple and literal meaning.

There is a rich abundance of scholarly literature on the NT parables. However, most is focused on theological aspects of interpretation. Only recently have some scholars begun to look at the methodology of the parables in light of their Hebraic nature. Therefore, the books and articles I am recommending below represent the theme of this book, which is the Hebraic nature and methodology of the parables.

## BOOKS

1. Robert Alter
*The Art of Biblical Narrative*
NY: Basic Books, 1991

Alter's book was a breakthrough for me as it may be also for you. I was working to understand the numerous linguistic devices that people of ancient Israel would have heard and the way in which they would have responded. Alter "hears" the linguistic devices as markers to a deeper understanding. He carefully explains these linguistic devices in some detail. He then demonstrates their use through numerous narrative accounts in the Hebrew Scriptures including the Jacob-Esau story, the type scene of meeting a wife at the well, and the account of Balaam the Gentile prophet. This book is required reading for my student who are pursuing certification for teaching First Century Methods.

2.  Mark Bailey
*Jesus through Middle Eastern Eyes: Cultural Studies in the Gospels*
Downers Grove: Intervarsity, 2008

Bailey spent his childhood in Egypt followed by 40 years teaching the New Testament in seminaries and institutes in Egypt, Lebanon, Jerusalem and Cyrus. This landmark book explores the parables in the light of Middle Eastern culture today. This approach has been met with significant interest and approval for two reasons. First, there are no ancient texts that describe the customs and manners of the ancient biblical culture. Second, attempts have been made to apply cultures of modern illiterate societies to the ancient biblical world. However, these comparative sociological studies have not been generally accepted. Bailey examines 32 passages in the New Testament gospels and provides a view of the ancient setting and its use of language.

3.  Craig L. Blomberg
*Interpreting Parables*
Downers Grove: InterVarsity, 1990

Published in 1990, Blomberg's incisive study paved the way for examining the linguistic structure of the NT parables rather than focusing exclusively or primarily on the theological message. He is most interested in the characters in each narrative, the roles they play, and the resulting linguistic structures, which he labels as simple three-point parables, complex three-point parables, two-point and one-point parables. Blomberg also examines the research at that time on the Kingdom of God, and demonstrates the growing understanding that Jesus believed the kingdom was in some sense both present and future. This is a good introductory book on the linguistic nature of the NT parables.

4.  C. H. Dodd
*According to the Scriptures: The Sub-Structure of New Testament Theology*
London: Nesbet & Co, 1952.

Although written over 50 years ago, this book remains a classic that is still useful in literary studies of the Bible. Dodd was the first one to suggest that a citation in the New Testament provoked a memorized block in the Hebrew Scriptures. His approach presupposed an ancient oral culture in ancient Israel, which is evident in his writing.

5.   Brad H. Young
*The Parables: Jewish Tradition and Christian Interpretation*
Peabody: Hendriksen, 1998

Young broke from the Christian tradition of viewing the parables as exclusively New Testament compositions, and convincingly argued that many of the NT parables are related to passages in the Jewish literature. For those who are not intimately familiar with Jewish literature, Young's work can be hard to follow. However, his reference to common themes is relatively easy to grasp and quite helpful.

## ARTICLES

ECONOMIC BACKGROUND
In the Parable of the Talents, many have perceived the talents as representing gifts and abilities. Others find theological meaning in faithful stewardship. Chenoweth, on the other hand, suggests that Matthew intended, by means of an extended verbal repetition, that the talents refer to the knowledge of the secrets of the kingdom of heaven. In other words, the disciples have been given inside information about the kingdom.

1.   Ben Chenoweth
"Identifying the Talents: Contextual Clues for the Interpretation of the Parable of the Talents (Matthew 25:14-30)"
*Tyndale Bulletin* 56/1 (2005): 61-72

THE UNEXPECTED AS A CLUE
De Boer is intrigued with the suggestion by J. Jeremias that parables often contain "an element of unexpectedness" and this element "was intended to indicate where the meaning was to be found." To test this proposal De Boer examines the Parable of the Unforgiving Servant because the extraordinary amount of debt demands an explanation.

2    Martinus C. De Boer
"Ten Thousand Talents? Matthew's Interpretation and Redaction of the Parable of the Unforgiving Servant"
*Catholic Biblical Quarterly* 50 (1988): 215-32

## SOCIAL AND CULTURAL BACKGROUND

An important contribution to parable research has been a growing interest in cultural studies as background information to fully appreciate the parables. A classic study is the work of Mark Bailey mentioned above. Another interesting article has been written by Harrill, who questions traditional theological conventions about the master-slave relationship. He examines what it was like to be a slave in antiquity and then suggests the power of irony in the Parable of the Overseer (Mat 24:45-51; Luke 12:42-46) where the abused becomes the abuser.

3.   Von J. Albert Harrill
"The Psychology of Slaves in the Gospel Parables: A Case Study in Social History"
*Biblische Zeitschrift* 55/1 (2011): 63-74

## PARABLES AS HAGGADIC MIDRASH:

Of the many articles I reviewed I found only one scholar, Isaac Kilimi, who suggested that the New Testament parables were related to the rabbinic haggadic midrash. Kilimi writes, "A parable or an illustrative tale [is] similar to the Rabbis' *aggadic* Midrashim, not a historical report." However, Kalimi does not pursue this idea with analysis nor does he offer examples.

4.   Isaac Kalimi
"Robbers on the Road to Jerusalem"
*Ephemerides Theologicae Lovanienses* 85/1 (2009): 47-63.

THEMATIC UNITS:
Lunn is moves toward an understanding derived from literary analysis in contrast to theological interpretation. He identifies thematic units within the parables by first viewing the entire parable as a thematic whole that generates a comprehensive meaning, which is generally called macro-interpretation. Then he examines linguistic details, which is micro-interpretation. Considering thematic units within a parable first requires an examination of the details, and then offers a structure of the parts that helps generate the macro-interpretation. I find the study of thematic parts quite helpful in revealing a deeper understanding of the message conveyed by the parable.

6.  Ernst R. Wendland
"Finding Some Lost Aspects of Meaning in Christ's Parables of the Lost-and Found (Luke 15)"
*Trinity Journal* 17NS (1996): 19-65

5.  Nicholas Lunn
"Parables of the Lost" Rhetorical Structure and Section Headings of Luke 15"
*Bible Translator* 60/3 (July 2009): 158-64

CLUSTERING OF PARABLES:
Thematic units occur within one parable. Clustering of parables, on the other hand, recognizes two or more parables that have been placed together in a cluster to convey the same basic message. Moreover, their placement coordinates the similar theme to build one comprehensive message generated by the entire cluster. Wendland examines such a cluster in the three closely related parables of the lost in Luke 15.

Made in the USA
Charleston, SC
04 December 2013